A-level Study Guide

Sociology

Steve Harris

Series Consultants: Geoff Black and Stuart Wall

Project Manager: Julia Morris

Pearson Education Limited

Edinburgh Gate, Harlow

Essex CM20 2JE, England

and Associated Companies throughout the world

© Pearson Education Limited 2000

First published 2000

British Library Cataloguing in Publication Data

A catalogue entry for this title is available from the British Library.

ISBN 0-582-43166-2

Set by 35 in Univers, Cheltenham

Printed by Ashford Colour Press, Gosport, Hants

Sociological methods

All the specifications cover the use of sociological methods at both AS and A2 levels. Some of the exam papers have separate questions on methods (OCR unit 3 and 6, AQA unit 3 and 5) either in the form of data response questions or essays. You will have to answer questions on methods.

Where coursework is chosen, the ability to employ methods successfully and evaluate their use is rewarded. A critical understanding of the use of research methods is helpful in understanding and criticising any topic you study. For some topics, such as deviance and suicide, the discussion of research methods is a central theme.

Exam themes

→ Should sociological research use scientific methods?

→ The strengths and weaknesses of quantitative and qualitative methods

→ The usefulness of secondary data

→ The reasons why sociologists choose particular research methods

→ The link between sociologists' theoretical approach and their choice of research methods

Topic checklist

	AQA Sociology	OCR Sociology	EDEXCEL Social Policy
O AS ● A2			
What is sociology?			
The scientific approach	O●	O●	O●
Quantitative methods	O●	O●	O●
Qualitative methods	O●	O●	O●
Secondary data	O●	O●	O●
Choosing research methods	O●	O●	O●

What is sociology?

Sociology studies human behaviour in a different way from other academic approaches. Sociologists look at a wider range of behaviour than economists or political scientists. Where psychologists study individual behaviour, sociologists study social behaviour. Where biologists focus on the importance of nature in explaining human behaviour, sociologists emphasize the role of culture.

What do sociologists do?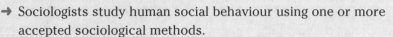

→ Sociologists study human social behaviour using one or more accepted sociological methods.

→ Many sociologists favour scientific methods. The essential feature of the scientific approach is doubt. Scientists do not believe anything until evidence has been produced, yet are prepared to change their minds when new evidence is produced.

→ Other sociologists try to explain human behaviour by attempting to look at social situations from the point of view of the people they are studying.

Divisions within sociology

Disagreement between sociologists is the basis of most questions and can form the framework for many answers. The reasons for disagreement do not just depend on the personal views of the individual sociologist but are more systematic. We can identify differences in perspectives, theories and methods:

→ **perspectives** are the different ways sociologists see the social world
→ **theories** are explanations of social behaviour
→ **methods** are different ways of gathering and interpreting information

Social action perspectives

→ Individuals create human society: they have motives and beliefs and choose how to act.

→ Individuals give a social meaning to their own behaviour and to the behaviour of others. These meanings tend to be shared within a group or society but differ between groups and societies.

→ Social meanings may change over time.

→ Social action theories try to explain how social meanings are learned and shared, e.g. labelling theories explain how the police define situations and are able to impose their meanings on those who are labelled as criminals.

→ Interactionist sociologists tend to use small-scale research methods to study how individuals or small groups make sense of the social world.

Structural perspectives

Society is a social system. Society exists independently of individuals. This can be shown by looking at the characteristics of a society which differ from other societies but persist over a long period of time, e.g. each society may have a characteristic divorce rate or murder rate that remains more or less the same over time. Society limits the behaviour of individuals. We learn norms (rules), values and beliefs and thus the expected way to behave in social situations.

Structuralist sociologists tend to use quantitative methods to study the effects of society on the behaviour of large groups.

Structural-consensus perspectives

Consensus means agreement. The consensus perspective sees a society united by shared and agreed values (aims), beliefs and norms (rules). Social life is based on co-operation rather than conflict. We give people, such as politicians and the police, the authority to maintain social order and look after the interests of us all. The most important theory is **functionalism**.

Structural-conflict theories

Societies consist of groups with unequal access to power and rewards. There is a conflict of interest between these groups. The strong impose social order on the weak. The most powerful groups use the institutions (such as schools, police and the mass media) to control others.

The most important conflict theories are:

→ Marxism, which focuses on social class inequalities
→ feminism, which focuses on gender inequalities
→ Weberian theories, which focus on inequalities in power

What's new?

The major divisions between structural and action theories and conflict and consensus perspectives go back to the early days of sociology. Changes in the social world have encouraged changes in the sociological theories used to explain social behaviour.

The newer sociological approaches include:

→ **feminism** – argues we live in an unequal society dominated by men
→ **New Right** – argues for traditional moral values and free market economics
→ **postmodernism** – argues that the modern world has been replaced by a new, i.e. postmodern, world

Example

In our society, both men and women learn the same language but there are different rules about how to behave, e.g. men are expected not to cry, women are expected not to be aggressive. These expected patterns of behaviour are *gender roles*.

Links

These approaches are explained in chapter 14 and used where appropriate in other chapters.

The scientific approach

You need to understand what is meant by scientific methods in order to understand some of the debates about the use of methods and the relationship between theoretical approaches and choice of methods. The big issues here are:

→ should sociologists use scientific methods?
→ what are the problems of studying social behaviour using scientific methods?

What is science? A conventional view

Science is usually defined in terms of its methods. The scientific method involves both *procedures* and *logic*, and the aim of scientific sociology is to be **reliable** and **valid**.

The procedures are the techniques used by scientists. These are most commonly experiments but they also involve observation and statistical tests. The logic is the way of thinking adopted by scientists. Popper explained this as a process of *conjecture* (i.e. a guess, an untested *hypothesis*) and *refutation* (test). The scientist has a hypothesis and tests it – usually using the experimental method. The best way to test a hypothesis is to try and find evidence against it (i.e. refute, falsify or disprove it). If no evidence against is found, the theory is accepted until it can be disproved. Therefore all scientific knowledge is temporary.

The experimental method

→ The *experiment* involves manipulating (changing) an **independent variable** (IV, a cause) and observing the **dependent variable** (DV, the effect), whilst controlling **extraneous variables** (EV, other factors which might influence results).
→ Natural scientists favour the use of experiments because of the possibility of control and thus reliability.
→ *Laboratory experiments* maximize control.
→ *Field experiments* are more natural.
→ Experiments are common in psychology and rare, but not unknown, in sociology.

Using scientific methods in sociological research: the case for

Early positivist sociologists, such as Comte and Durkheim, favoured the use of scientific methods because of their success in producing and testing knowledge in the natural sciences. They saw sociology as the study of social facts, which are the ways in which society influences the behaviour of individuals.

Durkheim argued that the comparative survey was an appropriate substitute for the experiment because the thinking behind both methods was similar. Scientific methods can produce sociological explanations which are generalizable and testable.

Examiner's secrets

This is a difficult section. If you are studying this at the beginning of your course it is probably sufficient to understand that some sociological methods follow natural science.
For the A2 course you need to be able to discuss 'Is sociology a science?'

The jargon

Reliable in this context means research can be repeated to produce the same results. *Valid* means true, i.e. the research measures what it intended to.

Checkpoint 1

Explain how you could use the experimental method to demonstrate racial discrimination in employment. Try to use the terms IV, DV and EV in your answer.

Checkpoint 2

Why don't sociologists use laboratory experiments?

Using scientific methods in sociological research: the case against

Theoretical problems

→ Interactionists argue that sociology should study social action, not social facts.

→ Social action, because it involves the social meanings given to behaviour, not just the objective behaviour, cannot be directly observed.

→ P. Winch said sociology needs to discover the '*reasons for behaviour*' (which exist in people's minds) rather than '*the causes of behaviour*' (which are external to individuals and are found in the structure of society).

Practical problems

→ The act of studying people may change their behaviour: this has been called the experimenter effect or **Hawthorne effect**.

→ The expectations of researchers may influence the behaviour of subjects: this is referred to as a **self-fulfilling prophecy**.

Both these problems also occur in the natural sciences. Sociologists try to minimize them by remaining detached from their subjects.

What is science? A critical view

The view that scientists are detached and open-minded seekers of truth has been challenged. *Kuhn* argued that normally scientists accept a basic framework of ideas and do not ask questions outside this framework. Evidence which challenges this taken-for-granted framework is ignored or distorted. When there is too much evidence to ignore, a scientific revolution occurs and a new framework is established. *Kaplan* argued that scientists write up their results as if they have followed the formal scientific method but actually do the thinking and research in a more haphazard way, e.g. discoveries may be the result of inspiration or accident. *Broad and Wade* pointed out that some scientists cheat to produce the results they want.

Conclusions

→ Some sociologists try to use scientific methods.

→ There are problems in applying scientific methods to the study of social behaviour.

→ Some sociologists reject the scientific approach.

→ There is some controversy about what scientists actually do.

Checkpoint 3

Suggest one social cause of and one individual reason for crime or divorce.

Example

The Hawthorne effect was described by Mayo in his study at the Hawthorne works. Workers included in research on the effects of lighting on production worked harder whatever the level of lighting.

Checkpoint 4

Explain briefly how studying people may influence their behaviour and why this is a problem for sociologists.

Example

Cyril Burt was a major figure in British psychology and education. His work on IQ, which supported the introduction of the 11-plus, was based, in part, on fictitious studies of twins.

Exam question   answer: page 16

Is it possible for sociology to be a science? (20 min)

Quantitative methods

Quantitative methods are favoured by sociologists who wish to take a scientific approach. They involve the systematic collection of data, and the results are usually expressed in a numerical way.

Social surveys

What is a survey?

A survey method involves both collection and analysis of data, usually by asking questions. Many 'cases' are studied; a case might be a person, a household, a school, a crime, etc. Data is quantified and analysed in a systematic way (often nowadays with the aid of IT). The survey can be used to test hypotheses by seeking correlations between variables such as religion and divorce or gender and educational success.

Types of comparative survey

→ **Longitudinal surveys** follow the development of the same subjects over a long period of time.
→ **Historical surveys** compare behaviour in different periods.
→ **Cross-sectional surveys** study different subjects, such as voters, at one moment in time, e.g. before an election.
→ **Cross-cultural surveys** study different societies and are useful in demonstrating that behaviours, such as gender roles, are not natural but are learned through socialization.

The sample survey

This involves selecting and studying a small proportion of the total population of subjects being researched. This saves time and money. If the sample is *representative*, the results can be *generalized* to the whole population. **The population** is all those who could be included in a study and all those whom the study claims to describe. As well as individuals, the population could be groups such as households. **The sampling frame** is the list of the population from which the sample is chosen.

Sampling methods are ways of choosing representative samples and include the following. **Random samples** are chosen so that each person has an equal chance of being chosen. **Quota sampling** involves choosing people from a variety of relevant groups, usually reflecting their proportion in the population. **Stratified sampling** involves dividing up the population into different strata and choosing at random from within each group. This ensures better representation where the sample size is small. **Purposive sampling** involves deliberately choosing an unrepresentative sample to test a hypothesis. **Snowball sampling** involves getting respondents to introduce other subjects. It is not representative but allows access to secretive groups.

Checkpoint 1

What social characteristics would you expect to correlate with
(a) voting Labour
(b) educational success?

Checkpoint 2

Identify two advantages of longitudinal surveys.

Examples

The NCB study filmed as *7 up* and *7 plus 7* is a continuing *longitudinal* study begun in the 1950s.
   Durkheim's study of suicide was both a *cross-cultural* and *historical* survey (see page 150).
   The national survey of sexual attitudes and lifestyles was a *cross-sectional* survey.

Action point

Make notes on types of sampling and choose examples to illustrate their use.

Evaluation of the techniques for data collection used in surveys

Questionnaires

These are lists of pre-set questions used to measure attitudes, opinions and behaviour. They can be issued face to face or distributed by post to a large number of widely dispersed people, e.g. *National survey of sexual attitudes and lifestyles, 1992*.

Uses

→ They can be pre-coded and **standardized** allowing easy analysis and use for **comparative research**.

→ They are easier than interviews to replicate later, which makes them more *scientific*.

→ Subjects may prefer to answer questions in private.

Limitations

→ They are artificial and do not record real behaviour.

→ Subjects may give expected answers or even lie.

→ Questions can be worded to produce the desired results.

→ The researcher can't be certain who completes them if it is done in private.

→ They are artificial situations so produce invalid data.

Interviews

Normally face-to-face conversations, they can be more or less structured and formal. Surveys tend to use structured interviews to produce easily quantified reliable data, e.g. Dobash and Dobash on domestic violence.

Uses

→ Interviewers can explain and probe.

→ In-depth interviews can explore sensitive topics (e.g. domestic violence) by encouraging subjects to talk.

→ Interviewing is quicker than (participant) observation and focuses on the topic to be researched.

→ Informal interviews allow subjects to talk about what they think is important and are more qualitative than quantitative.

Limitations

→ **Interviewer bias** can distort results.

→ Interviews, especially informal ones, are time-consuming and difficult to analyse.

→ Informal interviews are difficult to replicate and unscientific.

Secondary data

Sociologists can analyse data collected by somebody else, e.g. Durkheim on suicide.

Checkpoint 3

Identify one disadvantage of using postal questionnaires.

Examiner's secret

Interviews can be discussed in questions on qualitative methods (when they can be compared to observation) as well as those on surveys (where they can be compared to questionnaires).

Checkpoint 4

Identify an advantage and a disadvantage of using interviews to study sensitive topics.

The jargon

Interviewer bias occurs when the presence of an interviewer affects the response from the subject. There is evidence that the class, ethnicity and gender of interviewers influence responses.

Links

The uses and limitations of secondary data, particularly statistics, are discussed on pages 12–13.

Exam question   answer: page 16

Examine the advantages and limitations of using questionnaires. (25 min)

9

Qualitative methods

Qualitative methods can collect both objective and subjective data, which is descriptive rather than numerical. Exam questions tend to focus on participant observation, although you may have the opportunity to discuss the use of unstructured interviews as a qualitative method.

Much sociological research depends on observation.

Observation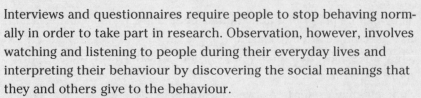

Interviews and questionnaires require people to stop behaving normally in order to take part in research. Observation, however, involves watching and listening to people during their everyday lives and interpreting their behaviour by discovering the social meanings that they and others give to the behaviour.

Where the involvement of the sociologist with the subjects is minimal we call it observation. Where involvement is deliberate we call it participant observation.

Uses and advantages of participant observation

→ Subjects are studied in their natural environment to produce detailed accounts of everyday life.
→ Sociologists can see what is important to the subjects rather than imposing their views through questions.
→ Sociologists can share the experiences of their subjects, enabling them to discover motives and understand the meaning the subject gives their behaviour. This is why interactionist sociologists favour PO.
→ PO, particularly when covert, minimizes the possibility of subjects changing their behaviour because they are being observed.
→ Covert PO allows the sociologist access to groups who might exclude outsiders because their behaviour is illegal, shameful or secret, e.g. research on gangs, freemasons and sects.

Problems and disadvantages of participant observation

In some cases, what is seen as an advantage by supporters of PO (particularly interactionists) is seen as a problem by critics who prefer scientific methods. The first five points below deal with these **theoretical issues:**

→ it is more scientific to be detached from your subjects and study objective behaviour from the outside
→ researchers may change the behaviour of their subjects
→ sharing the subject's point of view may encourage bias
→ PO cannot be replicated and the findings verified or refuted – this makes it unscientific

Links

Unstructured interviews are discussed on page 9.

The jargon

Participant observation involves joining in with subjects in order to understand as well as describe their everyday lives.

Checkpoint 1

Give one argument for and one argument against the view that a sociologist can successfully share the experiences of the subjects.

Example

J. Patrick covertly studied a Glasgow gang using a false name.

Checkpoint 2

Why can't research involving PO be repeated?

→ groups studied are unlikely to be a representative sample of the population.

There are also *practical problems* with PO:

→ PO is time-consuming
→ it is difficult to get access to some groups; sociologists have often studied low-class and low-status groups rather than the powerful
→ when doing covert PO, access may be limited to groups where the researcher can pass as a subject; thus class, ethnicity, age and gender may limit opportunities
→ the researcher will need to learn the language and behaviour of subjects to fit in with them, as well as to understand them
→ covert PO makes it difficult to ask questions and record behaviour; few studies have employed the secret electronic surveillance techniques favoured by some journalists and the police.

Finally PO, and particularly covert PO, raises a number of moral or *ethical issues*:

→ researchers may witness, or even be expected to participate in criminal behaviour
→ deception of subjects who are studied without their consent is generally seen as unethical research
→ the professional codes of conduct for medical, psychological and sociological research normally require consent of subjects
→ information may be published about subjects' private lives without their consent.

Checkpoint 3

How might sociologists gain access to groups of people with different social characteristics from the sociologist in order to study them?

Examiner's secret

PO is not the only covert method and not all PO is covert.

Checkpoint 4

How might a sociologist overcome the ethical problems of studying criminals?

Examiner's secret

The rules for coursework are likely to prohibit research where subjects cannot give consent.

Exam questions answers: page 17

1 What are the differences between studying the social behaviour of people and studying natural objects such as rocks, plants and animals? (12 min)

2 Explain the *practical* advantages and disadvantages of using covert research methods. (20 min)

3 Explain and discuss the view that participant observation can be criticized on ethical grounds. (12 min)

Secondary data

Secondary data is information that has been collected not by the sociologists conducting the research but by others. It exists in either a quantitative or a qualitative form.

Evaluation of the usefulness of secondary data is based on *practical concerns* about their reliability, completeness and accuracy and *theoretical concerns* about their validity (does the data tell us more about the people and processes involved in producing it than it tells us about the research subject?).

Types of secondary data

→ *Organizational records* – employers, schools, churches and other organizations keep records which may be of use to sociologists. R. Revans compared the level of morale and effectiveness of five hospitals by using their records of absenteeism, wastage of student nurses during training, labour turnover and patient recovery rates.

→ *Mass media output* – occurs in the form of print, TV, radio, recorded music, etc. Sociologists have been particularly interested in representation of gender and ethnicity and 'the news'. Analysis can be quantitative or qualitative.

→ *Diaries, autobiographies and other personal documents* – have been used to discover the lives and views of people in the past. The complex relationship between class, race and gender can be examined by reading accounts of domestic labour written by employers, owners, servants and slaves.

→ *Published sociological research* – can be used to compare the present with the past or to study a large number of subjects spread over a large area when time and/or funds are limited. G. P. Murdock argued the nuclear family was universal on the basis of other people's studies of about 250 societies.

Social statistics

These are produced by a variety of bodies. Those produced by the government are called *official statistics* and cover areas such as births, marriages, divorces, deaths, crime, employment, unemployment, educational achievement and health.

Non-governmental organizations produce statistics on some of the above and also on church attendance, racial disadvantage and job opportunities for women.

Evaluation – advantages of using social statistics

→ **Positivist sociologists** favour the use of scientific methods. They assume statistics can describe aspects of social life such as the extent of crime, the number of broken marriages or the suicide rate.

Check the net

www.upmystreet.com provides access to a range of data about where you live.

Checkpoint 1

Suggest two ways in which school records could be used in sociological research.

Checkpoint 2

Identify and explain two problems associated with the use of personal documents.

The jargon

Domestic labour refers to both paid and unpaid housework.

Links

Housework is discussed in the section on families and households. Nuclear families are discussed on page 34.

Examiner's secret

The usefulness of social statistics is a major issue in questions on several topics, including methods.

- Durkheim's study of suicide remains the model for research using official statistics.
- Statistics can be used in comparative surveys to test a hypothesis, e.g. Durkheim's *Suicide*, or to generate a new hypothesis such as those found in the Black Report once social class differences in health had been established.
- Using statistics allows sociologists to remain detached from their subjects and thus avoid influencing their behaviour.
- The data are reliable (others can use them to test conclusions).
- Statistics may be the only available source of data, as in historical studies of the family.
- Statistics provide a cheap, speedy source of large amounts of data, which nowadays can be easily analysed using computers.

Evaluation – disadvantages of using social statistics

Postivists do not accept the use of official statistics uncritically. They are concerned with the technical problems of gathering and interpreting data which may affect the accuracy of research.

Interactionists question the **validity** rather than the **reliability** of statistics. They claim that statistics are not neutral descriptions of social life but the result of negotiations which lead to the definition of certain acts as crimes or suicides. Similarly, suicide statistics tell us about the work of coroners rather than suicides, and health statistics about decisions made by doctors rather than patterns of disease.

The problem of crime statistics ●●●

Crime statistics may tell us more about the police and courts than about criminals. They may be incomplete as not all crimes are reported:

- victims may be afraid or ashamed
- victims may see reporting crime as a waste of time because the offence was trivial or there is little chance of detection
- victims are unaware or unconcerned, e.g. theft at work
- the crime is 'victimless' and thus requires police detection, e.g. drug abuse and prostitution.

This last point is important to interactionists who argue that the crime figures are the result of police actions and do not reflect real rates of crime. For example huge increases in the number of sex offences have been recorded as a result of decisions to place undercover policemen in public lavatories to catch homosexuals.

Checkpoint 3

Explain how a comparative study can be used to test a hypothesis.

Links

See page 34 for Lazlett and Anderson's use of statistics on the family.

Links

Questioning the validity of crime figures is a central part of the interactionist approach to deviance, see pages 144–5.

Checkpoint 4

If official statistics on reported crimes are not accurate, what alternative sources of data can be used to measure crime?

Exam question   answer: pages 17–18

Why do official statistics need to be used carefully? (20 min)

Choosing research methods

Bell and Newby's book *Doing Sociological Research,* asked contributors to describe how they *actually* undertook well-known pieces of research, (instead of asking how research *should be done*). The main issue is the extent to which sociologists' theoretical assumptions are a major influence on their view of validity and choice of methods.

Theoretical assumptions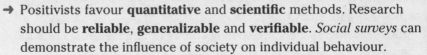

→ Positivists favour **quantitative** and **scientific** methods. Research should be **reliable**, **generalizable** and **verifiable**. *Social surveys* can demonstrate the influence of society on individual behaviour.
→ Interactionists favour **qualitative** methods which provide insights into the social meanings given to behaviour. This may involve **participant observation**.
→ Feminists often choose interactionist methods to allow women to speak for themselves.

Practical influences

Each method has its uses and limitations, depending on the circumstances in which it is used:

→ participant observation requires access to groups of subjects
→ sample surveys must compromise between cost and representativeness
→ different types of interview can be compared on the basis of reliability and insight.

The topic being studied

→ Historical studies usually require use of secondary data.
→ Large-scale studies often use sample surveys (e.g. on voting behaviour) or employ secondary data (e.g. use census data).
→ Initially, studies of deviants often use participant observation; later this method can be followed up with interviews.
→ The study of nonliterate societies often involves participant observation because of the absence of written records and the need to learn new languages.

Ethical considerations

→ Covert research may involve deception and invasion of privacy.
→ Studying deviants may involve joining in or having knowledge of crime.
→ Experiments, interviews and participant observation all involve interfering with the lives of subjects (these arguments can be countered if the research is intended to benefit the subjects/public).

The jargon

Generalizable means that the results of a study of a sample can be applied to a wider population. *Verifiable* means findings can be checked and proved right or wrong.

Checkpoint 1

Identify two types of subjects who might be difficult to access for research and explain your answers.

Links

See pages 8–11 for further details on these three methods of research.

Checkpoint 2

How might sociological research benefit
(a) the subjects
(b) the public?

Chance and inspiration

There are famous stories of chance scientific discoveries, and similar events have influenced sociological research. Malinowski was on his way to Australia when the Great War began. In order to avoid internment as an enemy alien, he stopped in the Trobriand Islands and began a lengthy participant observation study.

The sociology of sociologists

There are sociological explanations of the behaviour of sociologists, just as there are for any other occupation or social group. Bell and Newby thought that money and the organization where the sociologist was working were important factors.

Doing feminist research

Oakley's *Sociology of Housework (1974)* pioneered the view that actually doing sociological research involved feminist issues. This view has been developed by other feminist sociologists who are critical of conventional research, which they call 'malestream'. Their feminist alternative has the following characteristics:

→ women are subjects
→ gender relationships are important and are based on power
→ women are the researchers and treat subjects as equals
→ there is no best method but women subjects should be allowed to speak for themselves
→ 'malestream' sociology is not value-free and feminist research should try and improve women's lives.

Conclusion

Critical evaluation of sociological methods should involve consideration of theoretical, practical and ethical issues. Studies of large numbers of subjects are more representative and reliable but lack depth, insight and, some say, validity. Minimizing personal involvement reduces the problem of contamination but limits depth of understanding. High levels of control make research more reliable but less natural. There is no best method, and using more than one method may allow sociologists to check their findings (sometimes called triangulation) and combine the insights of both large-scale quantitative scientific research and small-scale, in-depth interactionist research.

Checkpoint 3

What do you think are typical social characteristics of sociologists? Explain your answer.

Example

Funding is usually easier to get for projects that seem useful, e.g. deal with social problems.

"I did not regard it as reasonable to adopt a purely exploitative attitude to interviewees as a source of data . . . Sisterhood an . . . important concept . . . demanded that women re-evaluate . . . their relationship with one another."

Oakley 1984

Checkpoint 4

How might sociological research benefit women?

Exam question answer: page 18

Examine the relationship between a sociologist's theoretical approach and her/his choice of research methods. (20 min)

15

Answers
Sociological methods

The scientific approach

Checkpoints

1 Discrimination in recruitment is the effect (DV). Race is the cause (IV). You can show that not getting a job is the result of racial discrimination by controlling other factors that might affect recruitment, such as qualifications or experience. Use black and white applicants who are otherwise identical (same age, education, experience, etc). W. Daniel (1968) did similar research on jobs, housing and services.

2 People don't behave naturally in laboratory situations. They may try to meet the expectations of the researcher.

3 Social causes of crime might include the level of unemployment, the amount of inequality in society, the decline of religious values, etc. Individual reasons might include taking risks, wanting excitement, desire for illicit sexual behaviour, etc.

   Social causes of divorce include the changing role of women and a decline in religion. Individual reasons may be sexual desire for another, incompatibility or domestic violence.

4 Some methods put the subject in an artificial situation. Subjects may try to conform to the sociologist's expectations or try to conceal shameful or deviant behaviour. This presents problems to sociologists as they may find there is nothing to observe or that they are unable to deduce cause and effect relationships as behaviour may be influenced by the sociologist.

Exam question

If the conventional definition of science is accepted (i.e. defining science in terms of the 'scientific method') then some sociology tries to be scientific. You need to explain: what positivists study (social facts); what their preferred methods are (comparative survey); and what their aims are (to produce testable theories).

   Outline the problems sociologists face if they try to use scientific methods, e.g. theoretical problems – interactionist criticism of what positivists study and how they study it.

   Conclusion, e.g. some sociologists think it's worth trying to be scientific because of the superiority of scientifically testable knowledge. Others do not.

   The definition of science can be questioned. Science may not be superior knowledge but socially accepted knowledge.

Quantitative methods

Checkpoints

1 'Social facts' are often identified by survey research. In addition, a correlation does not necessarily indicate a causal relationship.

(a) Labour voters are more likely to be found in the working class, amongst ethnic minorities, trade unionists, the Scots and Welsh, etc.

(b) Educational success correlates with higher social class, gender (boys did better until the 1970s now girls do better by most measures).

2 Following the same group over time removes the need to find two similar samples, i.e. it removes the need to control social characteristics of subjects, which might be extraneous variables.

   The life chances of the sample can be measured over time and correlated with a range of other factors.

3 The major disadvantage is probably the low response rate which affects the probable representativeness of the sample selected, e.g. those most interested in the survey are most likely to respond.

4 One advantage is that skilful interviewers may get their subjects to relax and reveal their true feelings. A disadvantage is that people may be embarrassed, e.g. in a sex survey.

Exam question

You should explain what a questionnaire is and how they are used in social surveys.

   Uses and advantages can be examined by explaining the value of scientific approaches (verifiable, reliable and generalizable) and quantitative methods. Refer to large-scale studies, the study of social facts and links to structuralist views of society.

   Contrast questionnaires favourably with other methods of data collection used in surveys, e.g. use of secondary data or interviews.

   Introduce the idea of limitations by linking to the previous paragraph and pointing out the relative advantages of interviews as a technique for gathering data. Other practical limitations might refer to low response rates, problems with questions, the experimenter effect, etc.

   So far you have assumed surveys are a good method and the scientific approach is desirable. Question this by employing interactionist criticism of scientific approaches. You can mention the advantages of qualitative methods – natural, valid, etc.

Qualitative methods

Checkpoints

1 *For*: PO is a skill. Those who have learned it will learn the language and meanings their subjects give to behaviour and be able to empathize. Sometimes sociologists do 'real' participant observation and study people like themselves

Against: Sociologists are not really the same as their subjects and their motives for joining in are to observe rather than participate.

2 PO can't be repeated because:
- another researcher may experience the same situation differently
- the same researcher may encounter a different situation
- researchers will have different impacts on those they study
- the recording of what is observed tends to be selective and impressionistic rather than systematic.

3 If the study is covert, the sociologist may try a disguise (Griffin dyed his skin black, Pat Moore disguised herself as an old lady). Covert PO can also be carried out by someone who has an acceptable reason to join in. Beynon pushed a broom to gain access to Ford assembly line workers. Overt observers can make themselves unthreatening and gain trust (Eileen Barker and the Moonies).

4 Ned Polsky made it clear to criminals that he did not want to learn of crimes to be committed, and studied their everyday non-criminal lives. The sociologist might study those committing petty crimes, of which they do not really disapprove, e.g. Young on drug takers. The evidence discovered may benefit society by helping crime prevention. Janet Foster has helped us understand both crime and policing through PO.

Exam questions

1 The behaviour of rocks, plants and animals appears to follow consistent and universal laws. They respond to external stimuli in a predictable way. The scientist who studies nature is studying what is objective, i.e. it is observable and measurable.

Some human behaviour is natural and follows the same pattern as other objects in nature. Socio-biologists and evolutionary psychologists see a large proportion of human behaviour as natural. Sociologists do not, particularly interactionists who study social action (i.e. social meanings given to behaviour).

Humans are reflexive – they think about their behaviour, are able to be aware of what others think about them and can choose to change their behaviour.

2 The most common covert method is PO. Other covert methods include covert non-PO, perhaps using video, and experiments where the subjects are unaware of research, e.g. Daniel on race discrimination.

The *practical advantages* of using covert research methods include:

- getting access to exclusive, illegal, or shameful activities
- researcher won't change people's behaviour

The *practical disadvantages* include:
- access being limited to situations where the researcher can pass as a subject; social characteristics which impose limits may include gender, age, race and class
- discovery may lead to the end of the study or even danger
- opportunities to ask questions and record data without arousing suspicion are limited

3 The following ethical issues may arise:
- invasion of *privacy* without informed consent (can be overcome is research is overt)
- *publication* of embarrassing data (can be overcome by disguising identity of subjects)
- often it is the relatively strong who invade the lives of the relatively weak (Becker says this gives the 'underdog' the chance to have their say)
- Humphreys justified covert PO by saying findings were useful; Polsky disputed this and says data can be gained by declaring your identity

Secondary data

Checkpoints

1 School records of pupils' achievements can be used in comparative surveys to test the relationship between results and other factors such as class sizes, social class of pupils, etc.

School attendance records can be used to test hypotheses explaining truancy.

2 They provide selective and *objective* data, which cannot be generalized from, as it is *not representative*.

They cannot be verified by repeating the research so they are *not reliable*.

3 A hypothesis is a tentative explanation – an untested guess at the causes of the social phenomena being studied.

A comparative survey can investigate the link between IV (cause) and DV effect. It is the equivalent of an experiment. Instead of the researcher changing the IV and observing the DV(s) he compares people who differ in terms of the IV. For example, you could test the relationship between ethnicity and educational achievement by comparing the performance of two different groups who were similar in other relevant respects such as class, age gender. (These would be EVs, which you are controlling.)

4 Alternative sources of crime data are:
- victim studies, e.g. British crime survey
- self-report studies where subjects report on types and extent of crimes committed
- observation and PO

Exam question

Positivists see caution as necessary to ensure representative data is collected accurately and fully. Illustrate this with reference to crime statistics. Interactionists are more concerned with the validity of statistics. Explain the argument that they are the result of interaction between those who label behaviour and the subjects being described. Use examples of police creating crime statistics.

Choosing research methods

Checkpoints

1 • Women from an ethnic minority, work in their homes and who may not speak English.
  • Children who have been abused and mistrust adults.
2 (a) Publication of research may help to define the experience of disadvantaged subjects as a social problem and encourage policies to help them.
  (b) Understanding a social problem such as football hooliganism or racial discrimination may encourage a solution and so benefit the public.
3 Sociologists tend to be middle-class in origin and/or destination because they are well qualified and have had a lengthy higher education.

The political views of sociologists in Britain tend to be left-wing rather than right-wing. This is because sociology is a critical discipline and Britain is a capitalist society. Older sociologists have been beneficiaries of the welfare state.

4 You can offer similar answers to the ones given for Checkpoint 2. Feminist research can identify and explain gender inequality and uncover latent problems such as domestic violence. It can provide a voice for disadvantaged women. It can raise the consciousness of women who do not understand their position in a patriarchal society.

Exam question

A theoretical approach is one influence on the choice of methods.

You should explain why positivists, interactionists and feminists tend to choose particular methods.

Explain, with examples, that there are exceptional cases. (Goldthorpe and Lockwood used a survey to research the motives for social action of workers.)

Explain, with examples, that there are other influences on the choice of methods.

Culture and identity

This section covers very traditional sociological concerns, such as socialization. It also contains some of the major debates from the 1990s about the existence and significance of living in a media-saturated postmodern society. This is no longer a distinct topic in the AQA specification but the concepts and theories should be used throughout your programme of study, particularly with regard to gender, ethnicity and the mass media. The concept of socialization is central to the study of the family, education and religion.

Exam themes

→ The different explanations of socialization and the acquisition of identity

→ Different views on the existence of a mass culture

→ The relative importance of social class and other sources of identity

→ The postmodernist view of popular culture

Topic checklist

O AS ● A2	AQA Sociology	OCR Sociology	EDEXCEL Social Policy
Introduction to culture and identity	O	O	
Theories of culture and identity	O	O	
Sources of identity	O	●	
Types of culture	O	O	

Introduction to culture and identity

Sociology offers explanations as to how humans learn to be separate individuals within a society.

Check the net

The very existence of the www is a significant part of the postmodernist case. Try *www.adbusters.org* a (very) good critical insight into the role of advertising and global capitalism. It also has a postmodern flavour, demonstrated in the way ads are doctored to make a point.

Examiner's secrets

You must be able to *define* and *explain* these concepts.
    You should use them to interpret the items in data response questions and apply them when answering questions.

Checkpoint 1

Give an example of how consumer goods are used:
(a) as status symbols
(b) to make statements about our identities (who we think we are)

Checkpoint 2

List two other social groups which may form subcultures.

Action point

List some of your social statuses. Describe the role associated with each. (Think about family, school, work, etc.)

Key concepts

The topic of culture and identity introduces important terms and concepts that help provide answers to some of the fundamental questions sociologists ask:

→ How do we explain people's behaviour?
→ What are the social meanings we give to people's actions?
→ What is the relationship between the individual and society?

Culture

Culture is the whole way of life of a social group. It includes language, customs, norms (rules) and values.

The relationship between culture and social structure

Culture has become important in explaining the different ways that individuals are influenced by structural relationships, such as in the family or at work. For example, people in different societies are all members of families (the family is a structural relationship) but the relationships between spouses and parents and children varies according to cultural differences.

Material culture

This refers to the objects produced and used in a society, including tools, which we use to produce things, and consumer goods, which may be used as status symbols or to make statements about our identities.

Subculture

This is an identifiable group whose members share a culture which is different from the wider host society. Subcultures may be based on ethnicity, age or other social characteristics.

Roles

Roles refer to the expected behaviour associated with a particular status (social position), e.g. gender roles are how women and men are expected to behave in a particular society.

Socialization

This is the process of learning the culture of a society. Sociologists believe most human behaviour is learned rather than biologically determined. It may be learned from informal primary socialization within families or formal secondary socialization in schools. Socialization continues after childhood, e.g. in university, work and through the media. We do not uncritically and passively accept all we are taught. Lessons may be rejected or adapted – culture provides continuity in society but it also changes.

Identity

A sense of self develops as children grow up and see themselves as separate individuals in their families and in society. It enables us to:

→ see ourselves as others see us
→ imagine what it is like to be someone else
→ anticipate the consequences of our behaviour on others.

Postmodernism has made identity an important concept by examining the ways in which individuals get their sense of self by identifying with a range of social groups based on, e.g. age, gender or ethnicity.

The main sociological debates

Is there a dominant culture?

Structuralist sociologists, Marxist, functionalist or feminist, tend to agree that societies are dominated by a single culture, while recognizing the existence of minority subcultures which differ from the dominant culture. Postmodernism celebrates cultural diversity and sees individuals making choices about identity by joining a variety of social groups and through consumption.

How do we respond to cultural diversity?

In Britain ethnic diversity may be creating a new culture or may be seen as a threat encouraging racism. In some nations, e.g. former Yugoslavia, renewed ethnic identity has led to the atrocity of 'ethnic cleansing'.

What are the main sources of identity?

The reduced influence of social class is a major feature of postmodernism, which identifies a range of sources and focuses on consumption of cultural products rather than production of manufactured products.

Is identity chosen or imposed?

Again there is a debate between structuralists, who emphasize the imposition of culture on individuals, and interactionists and postmodernists, who describe how individuals make choices and construct their own identities. Giddens' theory of **structuration** attempts to combine both perspectives.

How have sociologists explained socialization?

Marxists see the dominant ruling class culture being imposed on individuals and making them falsely conscious. Feminists see the dominant patriarchal culture being imposed on both women and men and making them falsely conscious. Functionalists see socialization as the process of learning a consensual culture which integrates society. Interactionists see socialization as a process of negotiation and labelling.

Exam question   answer: page 28

What is socialization? Explain two ways in which people are socialized. (20 min)

Checkpoint 3

Apart from social class, age, gender and ethnicity (which are discussed on pages 24 and 25) name two other sources of identity.

Examiner's secrets

You should be able to assess arguments and evidence used in these major debates.

Checkpoint 4

Explain, with examples, the meaning of multiple social identities.

Theories of culture and identity

There are different theoretical approaches to culture and identity. The first three summarized below are largely structuralist theories; the others put more emphasis on individual actions and freedom of choice.

Links

An introduction to theories is found on page 3. A fuller account of all these theories can be found in the chapter on theory and methods. (pp. 167–175)

Functionalism

→ Culture is based on consensual (shared) values.
→ Socialization is the process of transmitting this culture.
→ Identities are created in families.
→ The main functions of the family are socialization of children and stabilizing of adult personalities.
→ Identity develops as individuals interact with others beyond the family.
→ Culture integrates society; individualism in modern society threatens integration.

Checkpoint 1

How do functionalists explain the acquiring of gender identities?

Marxism

→ Economic production shapes cultural ideas.
→ Ideology is used to control the working class by keeping them falsely conscious (ideology means ideas or beliefs that serve the interests of particular groups in society).
→ Consumerism is the ideology of late capitalism.
→ Gramsci emphasized the importance of culture for maintaining ruling class domination; the struggle over culture is central to his work and that of the CCCS. (A group of sociologists who studied culture and media, see page 24.)
→ Cultural production is in the hands of the capitalist ruling class who produce for profit and seek to maintain social control.

Checkpoint 2

How is the ideology of consumerism transmitted to the working class?

Feminism

→ Feminists argue that popular culture has contributed to the domination of women by men.
→ Popular culture reinforces the patriarchal ideology, which defines femininity in terms of the housewife-mother role.
→ Other media stereotypes are discussed on page 76.
→ These stereotypes encourage both men and women to have limited expectations of women.
→ Women's bodies may be presented as 'objects' in popular culture for entertainment or to sell consumer goods.
→ A more optimistic view shows the way in which feminist ideas have become increasingly well-known and accepted in our culture and used to create new images of strong women.

Action point

List examples of representations of women in the media that challenge existing stereotypes.

Social action theories

→ Culture cannot exist independently of individuals.
→ **Symbolic interactionism** is a type of action theory that places great emphasis on the development and presentation of the self.
→ Identity is not imposed by society and is more or less permanent.
→ Individuals see themselves as they think others see them.
→ Identity is developed through interaction, and changes according to the individual's perception of a social situation.

Goffman's study *Asylums* describes how inmates of psychiatric hospitals have their identities stripped away so that a new self can be moulded to fit the needs of the institution. Many inmates resist this either overtly or by staying out of trouble but not accepting the rules.

Checkpoint 3

Suggest two ways in which an institution such as a psychiatric hospital might strip away the identity of a patient.

Structuration

Giddens has developed the idea of structuration to show that the major principles of structuralist and action theories can be combined. He argues that structures only exist because human actions have created them and only continue to exist and develop because of actions. He also acknowledges the influence of existing structures, e.g. language, on actions. English existed before any of us were born but we use it and can choose to use it in different ways, e.g. to challenge or reinforce ethnic and gender inequalities.

Postmodern theory and popular culture

A postmodern society?

A major feature of postmodern society is uncertainty caused by globalization, technological change (particularly ICT), the dissolving of the old class structure and the development of a media-saturated society. Uncertainty has resulted in:

The jargon

Globalization means societies have become related to each other on a world-wide scale (see page 136).

→ the **decentring of identity** The old sources of identity (e.g. family, occupation, religion, nationality) have been eroded; there are no stable replacements, only consumerism, which emphasises the individual and prevents new collective identities developing.
→ the **emergence of a postmodern popular culture** The distinction between high and popular culture has gone. There is an emphasis on style rather than content. Image is consumed. There is confusion over time and space. Videos and films are made without plot or narrative. Our sense of place and distance is provided by the media.

Checkpoint 4

Explain with examples how our sense of time and distance might be influenced by the media.

Exam question answer: page 28

Compare and contrast two sociological accounts of how individuals acquire their identities through the process of socialization. (20 min)

Sources of identity

There are four main social characteristics that shape our identities.

Gender and sexuality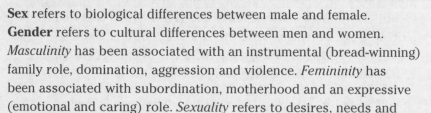

Sex refers to biological differences between male and female. **Gender** refers to cultural differences between men and women. *Masculinity* has been associated with an instrumental (bread-winning) family role, domination, aggression and violence. *Femininity* has been associated with subordination, motherhood and an expressive (emotional and caring) role. *Sexuality* refers to desires, needs and behaviour that are seen as specifically sexual.

Gender and the ways we express sexuality are socially constructed and influenced by culture as well as nature. Gender roles and sexual preferences vary from time to time and place to place. Feminine and masculine identities vary between social groups, and have changed over time. However, in any specific time and place there is a tendency to define existing norms and roles as 'natural' (fixed by biology) and thus 'normal' (the way people should behave). For example homosexuality as a separate identity (rather than just a pattern of desires and behaviours) emerged in Europe only after it was seen as a medical abnormality caused by biology or upbringing.

Age

Age also appears to be a purely biological characteristic. Different social meanings are given to chronological age, e.g. the old may enjoy high status in traditional societies yet be seen as dependent in modern societies.

Youth culture and subcultures

During the 1950s sociologists and others began to write about a distinctive **youth culture**, which was based on:

→ a generation gap between young people and their parents
→ the structural position of youth between childhood and the adult world of work and marriage
→ the growth in the newly affluent society of a distinctive youth market

There were also biological and psychological explanations.

During the 1960s and 1970s the focus shifted to deviant sub-cultures with a particular interest in style and fashion. The Centre for Contemporary Cultural Studies (CCCS) research emphasized the influence of social class (e.g. Hall and Jefferson 1976). S. Cohen's work on mods and rockers took a more interactionist approach to moral panics about youth.

During the 1980s studies shifted from exotic deviant youth to ordinary youth. Reasons for changing concerns included the following:

" . . . male sexuality is seen as a force or natural energy that seeks release . . . It is a bit like a missile; once launched there is no stopping it."

While female sexuality is seen as:

" . . . passive . . . submissive . . . associated with motherhood and reproduction".

(S. Lees 1986)

Checkpoint 1

Identify four different influences on our gender identities.

Example

Until 1972 homosexuality was defined as mental illness in the USA.

Checkpoint 2

Explain two reasons why some old people in modern societies may see themselves as helpless and dependent.

Links

The impact of distinctive youth cultures and subcultures is examined in the Education and Deviance chapters.

→ high rates of youth unemployment replaced affluence
→ feminism encouraged the study of girl subcultures
→ ethnic minority youth was recognized as having distinctive identities shaped by the diverse influences of parents, school and racism
→ the interaction of gender, age, class and ethnicity was recognized

Postmodernist approaches in the 1990s have suggested that current youth subcultures have little to do with resistance but are based on superficial styles, often taken from the past and mixed in a playful way.

Ethnicity

Ethnicity is a characteristic of social groups, which gives individuals a sense of identity.

Ethnicity involves a sense of belonging to a group with a common culture (including values, customs, language and religion). British sociologists have written about ethnic inequality and '*racial*' *discrimination*. It is likely that racism has strengthened existing identities and created new ones:

→ old identities may be based on tradition and country of origin
→ new identities may combine previously diverse groups under the new labels of 'Asians' or 'black British' or 'blacks'.

The **mass media** and **popular culture** also influence new ethnic identities, which also involve age, gender and class.

Ethnic identity has become a global issue as nations have been fragmented on ethnic lines and the media have shown scenes of war and 'ethnic cleansing' in Europe and Africa.

Social class

Social class has been seen as the major influence on identity. Hoggart (1958) argued that mass entertainment had begun to erode the working-class culture that he valued so highly.

The importance of class has also been undermined by the 'discovery' of gender and ethnicity and by postmodernist interpretations of changes in production and consumption.

Working together shaped people's lives in the past and this produced distinct class cultures, which influenced family life, voting, attitudes to education, etc. People today are less likely to spend their whole lives in one occupational community. Therefore new influences on culture, in particular globalized media images, become more significant.

Example

Patterns of consumption are often used in marketing to distinguish social groups (e.g. the Pink pound spent by homosexual men). It is arguable whether consumption can define people's identities.

Example

A. McRobbie wrote of the role of girls' magazines in creating a bedroom-based subculture and feminine identity.
C. Griffin and S. Sharpe wrote of the effects of subcultures on education.
M. Fuller wrote about black girls in school and C. Butler about Asian girls.

Checkpoint 3

Explain how youth learns about past styles (apart from studying sociology!).

The jargon

Humans are a single species. *Race* is a biological term for a distinct subgroup of a species. Despite the fact that dividing humans into 'races' has little biological foundation, real or imagined physical characteristics have been given social meanings.

Checkpoint 4

Explain one argument for and one argument against the view that social class has become less important as a source of identity.

Exam question   answer: page 29

Discuss reasons why migrant groups often undergo a process of cultural change. (10 min)

Types of culture

The main focus in this examination of different types of culture is on the production and consumption of mass culture.

Folk culture

Folk culture is the traditional culture of ordinary people. We still use the term to describe folk music or dancing. Folk cultures united rural societies but the **division of labour** associated with industrialization threatened this.

High culture

This is the culture of the elite. High culture was defined in literary terms by academics, such as T. S. Elliot and F. R. Leavis, who thought it could only be appreciated by the elite minority. They feared the threat of a commercial mass culture that would destroy 'real' culture and undermine the position of the elite who create and transmit it.

Mass culture

The mass society
Industrialization brought about the rise of the modern world. In addition to the economic features of the modern world (mass production and mass consumption) there were cultural changes. The traditional thinking of premodern society was replaced by scientific thinking and folk culture was replaced by mass culture.

Mass culture
Unlike folk culture, which developed from ordinary people, mass culture is a commercial product imposed on the masses who can only choose to buy or not buy. The mass culture identified by left-wing critics in the 1930s included Hollywood films, popular music and pulp fiction.

Critics of mass culture
The defenders of high culture, who are described above, worked in the field of English Literature. They criticized mass culture from an elitist right-wing position.

Left-wing criticism has been much more influential in sociology. Marxist writers, known as the **Frankfurt school**, fled the mass society of Nazi Germany and witnessed the mass society based on mass consumption in the USA. They condemned the brutal totalitarian society in Germany but also the liberal political system of capitalist America. They argued that advertising and the mass media created a mass culture for profit, which had the effect of reinforcing the **false consciousness** of the working class.

The jargon

Division of labour means people do different jobs and jobs are broken down into small tasks.

"Popular entertainments included brawling, cock-fighting and public executions as well as morris dancing and folk singing."

Kirby et al. 1997 suggest that some people have a romanticized view of folk culture.

Checkpoint 1

Identify two differences between mass culture and folk culture.

Action point

List all the uses of the term *false consciousness* that you have come across so far.

An evaluation of the mass culture approach

The function of popular culture

Some functionalists point to the integrative effects of popular culture. The mass population can feel included in society by sharing popular culture such as soap operas and the broadcasting of 'important' events such as royal weddings. Popular culture might also help to include immigrants in a multicultural society, like religion in the USA.

Working-class culture: resistance through rituals

Sociologists from the CCCS argued that groups within the working class did not always accept the dominant ideology found in mass culture. Subculture, such as youth subcultures based on styles, resisted this domination in a symbolic way ('resistance though rituals'). This contrasts with Hoggart's view that mass entertainment, often American, was destroying a warm and supportive working-class culture.

Postmodernist criticism

Postmodernism does not just reject the existence of mass culture but also argues that the class domination that produced it has also disappeared. In a postmodern society, individuals can choose to consume whatever cultural products they want to (presumably only if they can afford it: FM radio may be cheap, going to the opera is not). Hoggart regretted the way in which radio stopped the working class singing round the piano and making their own music. In postmodern society new technologies have encouraged people to produce as well as consume cultural products, e.g. football and music 'fanzines' and the use of electronics to produce dance music.

Conclusions

→ The postmodern position on mass culture has not been accepted without challenge.
→ The orthodox Marxist view that culture is the result of economic forces has been challenged, first by neo-Marxists and then by postmodernist sociologists.
→ However, many sociologists continue to believe that we still live in a capitalist society and making consumer choices about cultural products is simply part of that system and does not challenge or change it.
→ 'Home-made' or street popular culture is often incorporated by capitalism to remove its threat and to make money.

Checkpoint 2

Identify two characteristics of popular culture.

Links

This view was applied to a number of usually male subcultures such as skinheads. See youth culture on page 24 and the answer to checkpoint 3 on page 29.

Checkpoint 3

Give one reason, apart from technological changes, why individuals are producers of culture.

Checkpoint 4

Give two examples of the incorporation of street culture by capitalism.

Exam question   answer: page 30

Assess the view that capitalism produces a mass culture. (20 min)

Answers
Culture and identity

Introduction to culture and identity

Checkpoints

1 (a) Consumer goods can be displayed to indicate wealth or importance, e.g. expensive cars, designer clothes.
   (b) Dress may be used to indicate an ethnic identity or commitment to religious belief, e.g. Sikh men wearing turbans.

2 • Occupational communities, particularly those who may be isolated from the mainstream, e.g. the coal-mining communities of the recent past.
   • Pupils in a school may divide into subcultures. Willis described a working-class male anti-school subculture in *Learning to Labour*.
   (You could also mention deviant subcultures, subcultures based on religion, sexual preference, political views, etc.)

3 Religion, disability, occupation, nationality, parenthood, leisure activities and consumption may provide people with a sense of identity.

4 This is a postmodernist idea that developed to suggest that traditional sources of identity, particularly social class, had been undermined by social change. The concept of multiple social identities suggests that individuals see themselves in a number of different ways depending on the situations they find themselves in. The new identities may combine characteristics such as gender and ethnicity in new ways. Identification with ethnic groups within Britain has created new views of nationality such as British Asian. Some professional footballers may be able to discover a new identity when they choose which of four UK teams to represent.

Exam question

First define socialization in terms of learning culturally defined behaviour and contrast the process with biological influences on behaviour.

Argue that there are different explanations of socialization with similarities and differences in approach, e.g. Marxist, functionalist and feminist theories.

Choose and explain two ways, such as primary socialization in the family, formal education, religion or media. If you choose education you could discuss the impact of 'hidden curriculum' on socialization.

Theories of culture and identity

Checkpoints

1 They are learned in families. This is unlikely to be through formal teaching. Children may imitate the same sex parent and will be rewarded for appropriate behaviour.

2 The main means of transmission is advertising, although similar lessons may be learned in home, school and work.

3 • Taking away personal possessions, including clothes, and substituting some sort of uniform.
   • Taking away the patient's autonomy by controlling eating and sleeping times.

4 News events may be transmitted from overseas in real time. This undermines our understanding of distance.
   Stories may not follow a linear time sequence but use flashbacks, combine fiction with real historical events, or self-consciously deal with time travel.

Exam question

Organize your answer using two of the different perspectives explained in this section.
• Functionalism emphasizes what is done to a relatively passive child who learns roles and identity which conform to consensual values.
• Symbolic interactionism will see the actor as more active in acquiring an identity, see identities as more fluid and less fixed.
• Both would be criticized by Marxists for underestimating the importance of power to impose roles.
• Both might be criticized by feminists for paying insufficient attention to the importance of patriarchy.
• The two theories can be brought closer together by using Giddens' concept of structuration.

Sources of identity

Checkpoints

1 • family
   • school
   • workplace
   • mass media
   • religion
   Choose four from the above list. All of these influences are discussed in the relevant chapters in this book.

2 • It is customary to retire at 60–65 and this may make old people economically dependent on state benefits. Work may define the identity of men in particular and loss of work may undermine self-esteem.
   • Physical changes associated with ageing are often socially defined as ill-health.

3 Postmodernists stress the importance of the media in creating social reality. (Media images may recreate a past that never existed, e.g. the film *Grease* and the TV drama *Heartbeat* have reshaped idealized views and memories of 1950s America and 1960s Britain.)
   MTV and adverts have recycled styles and music and given new meanings to styles and fashions.

An example: Dr. Marten's boots, were – and still are – workwear, they were adopted by 1970s skinheads as weapons and perhaps as symbolic reminders of a lost masculine working-class culture. They have subsequently been remixed as gay fashion, goth, then grunge footwear and later catwalk chic. In 1998 they became sponsors of West Ham United football shirts with no overt reference to their past association with hooligans who were made to remove these 'weapons' when entering the football ground.

4 *For*: Most varieties of feminism assert that gender differences are at least as important as social class as sources of identity. Many feminists will see social class (and ethnicity) interacting with gender as an influence on the formation of identity (or identities).

Against: Marxists have rejected the postmodernist view that identity is a question of choice and still see strong structural and cultural influences on identity. Social class is seen as the major influence.

Exam question

Choose about four of the following reasons:

- The effects of different agents of socialization – education, mass media, youth subcultures. Most of these have a national character although they may be specific to an ethnic group or groups, e.g. religious education.
- They may experience racism and asserting a version of their traditional culture is a form of resistance.
- Consumerism.
- The move from rural to urban life. Most Bangladeshi immigrants live in big cities, many came from rural backgrounds.
- The move from traditional to a modern or arguably postmodern society.
- The impact of western ideas, e.g. feminism and its impact on family life.

Examiner's secrets

You only have ten minutes. You do not have to explain a long list of reasons. It makes sense to choose distinctive reasons and also to attempt to show that the process of change and the development of different identities is a complex process.

Types of culture

Checkpoints

1 Choose two of the following:
- Folk culture is characteristic of preindustrial rural society. Mass culture is a feature of modern industrial capitalist society.

- Folk culture is produced by participants. Mass culture is consumed by a passive audience.
- Folk culture is produced within a family, community or small locality. Mass culture is centrally produced by capitalist enterprises or the state.

2 Choose two of the following:
- Popular culture was distinguished from high culture or art.
- Popular culture is consumed by large numbers of people in society.
- Popular culture may represent resistance to imposed culture – rock music and street fashions.

3 • People don't like what's commercially available, e.g. there may be no broadcasting of ethnic music.
- Resistance to authority/capitalism, e.g. pirate radio or samizdat literature which was illegally produced and distributed in communist Eastern Europe.
- Need to satisfy creative/artistic impulses.

4 Incorporation means that businesses and government in capitalist societies use, rather than try to suppress, street culture in order to make money and/or neutralize a threat.
- Home-made punk clothing and piercing were quickly commercialized and sold in shops.
- Dance music, which was produced, performed and enjoyed in uncontrolled premises, was taken up by mainstream music publishers and organizers of licensed commercial events.
- Hip hop music and clothes which emerged from the black ghettos of the inner-city USA were later commercially exploited on a global scale.

Exam question

The question suggests that there is a single 'view' that capitalism produces mass culture. This is not so. An answer can contain at least two conflicting views on capitalism producing mass culture.

1 The Frankfurt school neo-Marxist explanation which condemned both:
- the state propaganda of Nazi Germany
- the alienation caused by the false needs which support consumer capitalism in the USA.

2 The elitist conservative view which sees capitalism as a threat to high culture.

Assessment can be based on the postmodernist view that the old structures of authority have disappeared and capitalism produces a variety of consumer cultures rather than a mass culture.

The *CCCS* work on the use of culture as a form of resistance to cultural domination can also be included.

Families and households

The traditional view of sociologists and the general public has been that the family provides benefits for members and serves the interests of society as a whole. This has been challenged from a variety of points of view, particularly following the growth of feminism as a social movement and sociological perspective.

Exam themes

→ Different aspects of the family, usually structure, roles and functions

→ Changes in the family

→ Sociologists' different views on the question 'What is a family?'

→ The social problems associated with family life, particularly divorce

→ Different theoretical approaches to the family

Topic checklist

	AQA Sociology	OCR Sociology	EDEXCEL Social Policy
○ AS ● A2			
The family in society: theories	○	○	●
Changes in family structure and functions	○	○	●
Changes in family roles	○	○	●
Family disorganization	○	○	●
What is a family?	○	○	●

The family in society: theories

Sociologists are interested in the relationship between the family and the wider society, particularly the economy. There are different views on how this relationship affects the family.

Functionalist approaches

Main assumptions

→ The **structure**, **functions** and **roles** of the family can be explained by examining the relationship between the family and other parts of society.
→ The family is a 'good thing': it is functional for members and the wider society.
→ The **isolated nuclear family** is dominant in modern society.
→ Roles within the family are becoming more equal.

Evaluation

→ Most critics question the functionalists' idealized view of happy families meeting the needs of society.
→ Marxists see the family serving the interests of the ruling class.
→ Feminists see the family as serving the interests of men.
→ A range of critics have identified dysfunctional, unhappy families, mentioning violence, abuse, mental illness, etc.

Marxist approaches

Main assumptions

→ Two main themes are the *influence of the economy* on the family – economic change causes changes in family functions, structure and roles – and the *role of the family in maintaining social class inequality* – the family reproduces labour power, children are raised at no cost to employers and learn to be obedient.
→ Married women are a *reserve army of labour*.
→ The family is a refuge from hardship at work, providing love and home comforts.
→ Families are the main consumers in modern capitalism, buying family homes, cars, etc.

Evaluation

→ Functionalists argue the family has a positive effect on members and society.
→ Feminists argue that gender, not class, is the major inequality and that men rather than employers benefit from family life.
→ It is questionable whether women will remain a reserve army of labour as employment rates for men and women equalize.

Checkpoint 1

State two arguments against the view that the family is functional for its members.

Checkpoint 2

Marxism and functionalism have some similar ideas. Explain two similarities

Feminist approaches

Arguably, feminism has replaced functionalism as the mainstream perspective on the family.

Main assumptions

The family creates and maintains the **economic dependence** of women on men. *Housework* is real productive work (Oakley) and the care of dependent children serves the interests of employers. The family is not based on free choice and love and does not perform functions efficiently – the disabled, sick, some children and many old people may rely on *state support.*

Evaluation

Women's power in the family may increase because more are in paid employment. Also women exercise control over the home and relationships with wider kin. Women may find housework a source of satisfaction – e.g. childcare, home improvements, autonomy.

H. Graham (1991) in a study of black domestic workers argued that time spent with their own families was seen as an escape from the exploitation of paid housework or slavery.

New Right approaches

These views have had a major influence on social policy during and since the 'Thatcher years' but have not been widely accepted.

Main assumptions

The conventional nuclear family is seen as an ideal and variations are seen as less functional. Single mothers are condemned and seen as responsible for poverty and crime, and state support for lone-parent families encourages rather than solves problems.

Evaluation

This approach takes a narrow view of the family. If mothers are discouraged from working this contradicts the New Right free-market approach to employment. The policies that have been developed by the New Right have been criticized for blaming, and punishing, the victims of social problems, e.g. lone mothers.

Links

Housework is discussed on page 63.

Checkpoint 3

Explain how the care of children benefits employers.

Checkpoint 4

All women do not have identical lives. With reference to H. Graham's study, explain the influence of ethnicity and social class on women's attitude to housework.

Links

See the New Right view on poverty (page 84) and the welfare state (page 88).

The jargon

The *free-market approach* means that the Government should not interfere in the labour market.

Exam questions   answers: page 42

1   Evaluate the contribution made by feminist writers to an understanding of changes in family roles and relationships. (20 min)

2   How far do you agree with the view that the family has sustained class inequalities and patterns of exploitation? (20 min)

Examiner's secrets

Often answers can be based on a critical discussion of functionalist approaches.

Changes in family structure and functions

Many sociologists have argued that industrialization has encouraged the development of the privatized nuclear family which is isolated from both the extended family and neighbours. This is because industrialization led to some family members leaving the extended family who worked together on the land to work for wages in factories in towns.

The jargon

Geographical mobility means moving to a different area, usually for a new job. *Social mobility* means changing your social class.

Stabilization of the adult personality is the positive effect of love and friendship in marriage.

Parsons ●●●

Parsons argued that the **nuclear family** is the typical modern family in that it 'fits' the needs of industrial society because it encourages **geographical mobility** and **social mobility**.

The nuclear family has two main functions:

→ socialization of children
→ **stabilization** of the adult personality

Historical studies of the family and industrialization ●●●

Examiner's secrets

These two studies are good examples of the use of secondary data, which can be used in methods questions.

Laslett studied population records of households and concluded that, contrary to the conventional view, people usually lived in nuclear, not extended, families in pre-industrial Britain.

Anderson used information from the 1851 census to argue that the insecurity that arose from industrialization encouraged the development of extended families which provided help with housing, care of the unemployed, old and sick.

Willmott and Young ●●●

Using historical information and their own social surveys, Willmott and Young wrote that the family had passed through four different historical stages.

Checkpoint 1

Explain the term 'mum-centred family'.

1 *The pre-industrial family* – the family worked together on the land. It was a **unit of production**.
2 *The early industrial family* – the family no longer worked together. Following the Industrial Revolution, they became wage earners. The 'mum-centred' extended family provided support in difficult times.
3 *The symmetrical family* – is an isolated, home-centred, nuclear family. Gender roles became more equal as more women went out to work.

Checkpoint 2

Give two reasons why the stage 4 asymmetrical family has not become more common.

4 *The asymmetrical family* – was only just beginning to emerge in the 1970s when the four stages were described. Work dominated the lives of managing directors (all men in the research) and women took the main responsibility for the home.

There is a relationship between changes in the functions of the family and other aspects of social change.

The functions of the family

A typical list of family functions includes:

→ *sexual, reproductive and legitimizing* – sexuality is controlled, children are born with a father who accepts responsibility
→ *socialization* – children learn the culture of the society, which helps to unify the society
→ *economic* – the family today rarely works together but they do consume products together, e.g. family house and car
→ *care and welfare* – families provide care and support for the young, old, disabled, sick, unemployed, etc.
→ *affective* – families offer love and companionship to members; compared to the past couples have children later, have fewer children and live longer

Functionalist approach	*Marxist Approach*
1 Sexual, reproductive and legitimizing	Women are oppressed Children are future workers
2 Socialization	Children raised as obedient future workers
3 Economic	Family produces workers Family consumes products of capitalism
4 Care and welfare	Care provided at no cost to employers
5 Affective	Refuge from work

The functions of the family and the state

The state is seen as a threat to the family:

→ the welfare state undermines the family by taking over functions such as childcare and creates and maintains poverty by encouraging single mothers to have children without supporting them.

The state supports the family:

→ through the law, e.g. women's property rights and legal recognition of marital rape and domestic violence
→ by providing contraception, abortion and child benefits in support of family policies – although critics see some of these actions as threatening the family.

The jargon

The *functions of the family* are the ways it meets the needs of society

Examiner's secrets

Questions may focus on the relationship between family functions and the welfare state or on whether the change in family functions is evidence of the declining importance of the family.

Checkpoint 3

You should attempt to give the feminist view of the five functions in this table.

Checkpoint 4

Identify and explain two ways in which the state might be seen as a threat to family life.

Exam question   answer: page 43

Using information from the paragraph on Willmott and Young above and other sociological studies, examine the relationship between industrialization and family life. (20 min)

Examiner's secrets

You should consider family functions and roles as well as structure.

Changes in family roles

Most research studies and exam questions focus on gender roles and the relationships between husbands and wives. However, recent research has looked at the role of the child. Instead of dismissing children as passive recipients of socialization, sociologists have begun to see them as people who make active choices about their own lives. Just as feminism made sociologists look differently at the role of women, the new sociology of childhood has questioned the subordinate role of children in families.

Functionalist view of family roles

Leader (parent)

Expressive role
Woman provides love in the family home

Instrumental role
Man works outside home to support family

Follower (child)

Checkpoint 1

This model illustrates Parsons' view of the two basic functions of the family. Explain with examples: (a) socialization (b) stabilization of the adult personality

The jargon

Socially constructed means that a phenomenon, like childhood, is not natural but the result of social interactions and the meanings given to behaviour.

The changing role of the child

Sociologists accept that children are biologically distinct from adults but claim that the social meaning given to these differences is socially defined. The social meaning of childhood varies from time to time and place to place. Thus childhood is a **social construction**.

→ In early industrial Britain, children were seen as an economic asset, as both present and future workers. Children were expected to care for the old.

→ In modern industrial societies, children have become the centre of family life. Gittins described children as a luxury to be enjoyed by adults – people talk of being able to afford children. Certainly, raising children is very expensive.

→ Many children still work within and outside the family.

→ Remember the differences between children – in some societies gender is a major influence on childhood. In others, class or ethnicity influence the child's experience.

The 'new sociology of childhood' (Hood-Williams, 1990), in contrast to the quotation from right-wing educationalists Cox and Boyson, believes children are controlled and even oppressed in the family and outside.

Checkpoint 2

Briefly state two arguments to support the view that some children in contemporary Britain are economic assets.

Changes in gender roles

→ Feminists argue that family relationships are based on **patriarchy**, i.e. the power relationship by which men dominate women.

→ Patriarchy is supported by **patriarchal ideology** learned in the family, school, workplace, from peer groups and through the mass media and religion.

→ This power relationship can be seen in: decision-making (studies, e.g Edgell, have focused on decisions over spending); the domestic division of labour (research, see below, has investigated who has responsibility for housework in different circumstances); and domestic violence (Dobash and Dobash pioneered research into domestic violence that involves the victimization of women and children by men).

Are gender roles in the family more equal? ●●●

Feminists have rejected the view that men and women are moving towards equality as suggested in the *Symmetrical Family*, Willmot and Young (1974).

The 1970s ●●●

Studies in the 1970s, such as Oakley's *Sociology of Housework*, argued that women still carried the main responsibility for childcare and housework.

Boulton pointed out that men thought they did do more in the home and that there should be a move to do even more. However, only 9 of her 50 subjects helped extensively. The men chose what they wished to do, largely childcare, and were advocating more equality after office hours.

The 1980s

The dramatic rise in unemployment, particularly for working-class males, meant unemployed men had far more time to participate in domestic labour. However, Morris (1995) suggested that the wives of men who did become unemployed did not necessarily seek paid work. If they did get jobs, men did not take over responsibility for housework. Both partners still saw being the breadwinner as the male role. Wives becoming unemployed had no effect on the domestic division of labour.

The 1990s

Far more married women are working and comprise an increasing proportion of the labour force. Wheelock (1990) argued against the commonly held view that men were still not doing much housework. She found that where men were unemployed and women in full-time work, men were doing more housework. However, the working-class families would have preferred a more traditional division of labour.

Exam question   answer: page 43

Discuss the view that childhood is largely a social construction.
Use material from the paragraph above on 'The changing role of the child' and your own knowledge. (20 min)

The jargon

Patriarchal ideology is the set of beliefs that support male domination.

> *"In truth being a housewife makes you sick"*
>
> Bernard (1976)

Checkpoint 3

What is a symmetrical family? Does it mean men and women perform identical tasks in the family?

Checkpoint 4

Briefly explain two arguments against the view that the housewife-mother role is natural.

Links

See unemployment on page 64.

Examiner's secrets

Sociological approaches explain the social construction of childhood differently but all agree it is not simply a biological stage.

Family disorganization

Many marriages and families do not live up to the high expectations that individuals and society have of them. This has led sociologists to study issues such as *divorce, lone-parent families* and *domestic violence*. Some sociologists believe these are exceptional problems whereas others, particularly feminists, believe that conflict is inevitable because of the inequality between men and women.

Family disorganization ●●●

Family disorganization is the term used to describe the breakdown of the family resulting from **functional failure** and **role failure**.

The causes and effects of family disorganization include:

→ death, disability and serious illness of one or more members
→ births outside marriage
→ divorce, separation, desertion or living in an 'empty-shell marriage'
→ conflict between members, including abuse or neglect
→ disruption caused from outside by unemployment, war, imprisonment or persecution.

Checkpoint 1

List two examples of functional failure in the family.

The jargon

An *empty-shell marriage* is one where partners live in the same household but the relationship is more or less finished.

Causes of an increasing divorce rate ●●●

Since 1960 there has been a massive increase in the divorce rate in Britain, which has the highest rate in Europe. One in three marriages end in divorce. Reasons given for this rise include:

→ changing attitudes to morality, marriage and divorce, related to **secularization**
→ the welfare state has encouraged a decline in the importance of the extended family and supportive functions – women can more easily afford to live without men
→ legal changes have made divorce cheaper and easier
→ women's roles and attitudes have changed
→ more women are in paid employment.

Oakley has argued a more feminist set of reasons:

→ marriage does not meet *women's high expectations* because their responsibility for childcare and housework makes them economically dependent on men
→ men rely on women to ease their anger and frustration, whereas women have no one to turn to
→ women are physically and economically less powerful than men: this may lead to feeling a lack of control or even to experiencing violence
→ men try to control women's sexuality and *fertility*: women are expected to 'please' their husbands and bear children. (Until the 1990s there was no legal recognition of marital rape.)

The jargon

Secularization is the decline in the influence of religion.

Checkpoint 2

Explain briefly why secularization might encourage a higher divorce rate.

Checkpoint 3

Give one reason why more women working might: (a) increase the divorce rate (b) decrease the divorce rate

The jargon

Reconstituted families are families where one or both parents have been married before and bring children to the family.

Consequences of an increasing divorce rate ●●●

→ More one-person households, **one-parent families**, co-habiting couples, remarriage, step-parents and **reconstituted families**
→ Increased welfare dependence

→ Disadvantaged children – the adverse effects of divorce on children's education or health is a subject of debate
→ A decline in the importance of the family

Is the family in decline?

The rise of divorce and other forms of family disorganization has led to a debate over the future of the family.

Arguments predicting decline

→ Critics of the nuclear family claim it has failed: it is oppressive (e.g. Leach); it encourages violence (e.g. Dobash and Dobash); it exploits women (e.g. Bernard).
→ Supporters of the nuclear family condemn the decline of traditional 'family values' (e.g. Marsland's attack on single mothers).

Arguments against decline (by functionalist supporters of the family)

→ Divorce is the result of higher expectations – marriage is more, not less, highly valued.
→ Divorce represents the failure of individual marriages, not the family in general.
→ Remarriage suggests discontent with partners, not marriage.
→ **Serial monogamy** and reconstituted families represent a change, not a decline, in the family.

Critics of the family argue that the family is changing as capitalism develops but continues to reproduce inequality (Marxist), and that the family is changing but continues to exploit women (feminist).

Check the net

www.jrf.org.uk
The Joseph Rowntree Foundation produces reports on family issues, e.g. *Divorce and Separation: The Outcomes for Children, 1998.*

Examiner's secrets

You can assess the effects of divorce by looking at effects on individual families, and the family and society.

The jargon

Serial monogamy is having several marriage partners, one at a time, during an individual's life.

Exam question

answer: page 43

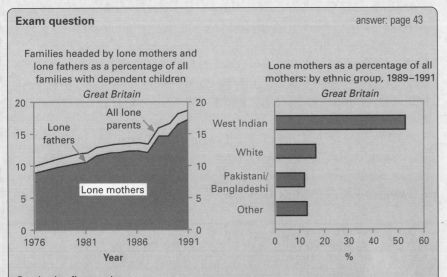

Families headed by lone mothers and lone fathers as a percentage of all families with dependent children

Lone mothers as a percentage of all mothers: by ethnic group, 1989–1991

Study the figure above.

(a) What was the percentage in 1976 of all families with dependent children in the 'All lone parents' category?

(b) What was the approximate percentage in 1991 of all families with dependent children in the 'Lone fathers' category?

(c) Which of the two categories of parents cited accounted for most of the increase of lone-parent families between 1986 and 1991?

(d) Assess the claim that the increase in the divorce rate since the Second World War has been mainly due to changes in the law. (20 min)

What is a family?

You need to be able to define and distinguish *family* and *household*. Be aware of the difference between the 'ideal family' and what families are really like. You should also be able to explain the existence of different types of family and recognize ethnic and other forms of diversity.

Defining families and households

→ There is no agreed definition of a **family**.
→ Common characteristics of the family are living together, economic co-operation, the reproduction and socialization of children.
→ A **household** is a group of people who live together under one roof and share certain aspects of their lives, e.g. eating together.
→ **Nuclear families** consist of parents and their immature children; Murdock argued that the nuclear family was universal.
→ **Extended families** add other kin to the nuclear family: these may be a third generation, or the families of adult brothers and sisters; members may or may not live together.
→ The '*ideal family*' is the model that is approved of by society. It follows then, that other types of family or living arrangements may be frowned upon or not even recognized as families. Feminists argue that the ideal family has been promoted by the media and supports the exploitation of women.
→ Attitudes and language change – **lone-parent families** were previously referred to disapprovingly as *unmarried mothers and children*.

Different types of family and household

There are many forms of household in addition to the ideal nuclear family, including: increasing numbers of one-person households; childless couples; unmarried couples cohabiting with or without children; remarried families with the children of one or both partners; single-sex couples – occasionally with children and other households of unrelated people.

Most people at any one moment in time do not live in nuclear families and many live in one or more nuclear families during their lifetime. Most people live in a variety of family and household arrangements during their lifetimes.

The ideology of the family

There are an increasing number of households that are different from the traditional family. At the same time the image of the ideal family has become more influential – Marxists and feminists have referred to the **ideology of the family**. There is increasing pressure on people to live in happy families and alternatives are condemned.

Checkpoint 1

Describe two kinds of extended family. You should refer to examples from sociological research.

Checkpoint 2

Identify two ways in which people learn about the 'ideal family'.

The jargon

Ideology refers to a set of beliefs that serve the interests of a particular social group.

Checkpoint 3

Identify two social policies which support the conventional nuclear family. Explain how each of the policies achieves this.

Ethnic diversity

Britain is a multicultural society. Sociological studies of ethnic minority families have frequently been written by outsiders and tend to confirm popular stereotypes such as father-dominated extended Asian families. The family life of minorities, like that of the majority, will vary on the basis of social class, religion, generation and individual factors.

Why do ethnic minorities have distinctive patterns of family life?

→ *Economic influences*   A history of slavery may have encouraged the development of female-led Afro-Caribbean families. Difficulties in finding employment and housing may have encouraged the persistence of extended families.
→ *Cultural differences*   Traditional patterns of family life are more likely to persist where a minority maintains a distinct language and religion.
→ *Discrimination and disadvantage*   Racism may encourage minorities to maintain a distinct culture. Westwood and Bhachu (1988) described the family as a source of strength and resistance against racism.

Ethnic minority families: reality or stereotypes?

J. E. Goldthorpe (1987) reviewed several studies of British 'Asian' families of different religions and national origin and identified some common characteristics:

→ men have authority over women
→ parents exercise control over children
→ the old exercise control over the young
→ marriage is arranged between kin groups
→ sexes are segregated, girls are chaperoned and family honour is important
→ families are extended, often in multigenerational households, often supporting each other in getting jobs and housing
→ in addition Westwood and Bhachu (1988) were able to confirm that households tended to be larger but that only Sikhs and families from East Africa were likely to contain three generations
→ only 21% of Asian households were extended families in 1991, however, extended family ties can be maintained through visits and by telephone.

Exam question   answer: page 44

Using evidence from above and other sources, assess the view that ethnicity is a major influence on family roles. (20 min)

Examiner's secrets

When considering research on ethnic minority families take note of the date. Older studies which describe first-generation immigrants may no longer be relevant.

The jargon

Asian here refers to people whose families originated from the Indian subcontinent.

Checkpoint 4

Are these characteristics common to all ethnic minorities?

Examiner's secrets

You'll probably concentrate on marital roles but you can also discuss the roles of children and the old.

Answers
Families and households

Checkpoints

1. • Feminists argue that the family is organized in the interests of men.
   • There is evidence of an increase in family disorganization, e.g. rising divorce rate.
2. • Both argue that the structure and functions of the family are related to the economy.
   • Both see the socialization of children as a key function.

Examiner's secrets

Marxist and functionalist explanations are often similar. A crucial difference is that Marxists argue that social arrangements benefit the ruling class, not the whole society.

3. Families raise future workers at no cost to employers. This involves socialization as well as feeding and clothing children.
4. Graham is pointing out that (working-class) women may do housework as employees. In the USA domestic labour was a major activity for black women, originally as slaves, later as employees. Such women would not view the work done for their own families as exploitation.

Exam questions

1. You must indicate an understanding of feminist theory and research studies and apply your knowledge to the issues in the question.

   In a data response question you will be able to refer to at least one source and then apply your own knowledge.

   Start by explaining the views of different feminist writers, indicating how they have changed previous views of family relationships:

   Feminists (Delphy, Oakley, etc.) have redefined housework as domestic labour involving the exploitation of women by men. Previously housework was seen as a part of women's natural role rather than work.

   Marxist feminists see the domestic division of labour as serving the interests of employers rather than the family as a whole or men in general.

   The unequal division of power in the family has been described by examining decision-making (J. Pahl 1989) and violence (e.g. Dobash and Dobash). Previously, families were seen as symmetrical and happy.

   More recently feminism has begun to refer to 'age patriarchy' to describe the subordination of children as well as women. Previously children tended to be ignored.

   Feminists have identified factors *outside* the family that have influenced roles:
   • changes in the occupational structure/more married women working; see studies by Wheelock (1990) and Morris (1995)
   • the role of the media in representing idealized views of gender roles and family relationships.
   Feminist approaches may be challenged by referring to:

• perspectives offering a more positive view of the family, such as functionalism
• other critical views such as Marxism.

Examiner's secrets

Remember to show an awareness of different feminist views. Ensure that your answer refers specifically to roles and relationships rather than the family in general.
A balanced conclusion based on the evidence and arguments in your answer should recognize the new insights that feminism provided but also note the continued debates between feminists and others – you could also mention briefly the attack on feminism from the New Right.

2. The question is asserting a Marxist view.
   You should explain this approach, emphasizing the importance of the economy and class structure in explaining the role of the family.

   The function of the family in reproducing labour power should be explained. This can be criticized by contrasting it with the functionalist concept of socialization.

   Feminism agrees with the view that the family sustains exploitation, but emphasizes gender rather than class inequality.

   Other explanations of exploitation focus on the school and work place rather than the family.

Examiner's secrets

You can refer to studies of housework to discuss exploitation.

Changes in family structure and functions

Checkpoints

1. The mum-centred family is an extended family where the dominant set of relationships is between mothers and their married daughters.
2. • More women are in full-time paid employment.
   • There are more job opportunities for educated middle-class women who are most likely to be married to those work-centred men described in stage 4.
3. 1. Men control women's sexual and reproductive lives.
   2. Children learn traditional gender roles.
   3. Women are exploited by men.
   4. Responsibility for care of children makes women dependent on men.
   5. His marriage is different from her marriage. Men benefit, women suffer.
4. • Easily available welfare benefits may discourage families from taking responsibility for their dependants.
   • More liberal divorce laws may encourage families to split.

Exam question

You should outline the case that industrialization has both encouraged and been encouraged by the development of the nuclear family (Willmott and Young and Parsons).

Evaluation should mention the persistence of the extended family, referring to Anderson, but also the contemporary (modified) extended family found, for example, in the South Asian community.

As well as considering changes in structure, i.e. replacement of the extended family, also discuss changes in roles, e.g. the move towards the symmetrical family.

You have the opportunity to get marks for evaluation by using feminist criticisms of the claimed move to more equal gender roles.

An overall conclusion might mention the diversity of family structure and roles at any one time, e.g. based on class and ethnic differences.

Examiner's secrets

AS questions may require less evaluation than A2 questions. See the list of words used in exam questions on page 187.

Changes in family roles

Checkpoints

1 (a) Socialization means transmission of culture, e.g. children learn language and morality at home.
  (b) Stabilization of the adult personality means partners provide emotional support for each other.
2 • Many children work in family businesses and can contribute to family income.
  • Children may be an investment for the future that provides money for care for ageing parents.
3 A symmetrical family does not mean men and women perform the same roles but that responsibilities should be equal.
4 If it were natural then:
  • there would not be differences in roles in different cultures
  • there would be no change in roles over short periods of time.

Exam question

Explain the term 'social construction', contrasting it with 'natural' or biological.

Either outline your arguments chronologically or use different sociological approaches such as:
• *Functionalism* – the role of the child adapts to meet the needs of society so that children stay dependent longer to acquire education for more complex jobs.
• *New Right* – conventional subordinate roles of children are natural and essential for an orderly society.
• *The new sociology of childhood* – presents a critical view of 'age patriarchy'.
• *Feminism* – could be used to draw the conclusion that the childhoods of boys and girls are socially constructed in different ways. The extent of the difference varies between different societies.

Examiner's secrets

This will *not* be a balanced answer. The sociological evidence and arguments are overwhelmingly in favour of the view in the question.

Family disorganization

Checkpoints

1 • Children will not be *socialized* effectively in abusive families.
  • Absent fathers may lead mothers and children into welfare dependence, undermining the *care* function.
2 The decline in the influence in religion removes restraints against divorce and permits remarriage, e.g. Roman Catholic Church doesn't permit divorce.
3 More women working means:
  (a) women seeking divorce can be economically independent
  (b) more independent women can negotiate more satisfactory relationships in families.

Exam question

(a) 10 or 10% (*all* lone parents means fathers and mothers).
(b) 'Approximate', so 1% or 2% or between 1% and 2%.
(c) Lone mothers.
(d) Causes of the rise can be discussed, perhaps within a theoretical framework, as follows:
Feminists
• (Challenges to) inequality and exploitation in the family
• Women's frustrated expectations
• Legal changes that have been fought for by feminists – property rights, recognition of domestic violence and marital rape as 'real' crimes
Functionalists
• Higher expectations
• Changes in attitudes to marriage
• More women are educated and working
• Legal changes which reflect changing attitudes to marriage and family
New Right
• Decline in morality and traditional values
• Too easy access to welfare benefits
• Misguided legislation from 'permissive and trendy' governments

Examiner's secrets

A simple list of causes of divorce will not score high marks. You must organize your answer so that it comes to a reasoned conclusion about the relative importance of changes in the law compared to other factors.

You can debate whether the legal changes are a cause or a consequence of the changes in marital relations and wider social changes (e.g. more women working) listed above.

A conclusion might argue that changes in the law are not a direct *cause* of higher rates *but an effect* of the demand for easier and cheaper divorce that has come about because of the factors listed above.

A final piece of evidence might be to point out that low rates can be found in countries with liberal divorce laws, e.g. Norway and high rates in societies with strict laws, e.g. USA in the 1950s.

What is a family?

Checkpoints

1 • The mum-centred family (see page 42) was described by Willmott and Young (1975).
  • The three-generation Sikh family is based on relationships between fathers and married sons (Westwood and Bachu).

2 They learn from their own family and through the mass media, e.g. in adverts.

3 • Benefits such as child benefit help families support children.
  • The law forbids same-sex marriage; this supports the view that the conventional family is 'better' and makes adoption difficult for same-sex couples.

4 The short answer is 'no', e.g. three-generation extended families are characteristics of Sikh but not Muslim families. Neither are they exclusive to minorities. Most feminists would argue that patriarchy is common in all cultures.

Exam question

The simple way to organize this, and similarly worded questions, is:

1 *Arguments and evidence in favour.*
Outline the three factors explaining the distinctiveness of ethnic minority families (economic, cultural and discrimination). Illustrate with reference to different minorities (various Asian, Afro-Caribbean and perhaps white minorities, e.g. R. Oakley on Greek Cypriots).

2 *Arguments and evidence against.*
Argue that it is not ethnicity itself which influences roles but other factors, e.g. immigration, social class, etc. Argue that distinctiveness is based on outdated stereo-types, not current evidence. For example, the proportion of white single mothers is fast approaching the once distinctively high proportion of black single mothers.

3 *Conclusion*
Yes, ethnicity is at least a short-lived influence on roles. Economic and other cultural factors may encourage assimilation. In any case these are generalizations – there is variation within as well as between minorities.,

Examiner's secrets

Focus on roles, not structure – references to extended families must be tied into the question, e.g. the relationship between extended family and the authority of grandparents.

Education

This is a topic where both students and teachers have first-hand experience. You can analyse your own experiences, using the ideas and theories in this chapter and evaluate sociological evidence and arguments, using your own experience.

Education is an area where sociologists have influenced policy-making. Sociological research has provided evidence of inequalities which governments have tried to address. Remember, things have changed and are changing very rapidly in the education world, so when you look at evidence you should note when it was produced.

Exam themes

→ The relationship between education and the economy

→ The relationship between education and inequality

→ Competing explanations of differential educational achievement by social class, gender and ethnicity

→ Research on classroom interaction between teachers and pupils and different groups of pupils

→ The formal curriculum and the hidden curriculum

→ The effectiveness of educational policies

Topic checklist

○ AS ● A2	AQA Sociology	OCR Sociology	EDEXCEL Social Policy
Education and society	○	●	○
Educational achievement: social class	○	●	
Educational achievement: gender and ethnicity	○	●	
Education policy debates	○	●	○

Education and society

Sociologists have studied the relationship between education and the wider society. They often see similar relationships but explain them in quite different ways.

The functionalist approach

Functionalists explain the development of the education system by examining the relationship between education and other social institutions, and the contribution education makes to meet the functional needs of the social system as a whole.

The economic function

Education systems respond to the demands from employers for educated and skilled labour. This investment in human capital produces economic growth which allows further investment in education.

The education system prepares people for the world of work by:

→ providing general training for work
→ providing specific training for particular jobs
→ allowing employers to use exams to select people for jobs
→ producing future workers with suitable attitudes.

The socialization function

→ Children are prepared for jobs and as members of society in general.
→ Education transmits culture. This may be deliberate and formal, e.g. in religious education classes, or informally through the study of literature and history. This includes consensual norms and values, shared beliefs and often a national or other cultural identity.
→ Pupils learn appropriate roles associated with age, gender and class.

The Marxist approach

Marxists see the education system, both the institutions and the ideology, as part of the superstructure of capitalist society. Socialization serves the interests of the economic role. Marxism is a structuralist-conflict theory, whereas functionalism is a structuralist–consensus theory.

Bowles and Gintis

They applied Marxism to modern capitalism in the USA. Their correspondence theory linked the home, school and workplace. Examples of the correspondence between school and work include:

→ pupils rely on teachers for knowledge as workers rely on managers
→ both school and work use external rewards rather than job satisfaction to motivate and control.

Links

See page 52 for discussion of vocational education.

Checkpoint 1

List any skills you have gained at school which are likely to be applied in the workplace.

Checkpoint 2

If more people pass exams how will this affect the way employers select staff?

Links

The Marxist view of workers is explained more fully on page 58.

A comparison of Marxism and functionalism ●●●

→ Both approaches study education by looking at its relationship with the whole social system.
→ Both link education with the economy. Marxism sees education as reproducing capitalism, whereas Functionalists see education meeting the needs of industrial society. Functionalists emphasize training and role allocation, whereas Marxists emphasize the production of deskilled obedient workers.
→ Both identify a cultural reproduction role. The functionalists stress the integrative effects of teaching consensual values, whereas the Marxists talk of the transmission of ruling-class ideologies which keep the working class falsely conscious.

Checkpoint 3

How would a feminist explain cultural reproduction?

The New Right approach ●●●

This approach has two, sometimes contradictory, elements.

1. They think that applying the principles of the free market will improve the standards and efficiency of education. This might lead to more parental choice and involving the private sector in the running of schools.
2. They believe in traditional teaching methods and curriculum. Anti-racism, anti-sexism and multiculturalism in the curriculum are condemned. The teaching of literature and history should emphasize English national glory.

Links

The introduction of market forces to education is discussed on page 53.

The hidden curriculum ●●●

The curriculum is the sum of learning experiences offered by schools. The hidden curriculum provides the unofficial and sometimes unplanned consequences of school experience. It includes:

→ knowledge, attitudes and beliefs gained in the classroom – this could include unintended sexism and racism in school books
→ the organization of the school which will have people at the top (often white middle-class males) exercising control; this also applies to relationships between teachers and pupils
→ rules – teachers control space and time; you need permission to pass time unless doing an approved task; some spaces are denied to pupils; lavatories may be a refuge but are liable to inspection.

Checkpoint 4

Give one argument for and one argument against the view that the knowledge in school books is ideological.

Examiner's secrets

The concept of the hidden curriculum was originally a critical Marxist term. Now feminists use it in a critical way and teachers in a neutral way.

Exam question   answer: page 54

Using the information above and your own knowledge, assess functionalist approaches to the relationship between education and the economy. (20 min)

Examiner's secrets

Remember to restrict your answer to the economy and don't talk about functionalism in general.

Educational achievement: social class

A major theme in education questions is the evaluation of sociological explanations of the different educational achievement of social groups. Different explanations (innate ability, out-of-school explanations and in-school explanations) are applied to social class inequalities. The next spread deals with ethnicity and gender.

Examiner's secrets

Although we consider class, gender and ethnicity separately, in real life they interact with each other in complex ways. You can use this information to evaluate explanations and studies.

The jargon

Innate characteristics are natural ones you are born with. These are largely genetic. Most people accept eye colour is genetic, but there is a long-standing dispute over the extent to which intelligence might be inherited.

Innate ability

This is a psychological rather than a sociological explanation. It suggests that achievement depends mainly on the natural ability with which the child enters school.

Evaluation

This may explain the performance of *individual* children but *not social groups* such as ethnic minorities or gender groups. It has been used to justify the low performance of groups or even to provide less education for them (e.g. sexist or racist societies and institutions have excluded girls and ethnic groups from education). The changing relative performance of social groups, particularly girls, over a short period of time demonstrates that natural differences are not the major influence.

Out-of-school factors

These are generally structuralist explanations which identify a number of causal factors under two broad headings:

Checkpoint 1

Explain the effects of bad housing on educational success.

→ **Material factors** are those related to family income and living standards. Research has focused on the underachievement of the poor rather than the overachievement of the rich. Material deprivation includes the effects of poverty and bad housing.
→ **Cultural factors** include parental expectations, values and child-rearing styles which vary between social classes. Language development and usage has been linked to class, ethnicity and even gender, and also linked to success and failure.

Checkpoint 2

If underachievement is caused by out-of-school factors, how can achievement be improved?

Evaluation

These explanations tend to play down the significance of individual differences and the experience of school.

In-school factors

Education provision can vary and influence success. Schools vary in the quality of staff, equipment and buildings. M. Rutter found that achievement amongst similar groups of children was influenced by good schools which depended on teacher's qualities. However, most of the studies which focus on the school tend to be: **interactionist** accounts of the relationships between teachers and pupils which draw on **labelling theory**; descriptions of **pupil subcultures** which associate anti-school attitudes with the working class; and descriptions of the effects of the hidden curriculum.

Evaluation

Interactionist studies tend to focus on what teachers do to pupils and may underestimate the active part played by pupils in making sense of school. There is a need to look at attitudes in the wider society to discover the source of teachers' low expectations of the working class.

Social class ●●●

Working-class underachievement was seen as a social problem long before British sociologists studied the relationship between ethnicity, gender and education. Despite real improvements in the performance of girls and some ethnic minorities, the problem of class remains.

Out-of-school factors

Douglas (1964) demonstrated a number of links between home and school. He saw the working class as experiencing both material and cultural deprivation. Rising living standards for most of the working class have done little to reduce underachievement.

Evaluation

This approach suggests that it is inequality rather than actual income that is important, and shifts the emphasis to culture. Bernstein's study of language suggests that *cultural difference* (language) rather than *cultural deprivation* is the key influence.

In-school factors

Ever since the Rosenthal and Jacobson experiment, sociologists have used small-scale studies to argue that teacher–pupil interaction is of crucial importance. Studies of subculture have explained the failure of working-class boys in terms of **anti-school subcultures**. In the past the ability of working-class boys to get well-paid jobs without qualifications was blamed. Later the high rates of youth unemployment led many pupils to believe that even with qualifications and training they would still be unemployed.

Conclusions

Halsey suggested that neither 'material circumstances' (housing, father's class, etc.) nor 'family climate' (parental encouragement, language competence, etc.) have a strong influence on achievement provided children were in the same school. The variety of evidence suggests that pupils' social background has an effect on the way pupils experience school, including how they are treated in school.

> **Links**
>
> Fuller's study of black girls shows how pupils can shape their own experience of school and succeed in spite of teachers' negative attitudes (see pages 50–1).

> **Checkpoint 3**
>
> Identify one reason for and one reason against the view that rising living standards would improve working-class achievement.

> **Example**
>
> Rosenthal and Jacobson (1964), in a controlled experiment, demonstrated that teachers' expectations influenced pupils' performance.

> **Checkpoint 4**
>
> Outline two reasons why schools combat gender and racial stereotypes but neglect to challenge class stereotypes.

> **Examiner's secrets**
>
> Assess the influence of the home. Don't just describe it or list alternative influences.

Exam question   answer: page 55

Using the information above and your own knowledge, assess the extent to which home background can influence educational achievement. (20 min)

Educational achievement: gender and ethnicity

> *"The most important myth that needs exposing is that girls underachieve at school."*
>
> Blackstone, 1985

Checkpoint 1

Explain one reason why girls might have become more career-minded.

The pattern of inequality described here is complex and subject to rapid change. Change has been caused by social policy, which has been influenced by the sociological research that identified differential achievement.

Gender and education

Out-of-school factors

The family, peer group and media can socialize girls into expectations of early leaving, marriage and what are seen as 'women's jobs'. These jobs, e.g. nursing and secretarial work, may have lower entry qualifications than equivalent men's jobs and this may encourage underachievement.

S. Sharpe (1976) described how girls learned the priorities of love, marriage, husbands, children, jobs and careers (in that order). She repeated the work in 1994 and found that although career was an increasingly important influence on identity, girls still anticipated the dual responsibilities of family and career.

C. Griffin (1985) suggested that working-class girls saw early leaving as an escape from responsibility for housework because paid employment raised their status in the family.

M. Fuller (1982) used the idea of subculture to explain the relatively high achievement of black girls in public exams (no need to please teacher!). Their subculture was not pro-school but valued success in education as a means to get on at work.

In-school factors

Comprehensive schools, the National Curriculum and the policies of government and individual schools have all encouraged boys and girls to take the same subjects. However, the hidden curriculum may still reinforce gender roles. Research into *teacher–pupil interaction* has suggested:

→ girls learn self-control earlier than boys and that hitting other children doesn't get attention
→ teachers pay more attention to boys
→ girls are taught to smile at male teachers
→ maths teachers perceive boys as being more able even when girls' results are better
→ government training schemes (YTS) pushed girls into 'women's jobs'.

Checkpoint 2

Outline one argument for and one argument against the view that language may be a factor in gender differences in educational achievement.

Research into *interaction between pupils* has suggested that boys denied girls access to bricks in nursery school and science equipment and computers in secondary schools. S. Lees (1998) wrote that sexist language such as 'slags' and 'sluts' is used by girls, as well as boys, to control the behaviour of girls. She also reports the physical intimidation of girls in school.

Ethnicity and education ●●●

Out-of-school factors

→ If social class differences are controlled this will eliminate a substantial proportion of inequalities related to ethnic difference. However, if ethnic minorities continue to be over-represented in lower social classes this might be an effect as well as a cause of educational underachievement.

→ Cultural differences have been seen as cultural deprivation and failure blamed on the 'victims'.

→ The higher proportion of black one-parent families has been identified as a cause of a range of problems but could also be seen as a positive motivating factor for black females who are overachievers and more likely to be in full-time work.

→ Language has been identified as a source of disadvantage where English is a second language. Some teachers see the increasing popularity of Caribbean dialects among black pupils as a problem, but there is little evidence of effects on exam performance.

In-school factors

Racism from teachers, pupils and in the hidden curriculum may seem an obvious explanation of underachievement. Coard (1971) saw racism as the explanation for the over-representation of black children in schools for children with learning difficulties, and the under-representation of Pakistani children. Performance in relevant tests did not explain this.

Evaluation

However, racism does not produce a consistent pattern of disadvantage, with Indians overachieving whereas other Asian minorities underachieve. Pupils may respond in different ways that help or hinder achievement. M. Fuller (above) has described gender differences in responses. Overt racism from teachers may be rare but low expectations may have detrimental effects.

Conclusion

The performance of girls and some ethnic minority groups has improved dramatically over a short period. But exam success does not mean that they now experience equal treatment. Performance of white working-class boys is now seen as social problem. Women have written extensively on gender inequality in schools. Most research on ethnicity and education has been conducted by white sociologists.

Checkpoint 3

How might a sociologist researcher control social class differences when conducting research into ethnicity?

Links

For comment on the link between ethnicity and family structure see page 41.

Checkpoint 4

If girls get better exam results, what disadvantages might they still experience as a result of sexism in school?

Exam question answer: page 55

Evaluate sociological explanations of the poor school progress made by some children from West Indian and Asian homes. (20 min)

51

Education policy debates

52

> *"Education, Education, Education."*
>
> The three priorities for New Labour according to Tony Blair

Examiner's secrets

Life's not as simple as this division between Labour. and Conservative. suggests.
Callaghan (a Labour P.M.) started the 'Great Debate' on standards and vocational training. Thatcher, as education minister, shut many grammar schools. New Labour has extended the role of the private sector in education.

Checkpoint 1

Explain why selective education might 'waste talent'.

Action point

Briefly explain and illustrate the operation of the 'self-fulfilling prophecy' in education.

Checkpoint 2

Outline two reasons why comprehensive schools have not eliminated social class inequalities in education.

Action point

List the points in this section on vocational training which support the functionalist viewpoint (explained on page 46).

The social problems associated with education, and the policies chosen to deal with them, depend to a large extent on the ideologies of political parties.

The political parties

Labour were keen on reducing inequality in the 1960s by promoting comprehensive schools and in the 1970s by tackling the disadvantages associated with gender, ethnicity and disability.

Conservatives have been concerned with training people for jobs, raising standards through the National Curriculum and testing and encouraging a 'market' in education with increased parental choice. Labour since 1997 has continued much of the Conservative agenda.

Selective or comprehensive schools

The 1944 Education Act introduced free secondary schooling for all. Children were selected by the 11-plus exam to go to: grammar schools, technical schools, or secondary modern schools. However, by the 1970s most children were in comprehensive schools.

Arguments for comprehensive schools (both *educational and social*)

→ The 11-plus was a poor predictor of later success.
→ The talent of many children was wasted.
→ Labelling failures may produce a self-fulfilling prophecy.
→ Social class divisions were reinforced and continued in the workplace.

Arguments against comprehensive schools

→ Social class divisions continue where schools recruit from the local area and there are distinct middle- and working-class neighbourhoods.
→ Streaming and banding within comprehensives had similar effects to separate selective schools.
→ The grammar school was an important means of upward mobility for the brightest working-class children.

School to work: education and vocational training

Both Labour and Conservative governments are convinced that the education system should contribute to economic growth by providing a more skilled and thus more productive workforce. This became increasingly important because of the high levels of youth unemployment in the 1980s and the decline in demand for unskilled and semi-skilled workers.

The Conservatives encouraged employer involvement in education and training by encouraging employer governors in schools and colleges and letting employers spend public money on education and training through Training and Enterprise Councils (now disbanded). There is disagreement as to how specific vocational training should be, particularly as the nature of jobs is changing so rapidly. New vocational qualifications were introduced, e.g. GNVQs in 1995.

The National Curriculum and testing ●●●

Since 1988 governments have increased control over education at the expense of local authorities. Through the National Curriculum Government now states what should be taught in school and what programmes pupils follow. In 1999 Labour added more rigid control over timetables in primary schools by introducing literacy and numeracy hours. There is more testing, which is also controlled by government rules. Results of tests in schools are published as league tables.

Checkpoint 3

What impact has the National Curriculum had on gender inequality in schools?

The expansion of higher education ●●●

The number of HE students doubled during the 1990s. Increasing proportions were mature, female, from ethnic minorities, from the working class and had not done A-levels. However, funding for universities was not increased in proportion, tuition fees were introduced and maintenance grants largely abolished. Dropout rates increased dramatically, particularly for non-traditional students, and there were fears of falling standards.

Checkpoint 4

Explain two reasons why more students drop out of university now compared to before the 1990s.

Market forces ●●●

According to S. Ball (1996) the introduction of market forces to education involves:

→ schools recruiting outside LEA catchment areas
→ league tables, which inform parental choice
→ competition between schools for (good) pupils
→ funding of schools based on pupil numbers
→ schools acting like businesses with budgets they can spend on staff, marketing, buildings, etc.

The Government encourages diversity, e.g. schools can specialize in technology, arts, etc. More religious schools have been state-funded.

Is there choice?

Ball doubts there is real parental choice. Popular schools may choose 'good' pupils and exclude 'difficult ones' who end up at less popular schools. Middle-class parents are better equipped to make choices since they have:

→ **economic capital** – the cars and child carers to transport children
→ **cultural capital** – the skills in collecting and assessing information to judge schools (Ball is using Bourdieu's concept of cultural capital)
→ **social capital** – the contacts to 'work the system' and win appeals.

Examiner's secrets

Independent schools provide choice for richer parents. They do not, however, usually provide education for profit so market forces are not the only influence on them.

Exam question   answer: page 56

Examine sociological arguments and evidence for the view that diversity and choice in education inevitably favour the children of the powerful and articulate. (20 min)

Examiner's secrets

Use the evidence on this page concerning selective education and market forces.

Answers
Education

Education and society

Checkpoints

1 You can distinguish the transferable skills learned through general education such as reading, writing and arithmetic, from vocational skills such as keyboarding and food handling. Learning specific workplace skills may not make you more employable, e.g. shops may prefer to employ part-time staff with higher levels of general education to those who have specific retail training and qualifications.

2 Functionalists identify role allocation as one of the functions of education. Employers may use qualifications to select people but could also regard people as overqualified and not employ them.

   There is evidence of 'grade inflation' where qualifications lose their competitive value because so many people have them. In the 1950s, entry to law and teaching was possible with the equivalent of five GCSEs. Both are now graduate professions.

3 Feminists have a similar approach to Marxists. Both identify a process where the powerful (men and the ruling class respectively) use ideology to justify their power and the exploitation of a weaker group (women and the working class respectively).

   Feminists see the family as the main location for the reproduction of patriarchal ideology but see the school reinforcing this ideology through the hidden curriculum.

4 Ideology refers to ideas which serve the interests of a particular group. Often ideology is used to legitimize (i.e. justify) inequality and oppression. Loban found evidence of sexism in children's reading schemes where characters consistently played conventional gender roles. Wright found the perpetuation of racist stereotypes in popular school geography texts as recently as the 1980s.

   Arguments against this view could point to neutral, value-free knowledge found in maths and science texts. It all depends on your point of view.

Exam question

Outline the functionalist approach, referring to investment in human capital and the importance of role allocation.

   Agree there are links with the economy but explain comparisons and contrasts with Marxist approaches. Use Bowles and Gintis.

   Question whether there are close links between education and the economy by arguing that education sometimes acts independently of purely economic forces, e.g. the demand for equal opportunities may have encouraged more women to go into HE rather than the demand for a more educated labour force.

Examiner's secrets

This isn't a full-length essay so you don't have to include everything you know about functionalism and alternatives. The examiners want a few well-explained and developed points and a focus on the strengths and weaknesses of the functionalist accounts.

Educational achievement: social class

Checkpoints

1 You should be able to explain that:
   - poor housing could directly affect educational performance (e.g. by damaging health and thus leading to absence from school; by not having an appropriate place to work at home, etc.)
   - and that *indirectly* poor housing is associated with the more general disadvantages of lower income and social class.

2 • The out-of-school factors could be changed, e.g. through tax and benefit policies, which affect income distribution or housing aid.
   - These factors could be compensated for. Compensatory education has taken the form of extra nursery provision and spending more money on schools in deprived areas.

3 *For:* Rising living standards may remove the pressure to leave school as soon as possible *or* improve health *or* mean more money is available for educational experiences.

   Against: If the underachievement is the result of cultural deprivation or in-school factors, more money may make little difference.

4 There have been social movements campaigning for equality of opportunity for both gender and racial equality.

   Biological differences between gender and ethnic groups are more obvious and the stereotypes cruder and easier to challenge.

Exam answer

Explain the impact of home background on educational achievement. Distinguish material from cultural factors.

   Assessment involves both strengths and weaknesses of this type of explanation.

   Strengths involve the reliable quantitative evidence of a correlation between social class and achievement and the success of some (but not all) compensatory education programmes.

   Weaknesses include the underestimation of the importance of in-school factors and the sociological evidence (both quantitative, e.g. M. Rutter, and qualitative accounts of labelling) that schools matter.

   Conclude that although controlled research can isolate and measure separately the in- and out-of-school factors they interact with each other in real life. (E.g. the research of Willis, which discusses the active behaviour of working-class boys whose response to school is influenced by the culture of, and the employment opportunities for, the working class.

Examiner's secrets

Remember to concentrate on home background rather than all out-of-school factors. You should refer to gender and ethnicity in addition to social class.

Educational achievement: gender and ethnicity

Checkpoints

1 Your answer can refer to either:
   - changes in the labour market producing more opportunities and successful role models
   - changes in girls' aspirations because they perceive a need to be financially independent because of divorce, male unemployment, etc.
   - changes in schools have encouraged girls to become more career-minded.

2 *For:* School tests show girls have superior language skills from an earlier age. Bernstein has shown the impact of language differences on overall achievement.

   Against: The relative performance of gender groups has changed dramatically since the 1960s – it is unlikely that language skills have changed in a short span of time.

3 Control of the extraneous variable social class can be achieved by choosing samples that have been matched for social class differences. This can be done by looking at father's occupation or using groups from different ethnic groups with the same postcodes.

4 Disadvantage and discrimination in schools may be overcome. Girls (and some ethnic minorities, e.g. Jews, Chinese, Asian and East Africans) have higher than average performance in exams. However, sexism in the school may lead to girls limiting their experiences in-school and lowering their career aspirations after school. S. Lees has argued that the physical threat from boys limits girls movements in school and the attitudes of other girls limit their relationships with boys.

Exam question

You can use the same structure that has been used in this chapter, distinguishing in-school from out-of-school factors.
Out-of-school factors
There may be different material circumstances. Asian and black minorities tend to live in certain parts of particular cities – often in the relatively deprived 'inner city'. (However, any impact of these patterns of residence may be more the result of social class than ethnic differences.)

Cultural deprivation might include speaking English as a second language or using *patois* (Caribbean dialect). (However, this would not explain the differential performance of boys and girls or the overachievement of some minorities.)
In-school factors
Discrimination from pupils, teachers and through the hidden curriculum can disadvantage minorities. (However, this would not explain the differential performance of boys and girls or the overachievement of some minorities.)

Conclusion may (as usual) say home and school interact. In addition, question the view that progress is indeed poor and point out minorities perform differently and the pattern of achievement varies over time.

Education policy debates

Checkpoints

1 Selection at an early age, i.e. by the 11-plus, is based on the unlikely and unproven assumptions that educational potential is fixed by the age of 11 and is measurable on one day using pen and paper tests. The children who pass and those who fail may receive an unsuitable education. In many secondary modern schools expectations of 11-plus 'failures' were unjustifiably low.

2 • The explanation for the inequalities may lie outside the school.
   • Comprehensive schools may vary according to the social class profile of the neighbourhood.

3 Actually measuring the effects is problematic as other factors would need to be controlled. However, girls are now less likely to be excluded from or choose to give up subjects such as the natural sciences.

   The achievements of boys and girls are still different and girls have different experiences at school from boys.

4 • Different types of students attend. Adults may have different demands on their time from 18-year-olds.
   • Tuition fees and the stopping of maintenance grants create financial problems, particularly for non-traditional students.

Exam question

Arguments for this view can follow the pattern presented in S. Ball's writing on market forces and choice. (The concept of cultural capital has been taken by Ball from Bourdieu and applied to the question of choice.)

Both ethnicity and class may influence how articulate parents are.

You can also refer to the ability to buy private education.

Arguments against this view might include the positive effects on educational achievement of diversity in the form of separate girls' schools and schools for religious (which may coincide with ethnicity) groups.

Children with special abilities may benefit from attendance at schools which concentrate on the arts or technology. Such schools are often more generously funded than others and have a longer teaching day.

The theoretical approaches to this topic may seem rather old-fashioned. Marx was writing about early capitalism when the life of the working class in the world's richest country (Britain) was short and miserable. Blauner wrote about the technologies of the first half of this century and Goldthorpe and Lockwood describe the rise of an affluent working class. However, each of the four topics discussed in this section is undergoing rapid and dramatic change. Much of this change is driven by the revolution caused by information and communication technology which has transformed both work and leisure.

Exam themes

A good starting point for discussion of issues might be the view of the Marxist-influenced American sociologist C. W. Mills
'Much work is merely a way to make money. Much leisure is merely a way to spend it.'

→ How different types of workers experience different types of work

→ Job satisfaction and improvements (or otherwise) in working conditions

→ How technology affects job satisfaction

→ Happy, efficient employees or obedient workers? – a choice for employers

→ The factors influencing leisure activities

→ Definitions and analysis of unemployment

→ The causes and consequences of unemployment

Topic checklist

	AQA Sociology	OCR Sociology	EDEXCEL Social Policy
O AS ● A2			
Alienation and conflict	O	O	O
Management theories	O	O	O
Work, non-work and leisure	O	O	O
Unemployment	O	O	O

Alienation and conflict

For many, work is a boring and tiring experience which brings little or no reward, except for payment. Sociologists have called this lack of job satisfaction *alienation* and explain it from different sociological perspectives.

Marxist theories: the influence of capitalism

Alienation describes the difference between the creative and satisfying working lives we should have and the miserable experience at work we actually have. It is the separation of the individual from his true human self. Capitalism separates workers from their tools, from what they produce, and from other workers. Alienation is caused by the workers' experience of being forced to sell their labour for wages. There are two aspects of this relationship: *exploitation* (workers only receive a small part of the value they produce); and *the nature of (factory and later office) work itself* (work tasks are designed and controlled to produce profit rather than socially useful products and satisfying working lives).

Blauner: the influence of technology

Blauner (1964) explained lack of job satisfaction on production technology. He said workers experienced alienation in four ways.

1 **Meaninglessness** – jobs are broken down into tiny, repetitive tasks and the worker **deskilled.**
2 **Powerlessness** – workers have no control over what is produced, how it is produced or the pace of work.
3 **Isolation** – workers feel cut off from their workmates and bosses, because they stand in a fixed position on a noisy assembly line.
4 **Self-estrangement** – workers deny their true selves and pretend to be someone else, e.g. shopworkers must pretend to like customers.

Goldthorpe and Lockwood: an instrumental attitude to work

This *interactionist* approach rejected the views that alienation was the result of the structure of society or the organization of the workplace. Instead they said that the workers' experience of work depended on *the meaning workers gave to work* and their motives for doing it. They said that the workers' attitude to work could be formed by previous experiences inside and outside work. They studied workers in three factories in Luton and concluded that they had an **instrumental attitude** to work. They saw work as a means to an end – a way of earning money to support their 'privatized', home-centred, family life. Thus the workers were not alienated, as they did not seek job satisfaction, only secure jobs and high wages.

Action point

Make notes on the different ways Blauner and Marx use the term *alienation*.

Checkpoint 1

Who owns the tools and how does this affect the relationship between bosses and workers?

Checkpoint 2

Choose a job you know well and analyse it using Blauner's four aspects of alienation.

"Shop staff experienced . . . a feeling of powerless depression. The hatred of customers, often in an intense form, is one result."

C. W. Mills, 1955

Checkpoint 3

Describe two different meanings workers may give to their work.

Evaluation

→ Blauner argues that the problem is industrial society, not capitalism. He indicates that technology can have negative or positive effects on job satisfaction and he is optimistic about new technology.
→ Marxists argue that whether and how technology is introduced depends on the employer's need to control/exploit the workforce.
→ The interactionist view rejects structural explanations that suggest that workers react uniformly to conditions in the workplace. Individual workers may have different attitudes to work.
→ Feminists focus on the distinctive experience of women at work and at home. They are seen as doubly exploited by men in the family as well as employers outside. Oakley revolutionized the attitude to *housework* by treating it as real work and comparing its monotony and meaninglessness to factory work.

Conflict at work

Types of conflict at work

Individual workers may be absent from work or leave the job. Collectively, workers may strike, work to rule, and *sabotage* equipment or products. Theft can be individual or collective. Employers and managers may initiate conflict through imposing new contracts or conditions, sacking individuals or groups or temporarily locking out workers. Unemployment, fear of unemployment, declining membership and influence of unions, and legal restrictions on unions have led to a decline in strikes. These types of conflict are alternatives chosen by workers or bosses, e.g. where strikes are illegal, more individual or covert forms of conflict may be chosen.

Reasons for conflict

Pay is the most common reason for disputes. Employers seek to reduce wage costs and employees want higher pay. A more productive workforce can achieve both these aims. *Alienation* caused by the frustration of doing meaningless work can cause disputes or encourage absenteeism, leaving or sabotage. *Employers* may worsen conditions by increasing the workload. *Fear of redundancy* led to the biggest strike of recent years when miners went on strike for nearly a year in 1984–1985.

Links

Sabotage at work is an example of deviance (see the section on crime and deviance).

Checkpoint 4

Why is pay the cause of disputes at work?

Examiner's secrets

You can use the three approaches above to explain the causes of alienation. 'Nature' reminds you that there are different views on what alienation means.

Exam question   answer: page 66

With reference to the work of Blauner and others assess sociological explanations of the nature and causes of alienation. (20 min)

Management theories

This section deals with the impact on work of organization and management theories and of new technology.

Scientific management: F.W. Taylor 1911 ●●●

There is a science of work which can establish the best way to do a job. Workers want high wages and bosses want low labour costs. These apparently conflicting aims can be achieved if scientific management increases **productivity** and employers pay **piece rates**. Without scientific management workers will restrict work to have an easy life and protect jobs. Employers should select and train workers who accept control because they want the money.

Human relations: Mayo (1920s) ●●●

Mayo put forward the view that the work group influences workers' attitudes and behaviour. Workers have social as well as economic needs, so piece rates don't work, whereas attentive management can reduce conflict and increase productivity.

Fordism ●●●

Named after Henry Ford who pioneered the assembly line mass production of cars in the 1920s, it is used to describe the use of technology for the mass production of cheap standardized products. (All model T Fords were black and were bought in the 1920s by millions of families). According to Blauner, assembly line work is **fragmented**, **deskilled** and alienating.

Post-Fordism and the new technology ●●●

Post-Fordism describes new forms of work resulting from new technology. *New Technology* involves the use of information technology for:

→ computer-aided manufacture (CAM), such as the use of robots
→ computer-aided design (CAD), which can test buildings and cars before they are built
→ information processing in offices (and at home), e.g. for communication, information storage and retrieval, and calculations.

Workers can be replaced. New specialized products can be produced and sold in new markets. (Benetton in the 1980s combined traditional production methods with computerized information processing to sell non-mass-produced clothes in shops throughout Europe.)

Evaluation of organization theories

→ Discussion of Taylorism still dominates the work of many, particularly Marxist, sociologists.

Links

You should be able to see a link between Taylor and Marx and Goldthorpe and Lockwood. All see workers motivated by money (page 58).

The jargon

Productivity is output per head. *Piece rates* are pay based on work completed. Piece rates are a type of performance-related pay.

Checkpoint 1

Identify one similarity and one difference between the theories of Taylor and Mayo.

Checkpoint 2

Briefly explain the terms 'fragmented' and 'deskilled'.

Links

Refer to the impact of technology on employment on page 65.

- → Although much criticized, 'Taylorism' was and remains a major influence on work organizations. Tasks are scientifically designed and workers strictly controlled. This applied to Ford in the 1920s and applies to McDonalds today.
- → Mass production, developed by Taylor and Ford, produced cheap goods for consumers but arguably alienated workers.
- → The human relations movement claims to have improved the quality of working life.
- → Marxists have condemned human relations as being just a more subtle and covert way to control and exploit workers.
- → Interactionists argue that the relative importance of high pay and job satisfaction depend on the motives of individual workers.
- → Optimistic post-Fordist approaches suggest that workers who think are more efficient and can improve production methods. Routine office work can be replaced by computers, leaving more interesting work for the workers.
- → Pessimistic post-Fordist approaches see new technology as increasing surveillance and control of workers.

Checkpoint 3

Give two reasons why Marxists might criticize Taylorism.

Checkpoint 4

Explain one reason why you expect new technology to improve the experience of work and one reason why it will cause alienation.

The flexible workforce ●●●

Post-Fordism has been associated with the development of a *flexible workforce*. *Numerical flexibility* means the total size of the permanent ('core') workforce is kept to the minimum required yet can expand when necessary. This involves the use of 'peripheral' workers who may be part-time, casual, employed by agencies, on temporary contracts and working flexi-time. *Functional flexibility* means workers have a wide range of skills and can be deployed to do a variety of (new) tasks, e.g. teams of car workers are not tied to one deskilled assembly line job but can do a variety of tasks.

Evaluation

- → A flexible workforce is favoured by employers, who see it as a way of reducing labour costs.
- → Some writers have claimed that jobs can become more interesting as workers are empowered and no longer deskilled.
- → Critics say flexibility has led to job loss, insecurity, casual and part-time work and more demands being made on workers, e.g. Sunday work without overtime.

Examiner's secrets

You should present positive and negative effects and come to a conclusion.

Exam question   answer: page 66

Assess the impact on workers of more flexible ways of organizing work. (20 min)

Work, non-work and leisure

> *"Leisure is time free from obligations either to self or others – time in which to do as one pleases."*
>
> S Parker, 1983

Checkpoint 1

Outline two criticisms of Parker's definition of 'work'.

Examiner's secrets

S. Parker was a pioneer in the study of leisure and the evaluation of his work is a useful framework for studying and answering exam questions.

Links

Parker classifies jobs according to the extent of job satisfaction experienced by workers. See page 58.

Leisure was usually studied as part of the sociology of work. Increasingly, it is a topic in its own right and related to consumption and identity. It has been predicted that leisure will become increasingly important as people have more free time and money to spend on leisure products.

Defining work and leisure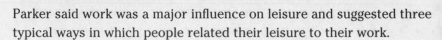

S. Parker (1983) offered the following definitions:

→ **Work** is paid employment; in modern industrial societies people usually work set hours in a place away from home.
→ **Work obligations** are work-related activities performed outside normal working hours and usually not in the workplace.
→ **Existence time** is devoted to fulfilling essential needs such as eating and sleeping.
→ **Non-work obligations** are domestic duties such as childcare and housework.
→ Parker sees leisure as **free time**.

The relationship between work and leisure

Parker said work was a major influence on leisure and suggested three typical ways in which people related their leisure to their work.

→ *The extension pattern* Leisure activities were often similar to work. The function of leisure was to 'develop the personality'. This was found where work was 'the central life interest' and often associated with workers who enjoyed their work, e.g. musicians.
→ *The neutrality pattern* Leisure activities were different from work. Either the family or leisure, and not work, were central life interests. Typically work was not satisfying. The function of leisure was relaxation. This pattern was associated with workers in routine office or factory jobs.
→ *The opposition pattern* Leisure activities were very different from work. Work was likely to be alienating. The function of leisure was escape and recovery from work. This pattern was associated with workers in extreme occupations, e.g. mining and deep-sea fishing.

Evaluation and alternative explanations

Parker himself recognized that these three patterns were not always useful. He defined leisure as time free from working, and this is obviously more appropriate for men in full-time work than it is for housewives and the unemployed, whom Parker saw as special cases. Parker also saw education and the amount of time available as factors influencing leisure.

Rapaport and Rapaport (1975) saw *age and family lifestyle* (marital status and parenthood) as more significant influences than work on leisure. They identified a fixed sequence of four phases from adolescence to retirement. They also saw class, gender and health as potential influences.

Roberts used the term **domestic age** to describe a concept that combines age with family relationships and responsibilities. Adolescence was exceptional in that the family was not the focus of leisure activities.

Deem (1986) replicated the Rapaport's study with women in Milton Keynes. She identified four life stages that influenced leisure, and saw sexual orientation and ethnicity as factors influencing the extent to which boys were the major leisure interest for teenage girls.

Feminist criticism

→ Housework is real work usually performed by women for men.
→ Women may not have 'free time'. They may enjoy leisure whilst performing an obligation, e.g. watching TV whilst ironing.
→ Age, marriage and children influence leisure. Single and childless women are more likely to work, have more money and free time.
→ Women may be limited in their freedom of movement. Fathers, husbands and women themselves may have views on what are safe and suitable places for women to go.
→ Deem suggested that leisure might be a state of mind rather than specific activities, e.g. cooking and eating could be work, non-work obligations or leisure depending on why they are done.

Marxist criticism

Marxists reject the view that leisure is free time because it is usually paid for and it involves *social control*.

Leisure takes the form of products which consumers are persuaded to buy, e.g. sport has moved from the park to the leisure centre and requires expensive kit.

Leisure is a means of social control, e.g. the young, particularly the young unemployed, are provided with or sold leisure activities to keep them off the streets. Many leisure activities are controlled by the state, e.g. where and when you can drink, dance or even walk.

Checkpoint 2

How does age influence leisure activities?

Checkpoint 3

Why might bingo halls or churches be seen as more suitable places than pubs for women to spend their leisure time?

"Leisure is now central to capitalist economic and cultural domination."

Clarke and Critcher, 1985

Checkpoint 4

Outline briefly how (a) feminists and (b) Marxists have challenged the view that leisure is 'free time'.

Examiner's secrets

You don't have to include all the factors mentioned here – select two or three factors which can be used to challenge the importance of work.

Exam question   answer: page 67

Examine the role of work and other social factors in influencing leisure patterns. (20 min)

Unemployment

Sociology syllabuses rarely mentioned unemployment until the 1980s, probably because it was seen as a social problem of the 1930s that had been solved by post-war government economic policies. The main issues are: the problems of defining and measuring unemployment; the causes of unemployment; and the effects of unemployment.

The definition and measurement of unemployment

Unemployment has been a major topic of party political debate since at least the depression of the 1930s. During the 1980s the definition and measurement of unemployment became a source of controversy. The Conservative Government was accused of changing the way unemployment statistics were collected in order to reduce the total figure. The 1982 Government decision to count *claims for benefits* rather than those *seeking work* reduced the apparent level.

Links

You can use unemployment statistics as an example when discussing the validity and reliability of official statistics (page 12).

Checkpoint 1

What's the difference between unemployable and unemployed?

Underestimating unemployment

Government critics from the left and feminists have argued that:

→ married women are unlikely to be eligible for benefit but could be seeking work
→ those under 18 are not normally eligible for benefit; they may be compelled on to training schemes or may be reluctant students
→ people with disabilities, the sick and those over 60 were encouraged to claim other benefits
→ those 'not actively seeking work' may be refused benefit; the Government decides what this actually means
→ when jobs are scarce, marginal workers, e.g. people with learning difficulties, may be seen as unemployable rather than unemployed.

Checkpoint 2

Why might some people decide against 'actively seeking work'?

Overestimating unemployment

The press, some politicians and New Right sociologists have argued that there are fraudulent claimants, some of whom work in the black economy, and that high levels of benefits encourage the 'work-shy' and welfare-dependent.

Evaluation

→ A consistent measure of unemployment would permit comparisons of rates between different groups and over time.
→ Pahl estimated that workers in the black economy were more likely to be employed than unemployed as they had more work opportunities and were less likely to be under official surveillance.
→ Rather than high benefits it is low wages and deductions from benefits which create the **poverty trap** which discourages working.

The jargon

The *poverty trap* exists when people cannot afford to take work because of loss of benefit income. Some benefits now top up wages.

The causes of unemployment

New technology causes structural unemployment by replacing jobs, e.g. computerization has reduced the number of bank workers. (The cure: technology creates jobs through new/cheaper products.)

International competition has reduced the market share of some UK firms, such as car makers, in both domestic and international markets. (The cure: be more efficient and competitive at home and abroad.)

Changes in the occupational structure, resulting from changing markets and technology, have led to a shift from manufacturing to service industries. The impact varies geographically and between different groups of workers. (The cure: education and training to provide new skills and encourage new investment in depressed areas.)

Cyclical changes in demand for goods and services at home and abroad lead to fluctuations in the total level of employment. (The cure: used to be increasing public spending to stimulate demand but this method was rejected as causing inflation and further job loss.)

Changes in the money supply influence inflation, thus competitiveness and thus unemployment. (The cure: control inflation and interest rates by cuts in taxation and public spending and keeping wage costs down.)

The social effects of unemployment

The unemployed and their families   The disadvantaged are most likely to be unemployed. The main consequence is poverty. Age and gender influence the experience of unemployment, which may lead to ill health and family breakdown. The proportion of women in the workforce has increased.

Workers feel less secure and stay where they are, unions are weaker, which permits more employer control and keeps wages down.

Regional unemployment – whole communities can be affected by job loss in one industry, such as coal, as local businesses suffer from reduced demand. This has led to similar problems in inner-city areas.

Unemployment and social control – unemployment is experienced disproportionately by the young and ethnic minorities and concentrated in specific locations. It has been linked with crime and political protest.

The welfare state – families tend to be work-rich, or work-poor and benefit-dependent. When unemployment is high, fewer workers may be supporting more claimants. Worse health costs the NHS more.

Checkpoint 3

Give an example of how new technology has led to (a) unemployment (b) new jobs.

Action point

Watch these films from the 1990s and make your own notes on the causes and effects of unemployment: *The Full Monty* and *Brassed Off*.

> *"What unemployment does before anything else is to make those who experience it poor."*
>
> Clarke and Critcher

Checkpoint 4

Explain briefly how age and gender might influence the experience of being unemployed.

Links

Unemployment has been identified as a cause of poverty (see the section on wealth, poverty and welfare, pages 85–6) and ill health (page 158).

Exam question   answer: page 68

Identify and briefly describe *two* ways in which unemployment statistics may be misleading. (8 min)

Examiner's secrets

Keep your answer brief; there are no extra marks for discussion.

Answers
Work and leisure

Alienation and conflict

Checkpoints

1 In capitalist society the employers own tools and all the other means of production. This, Marxists argue, means that in order to earn wages to live workers are forced to sell their labour to the employer. The employer pays workers less than the value of the goods they produce. Marxists see this employment relationship as exploitative.

2 You'll have to check this answer yourself. Most jobs are alienating in some respects but few are as extreme as the assembly line work Blauner identified as the worst case. On the positive side, teaching, for example, has a long job-cycle, requires skill and usually teachers exercise control in the classroom. In contrast, control over the curriculum is imposed from outside the classroom and school, increasing teachers' feelings of powerlessness.

3 The various meanings of work include:
   - a means to earn money
   - a source of positive satisfaction
   - a source of identity
   - a chance to get away from the home (this is often a reason given by mothers).

4 This may not be as obvious as it seems.
   Workers want/need more money to support themselves and families. Employers want to keep down wage costs, particularly as global competition increases.
   Money is seen as something workers are entitled to argue about. Who owns and controls the workplace is not seen as a legitimate source of dispute.
   The level of pay is a measure of relative success; being paid more than others is important to some.

Exam question

The 'nature' of alienation can be examined by looking at different definitions and the 'causes' assessed by discussing explanations.
- Blauner defines alienation in terms of the worker's subjective experience. The main cause is technology. You should outline his four dimensions of alienation
- Marxists say alienation is objective – workers are alienated whether they realize it or not. (Feminists share this view.) The causes are the design and control of work in an exploitative capitalist society, rather than just technology.
- Interactionists reject the Marxist view that working for money is necessarily an aspect of alienation. Instrumental workers may be content with a well-paid but boring job. Marxists see this as false consciousness. They also reject Blauner's view that technology has the same effects on workers regardless of their individual experience of work.

Examiner's secrets

'Assess' means you must identify the strengths and weaknesses of the explanations you choose. Time is limited so use it to assess views rather than give detailed accounts of Blauner and others.

Management theories

Checkpoints

1 You need only one example of each.
   Similarities
   - Both theories suggest there is one best way to manage work and workers.
   - Marxists say both theories are concerned with control and exploitation of workers.
   Differences
   - Taylor assumes workers are motivated by money.
   - Mayo says workers have social needs.

2 'Fragmented' means work is broken down into very short and simple repetitive tasks, e.g. boxes of chocolates might be filled by hand.
   'Deskilled' means the worker no longer requires any skill to perform simple routine tasks. This is because the job has been simplified or the skill and knowledge lies with managers or those who design machines.
   Both are the result of the division of labour and result in meaningless, alienating work.

3 Marxists say:
   - work is not designed to be efficient but to deskill and control workers; this maintains owners' profits and their domination of the working class
   - workers who do meaningless work for money are alienated; Taylor thought that higher pay would motivate them.

4 Satisfaction at work might improve as new technology removes the need to do boring, repetitive jobs such as copy typing, assembly line work, routine calculations, etc.
   New technology means work can be continuously observed and controlled, e.g. workers may be inputting data to a computer using a keyboard. The number of key-strokes per minute can be calculated and interruptions to work identified.

Exam question

Advantages
- Skilled workers can choose interesting work on short-term contracts.
- Learning from varied experience helps workers to become more employable.
- Deskilling and fragmentation are reversed, workers need more skills.
- Technology replaces routine work.
- Workers can choose work which fits in with their family needs; they can choose job sharing and part-time work.
Disadvantages
- Jobs become insecure.
- Technology causes unemployment.
- Workers may lose rights to overtime or holidays.
- Workers may have to work long or antisocial hours.

A reasoned conclusion should point out that some (core) workers may benefit at the same time as other (peripheral) workers suffer.

Considering both functional and numerical flexibility and a variety of jobs (e.g. skilled or unskilled in the factory, office or home) may help you think of a number of relevant points.

You could refer briefly to effects on the workers' non-working lives. These could include positive or negative effects on family life of flexible hours.

Work, non-work and leisure

Checkpoints

1 • Work may be unpaid, e.g. voluntary work.
   • Workers may be self-employed.
   • There are increasing numbers of home workers.
2 Age does influence choice of activities and the ability to participate, e.g. there are biological, legal and, above all, social restrictions based on age.

   Chronological age may be less important than the stage in the family life cycle that has been reached.

   Adolescence may be distinguished from adulthood by family obligations rather than simple age.
3 • Because the activities are seen as feminine.
   • Because women may feel safe from the threat of men.
   • Because husbands and fathers may not want women to meet other men (presumably the few men in church or bingo halls are seen as safe).

The emphasis in this question is on how church and bingo are socially defined as safe and suitable, not what these places, nor for that matter, women, are really like.

4 (a) Feminists argue that:
   • women, because of their domestic responsibilities, have no free time left over
   • women are socially controlled by men in their families and by strangers, and this limits leisure opportunities.
  (b) Marxists challenge the views that:
   • leisure is without cost – it has become a consumer product
   • leisure is based on freedom of choice – there are many social and even legal restrictions.

Exam question

Numerous research studies have shown a long list of factors that influence leisure patterns.

Parker demonstrates the role of work, with perhaps gender (Deem) and capitalism (Clarke and Critcher) providing critical alternative factors.

If you find yourself short of material you could refer to the research on family life cycle to develop the feminist view.

Using a framework based on theoretical approaches will help to produce a coherent answer with a conclusion rather than a long list of studies.

Unemployment

Checkpoints

1 *Unemployed* can be defined in different ways. Generally, it involves two characteristics:
   • not being in paid employment
   • seeking work

Unemployable means not able to work because of a number of factors including lack of skill, ill health, disability, learning difficulties, lack of experience, etc.

Who is 'unemployable' is socially defined, i.e. it varies from time to time and place to place. It depends on the demand for workers in general and in specific jobs. Also the way in which potential workers are perceived – e.g. is it seen as normal for people with particular disabilities to work and are workplaces accessible to, e.g. people with mobility problems?

2 Reasons include the following:
   • They don't want to work.
   • They live in an area where unemployment is so high that job seeking appears fruitless.
   • They have family obligations that make them unavailable to work away from home.
   • Expected wages are lower than the benefits they currently receive.
   • They work unofficially or illegally and may wish to avoid taxes and claim benefits.
3 (a) *Unemployment*
   • Computerization and cash machines have led to the loss of over 100 000 banking jobs.
   • Robots have massively reduced the number of car assembly line workers.
  (b) *New jobs*
   • Cheap personal computers have become household consumer goods.
   • Jobs are created in manufacture, sales, training and technical support.
4 The sociological point here is that not everyone experiences unemployment in the same way. You can consider both objective and subjective factors.

   Age influences your chances of getting a new job. The 'old' may be considered (and consider themselves) as retired, not unemployed, and withdraw from the labour market.

   The young school leaver may not expect to work and stay in full-time education or training. The young may drop out and become unemployable.

Women may consider themselves and be considered by others as full-time housewife-mothers and thus not unemployed. Women rely less on work as a source of identity and are therefore less likely to experience a sense of worthlessness and mental health problems. Depending on time and place, women may rely on men for income.

Men who are unemployed may feel worthless.

Exam question

Your answer should focus on the following two issues:

Validity

What do the statistics mean? The issue is the various definitions of unemployment. Do they count people wanting work or those eligible to claim? Distinguish unemployed from unemployable.

Reliability

Overestimates occur by counting those who don't want to work or illegal workers who may claim to be unemployed.

Underestimates occur because the statistics may omit housewives, the old, the young and people with disabilities, who may not be entitled to benefit or who are seen as not entitled to a job.

Examiner's secrets

The reliability and validity of social statistics are popular examination themes in methods questions and for a number of other topics. Particular favourites are statistics on crime, suicide, divorce, poverty and church attendance.

The main concerns when studying the mass media are:

→ who owns and controls the mass media?

→ how can we explain the content of the mass media?

→ how do the mass media affect their audiences?

There are close links between the study of the mass media and some aspects of culture and identity. The role of the media in the amplification of deviance is discussed in the crime and deviance chapter.

Exam themes

→ The relationship between ownership, control and media production

→ Bias in the selection and presentation of the news

→ Media representation of different social groups

→ Studies of the effects of the media on the audiences' attitudes and behaviour

Topic checklist

O AS ● A2	AQA Sociology	OCR Sociology	EDEXCEL Social Policy
Perspectives on the mass media	O	O	
Mass media: effects and audiences	O	O	
The news	O	O	
Representation in the mass media	O	O	

Perspectives on the mass media

The following perspectives all explain the relationships between the ownership, control and output of the media and the audience.

The mass manipulative model

→ This term is used by Cohen and Young to include not only Marxism, the dominant mass manipulative theory, but also conservative critics who fear the power of the media to create a mass culture and morally corrupt society.
→ Audiences are passive and uncritical receivers of media messages.
→ Marxists argue that the media transmit the dominant **ideology** to keep the working class falsely conscious.
→ Audiences are persuaded to consume.
→ Audiences are fed fantasy to distract them from the inequalities and miseries of capitalism.
→ There is debate between Marxists. **Instrumentalists** see the ruling class directly controlling the media. **Structuralists** explain how journalists and editors are themselves influenced by ruling class ideology and willingly conform to the interests of capitalists.

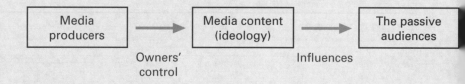

Evaluation

Interactionists challenge the view that audiences are passive 'sponges' who absorb everything they are told. Concentration of ownership may not lead to manipulation of audiences. If audiences seek choices they may be provided if profitable.

The market model

This model takes an uncritical view of the media.

→ The audience is made up of consumers who influence the content of the media by choosing what they like and thus providing profits for the producers.
→ The media producers (owners, managers, editors, journalists, musicians, film producers, etc.) seek audiences. They compete to provide what the public demand.
→ A wide range of opinions is offered; only the illegal and unsaleable are excluded.

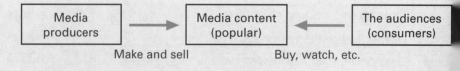

Checkpoint 1

Give examples of the fears that are expressed about media effects.

Links

See the reference to the Frankfurt school and mass culture on page 26.

Checkpoint 2

How can the market model explain the output of non-profit-making media organizations?

Evaluation

→ Support for this view comes from **pluralists** who support a free press as an important watchdog in a democratic society. They fear the domination of the media by monopolistic corporations or by governments.

→ Fear of government is a view shared by the New Right; they oppose government regulation of the media. However, the political and religious right may hold the contradictory view that the content of the media must be censored if it corrupts audiences.

The interactionist model   ●●●

This model combines some elements of the two previous approaches. Culture is not dominated by a ruling class ideology but does reflect the interests of the more powerful groups in society. This culture is accepted by most people, partly because the media does not just reflect cultural values and attitudes but also reinforces them. The prevailing culture is identified as pro-capitalist, sexist and racist (these themes are discussed below). The selection and presentation of news is influenced by ideological and technical factors.

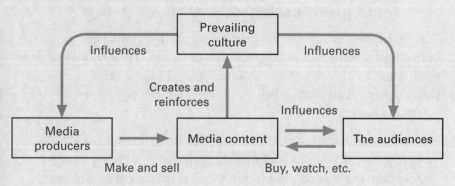

Evaluation

→ Because of the issues the interactionists have studied (sexism, racism, bias in the news against unions and the Labour Party) critics accuse them of having a left-wing bias.

→ The methods used to identify the prevailing culture and bias in the news involve sociologists interpreting what is in the media. They see stories and images according to their own cultural expectations.

The jargon

Pluralists believe that power in democratic society is widely dispersed, not concentrated in the hands of a small minority.

Checkpoint 3

Who are 'the more powerful groups in society'? What is the evidence that the media reflect their values and attitudes?

Checkpoint 4

Explain the second point of the evaluation of the interactionist model.

Exam question   answer: page 78

Assess the extent to which the ownership of the mass media can influence the content of the mass media. (20 min)

Mass media:
effects and audiences

The Marxist view of a dominant ideology transmitted by the media and the mass culture argument (see the culture and identity section) both assume that the media directly influence attitudes and behaviour. Alternative views do not deny that the media affects audiences but the process is seen as dependent on the characteristics of the audience.

Hypodermic syringe model ●●●

This assumes that a passive audience can be directly influenced by media messages. The audience is seen as an undifferentiated mass whose existing beliefs are overcome by the new message. This view was popular in the 1930s when the mass media, particularly radio, could easily be controlled by dictators and used for propaganda.

Evaluation

Although this view is argued more by psychologists than sociologists, it is accepted by some Marxists and also right-wing and religious groups who fear moral corruption.

Uses and gratification approaches ●●●

This developed as a pluralist critical view of the hypodermic approach. Individuals use the media for their own purposes. They choose what to read, listen to or watch. The media are more likely to reinforce rather than change existing attitudes.

Effects are limited by:

→ **selective exposure** – we choose to read or watch only a selection of output, usually what fits our existing views
→ **selective perception** – we interpret messages according to our existing views
→ **selective retention** – we remember and repeat what we agree with.

Katz and Lazarsfeld proposed a two-step flow model where opinion leaders, who may be more exposed to media, influence others. The media do not usually influence the public directly.

Evaluation

These approaches may overestimate freedom of choice for audiences and underestimate how much most people are now exposed to the media. The research which supports this theory is based on examining the immediate and short-term effects of the media, e.g. political broadcasts before elections. Longer-term effects weren't measured. Morley updated this approach by examining the effects of national TV news. He concluded that the social characteristics of the audience, e.g. occupation and ethnicity, influenced the effects that news programmes had on audiences. However, he did argue that watching national news helped 'construct the nation'.

Action point

Read the mass culture section on page 26 and the Marxist perspective on page 70. Note any similarities with the hypodermic model.

Checkpoint 1

Suggest how selectivity in exposure, perception and retention might influence voting behaviour.

The cultural effects approach

This approach argues that the media have long-term effects on the audiences. It is based on research into the content of 'the news' by the Glasgow University Media Group (GUMG). Their research also demonstrated effects on the audience. These effects were not simply believing what you see at a particular time, but more a case of setting an agenda of what is important (newsworthy) and how we should view issues.

The way that the media define issues has been argued by *Hartman and Husband* who said the media provided 'a framework for thinking about issues' rather than forming attitudes and opinions. Their study of race and the media concluded that negative stories (about violence and the alleged 'problem of immigration') were newsworthy because of the prevailing culture of our society and its imperialist past.

Schoolchildren saw immigration rates as high, rising and threatening. Those living in areas with few immigrants derived their knowledge from the media and saw riots as a problem. Those in areas with higher numbers of immigrants relied less on the media, saw less conflict and saw housing and jobs, rather than violence, as problems.

Measuring media effects ●●●

The methods used to study media effects have strengths and weaknesses, which limit the reliability and validity of research.

- Social psychologists, e.g. Eysenck and Nias, have conducted *experiments* demonstrating a link between violent films and aggression (though not real-life violence).
- Studies of short-term effects involved presenting messages to audiences and surveying effects on attitudes and behaviour, e.g. Belson correlated violent behaviour with watching violence on TV (without showing a causal relationship). He questioned boys about viewing habits and violent behaviour.
- Sociologists have used **content analysis** to measure, both quantitatively and qualitatively, the content or message of the mass media. Stories and their particular perspectives can be counted and the language used analysed. The problem with this research is that it may reveal the bias of the researcher as well as the bias in the media.

> *"The mass media may not tell us what to think, but they do tell us what to think about."*
>
> From an old AEB exam question

Checkpoint 2

What does Hartman and Husband's research tell us about different audiences?

Checkpoint 3

Explain why watching violence on TV might correlate with violent behaviour but not cause it.

Checkpoint 4

Why should we treat Belson's data with caution?

Exam question   answer: page 78

Assess the sociological evidence for and against the view that the effects of the mass media vary according to the social characteristics of the audience. (40 min)

Examiner's secrets

You can challenge the view that the media have any effects as well as considering the influence of different audiences.

The news

The main argument running through this section is that news reporting is not an impartial description of real events. Cohen and Young in the 1960s used the phrase the *'manufacture of news'* to describe the processes involved in choosing what was newsworthy and how it should be presented.

Introduction

Hoggart wrote that there were four filters through which TV news must pass:

→ the effects of time and resources
→ the visual value
→ the news value
→ the prevailing culture.

The first two filters are **practical** or **technical factors**.
The second two filters are **cultural** or **ideological factors**.

Technical influences

Deadlines
The press is governed by deadlines, which mean that events can only be covered if they happen a sufficient time before the paper is printed. This contrasts with TV and radio, which can broadcast in real time. In fact, newspaper content may be planned by editors weeks in advance.

Space and competing events
Newspapers tend to look the same every day in terms of layout, e.g. a fixed number of pages for sport, TV schedules, letters, etc. Thus decisions are made about what is most important that day. This also applies to TV and radio news if the programme has a fixed duration.

Placing of cameras
Some planning is required to deploy TV cameras and crews to places where 'news' is happening or expected to happen. This is why you often see reporters standing outside Parliament commenting on what politicians have said.

Access to events
Access to events and people may be physically, legally or politically limited. Reporting of the Falklands war in 1983 was limited by the desire of the Government to control it. This was possible as journalists relied on the Navy to provide reporting facilities. Crime reporting is limited by legal restraints about naming victims and offenders.

Checkpoint 1

Identify two ways in which the presentation of TV news has changed.

Checkpoint 2

How do the restrictions imposed by deadlines and space influence politicians who wish to manage the news?

Action point

Make notes on the ways in which governments can control media output.

New technologies

Satellite and portable cameras allow the broadcasting of events such as war in real time. The *globalization* of news is technically possible but may be culturally limited. Americans still read local newspapers and have less interest in international affairs than people in the UK.

Cultural influences ●●●

These work at different levels.

The prevailing culture

There may be a consensual view in the whole society of what is important and thus newsworthy. This consensual view may be based on genuine agreement and shared values, or a consensus 'manufactured' by those with power or influence. Marxists use the term 'dominant ideology' to describe the prevailing culture. The mass media themselves help to create and reinforce this 'consensus'.

The media professions

Tunstall focused on the professional culture of journalists and editors to explain the selection and presentation of news. Journalists are socialized to learn what are currently the characteristics of a news-worthy story. They often agree with rivals on what angle they will use to present the story. *Agenda-setting* is a term used to explain the selection or rejection of items for the news. They are the *gatekeepers* who control the information that is revealed to the public.

Rock, Cohen and Young and others have all argued that familiar stories get recycled (e.g. moral panics about drugs, hooligans, and the failures of education, etc.).

News is *personalized*. Political issues and policies are debated in terms of individual politicians who represent the ideas and policies. Newspapers and other mass media rely on celebrities who are often famous because they are in the media.

Examples ●●●

Glasgow University Media Group (GUMG) research analysed news stories and claimed to have identified bias in the selection and presentation of news. Within *industrial relations* they saw evidence of systematic bias against trade unions and employees. Regarding *war and peace* they showed that the women at Greenham Common in Berkshire demonstrating against nuclear missile bases were attacked for their failure to be feminine.

"News as Eternal Recurrence"

Title of article by P. Rock, suggesting that the same old stories get recycled

The jargon

A *moral panic* exists when people or events become defined as a threat to society.

Links

Moral panics about crime are described on page 148.

Checkpoint 3

Outline briefly how (a) Marxists and (b) the market model would explain the 'personalization of news'.

"Management are invisible heroes."

Littler and Palmer
They said the management view was often presented in the news as the objective view whilst the workers' view was presented by union leaders and thus seen as one-sided.

Checkpoint 4

In what sense could the Greenham Common women be seen as 'unfeminine'?

Exam question   answer: page 79

Using the information above and your own knowledge, outline the evidence and arguments which suggest that the reporting of news is selective. (20 min)

Representation in the mass media

Particular social groups may be represented differently in the media. The main argument is that ethnic minorities and women are disadvantaged groups, their lack of power being both a cause and effect of the unfair and inaccurate ways in which they are portrayed in the mass media.

Representations of ethnicity and 'race' ●●●

Hartman and Husband (1974) demonstrated that the media defined the way we thought about race rather than simply influenced our attitudes. (Their work is described further on the next page.)

Troyna (1974), in a study of press reporting of race, found different attitudes expressed in the *Guardian, Times, Mirror* and *Express* but agreement on the issues. The agenda comprised immigration control, hostility and discrimination and Enoch Powell.

S. Hall et al. (1978) produced a critical account of a moral panic created by the press about 'mugging'. They presented mugging as a new crime perpetrated by black offenders on white victims. The official crime figures did not justify this interpretation but it resulted in repressive policing of black communities.

Jones and Jones (1996) argued that science fiction draws on familiar racist imagery by portraying aliens from other planets as primitive savages who need civilizing. This they see as reflecting old attitudes about people in societies dominated by imperialist powers. They also pointed out that ethnic minority actors are used to portray aliens.

Van Dijk (1991) argued that the British press still presented a 'white voice', with minorities often invisible. The authorities who speak on race issues are often white politicians, police or experts. The agenda is not explicitly racist but represents minorities as 'a problem'.

Solomos and Black (1996) analysed the changes in media stereotypes of ethnic minorities over a long period.

→ 1960s 'welfare scrounger' rather than 'NHS worker'
→ 1970s 'mugger' rather than 'victim of race attacks'
→ 1980s 'rioter' rather than 'victim of repressive policing'.

However, they maintained that there were two consistent themes:

→ the cultures of Asian and black people are alien to the 'British way of life'
→ the presence of ethnic minorities represents a threat to 'British culture'.

In both cases the press tend to have a narrow view of British culture which ignores the contribution of minorities to the culture and identity of our society.

Representations of gender and sexuality ●●●

The mass media tend to represent gender in stereotypical ways:

→ men are seen as workers and active in public life (rather than as fathers and husbands)

Action point

With the exception of Enoch Powell, Troyna's agenda is still familiar. Choose a day, study a selection of newspapers and see if there is a new agenda.

Checkpoint 1

Apart from crime, identify and explain another moral panic which labelled ethnic minorities as a problem.

Links

See page 148 for a discussion of the role of the media in the amplification of deviance.

Example

The reporting of the racist murder of Stephen Lawrence in the late 1990s was consistently critical of the police and represents a shift from previous reporting of racist violence.

Checkpoint 2

Challenge the scrounger stereotype by giving two reasons why ethnic minorities in the 1960s were less likely than the majority to be welfare-dependent.

Examiner's secrets

You may find *all* these statements stereotypical and emphasizing inequality and conflict. Sociologists, however liberal, may also fall into the trap of seeing ethnicity as a social problem.

→ women are seen as wives and mothers who are active in their private lives (rather than as workers in paid employment)
→ women are portrayed as sex objects to sell sex products or other consumer goods.

Tuchman (1981) was one of the first feminists to analyse the representation of women in the media. She concluded that as well as the focus on sexual attractiveness and the housewife-mother role, women were shown doing jobs which were extensions of their domestic roles.

Cumberbatch (1990) analysed TV adverts. He found, as expected, that men were shown more often in paid employment. Women were younger and attractiveness was part of the message. Surprisingly, men were more likely to be shown cooking.

Ownership and control

Perspectives described earlier in this chapter provide explanations of the process of **reproducing patriarchal ideology** through mass media. Men still dominate ownership and control of the media and fill the majority of journalist jobs. Where women are in control there is little evidence that a feminist agenda is followed. Interactionists argue that the media reflect as well as create gender stereotypes.

Has anything changed? ●●●

There have been major changes at the end of the 20th century in the lives of women, both at home and in the workplace. It is therefore not surprising that the view that the media still portray women in crude stereotypes has been challenged.

Frazer (1987) and Barker (1989) have revisited McRobbie's famous 1970s study of *Jackie* (a magazine for teenage girls). McRobbie saw the magazine as reinforcing an ideology of femininity which encouraged girls to be attractive to boys in order fulfil a dream of romantic love. Her critics argued respectively that:

→ girls did not identify with the fictional characters
→ girls no longer saw romantic love as their major aim in life.

'Strong women' have been featured for a long time in TV police dramas (e.g. *Cagney and Lacey*, 1980s) and films (*Alien*, 1979).

Adverts have deliberately used gender role reversal to sell familiar products (e.g. 'Dad' using Oxo to make dinner).

Exam question   answer: page 79

Using material from this page and your own knowledge, assess the view that the media perpetuate gender stereotypes. (20 min)

"The symbolic annihilation of women"

Tuchman dramatically describes the effects of trivializing women's lives in the media or excluding them altogether

Action point

Find the most recent information you can on who owns the mass media.

Checkpoint 3

Explain what sociologists mean by 'reproducing patriarchal ideology through the mass media'.

Links

Sue Sharpe's updated version of *Just Like a Girl* identified a similar change in girls' attitudes (see page 50).

Checkpoint 4

Media stereotypes are based on outdated views of women's roles. Give one argument for and one argument against the view that there have been 'major changes in the lives of women'.

Examiner's secrets

You don't have to restrict your answer to women.

Answers
Mass media

Checkpoints

1 Public debate, press reporting, political speeches and research by psychologists and sociologists suggest that the main fears are that the media encourage:
   • violent behaviour
   • sexual immorality
2 Public service broadcasters may seek large audiences to justify licence fees (e.g. the BBC) or to solicit subscriptions (e.g. public service TV in USA and Canada).

   The free market permits those who produce media content to do so to make artistic, moral or political statements without interference from government.
3 For Marxists the 'powerful groups' are the ruling class of owners.

   For feminists powerful groups are those men who can maintain patriarchy.

   For interactionists the media mangers and professionals are seen as having the power to create and reinforce apparently consensual values.

   The evidence supporting these views would come from studying the concentration of ownership and the output of the mass media.
4 Sociologists have their own political and moral values. They judge what they see and read in the light of their own experience. They may see political bias, sexism or racism because they are looking for it.

Exam question

Outline trends in ownership, mentioning: concentration, globalization, public ownership, and development of new media, particularly the internet.

   Explain the Marxist approach, which asserts the closest links between ownership, control and content. The content produces profit for the owners and helps to control the working class by transmitting the dominant ideology.

   Criticize the Marxist view by questioning evidence of effects on the audience. Propose the market model as an alternative.

   Conclude with the interactionist model, which sees both audience and producers influencing content within the prevailing culture. Both technical and ideological influences can be identified.

Examiner's secrets

Make sure that each section is explicitly related to the question by stating clearly that the theory does or does not regard ownership as a major influence on media content. It's only the Marxists who see ownership as crucial.

Mass media: effects and audiences

Checkpoints

1 • Exposure – many people switch off or don't read party political messages.
   • Perception – faced with a single message, supporters of different parties will interpret it differently.
   • Retention – we are more likely to remember ideas and evidence which reinforce our existing views.
2 Audiences who have personal experience of events interpret media representation of the events in a different way. Those with little or no first-hand experience of ethnic minorities may have greater fears or hostility.
3 People who are already predisposed to violence may choose to watch violent films. Watching violent films may be more common in groups where violent behaviour has always been more common, e.g. young working-class males.
4 He did not directly observe either the watching of films or the violent behaviour.

   Children may claim to have watched notorious horror films to gain status with friends. Research has shown that they may claim to have seen films that don't exist when presented with a list of titles.

   As argued in Checkpoint 3, even if a correlation could be demonstrated it doesn't prove that the media cause the violent behaviour.

Exam question

This question requires an emphasis on the diverse nature of audiences. You could mention social class, gender, ethnicity, age, political viewpoint, educational background, etc.

   You can use the approaches in the order they are described in this section.
• The hypodermic approach assumes a mass audience rather than diverse audiences. It emphasizes passivity rather than active interpretation, but does claim the media influence the audience.
• The uses and gratification and two-step flow models argue effects depend on the mediation of opinion leaders, and membership of different social groups influences how messages are received, e.g. Morley's *Nationwide* research.
• The absence of convincing evidence of immediate effects has led to the development of the cultural effects approaches which see class and gender as important influences on audiences.
• Marxist and feminist approaches would emphasize the importance of the relative power of producers and different audiences.

Examiner's secrets

The best answers will evaluate the evidence raising theoretical and methodology issues. Use concepts such as ideology.

The news

Checkpoints

1 Select two from this list or reasonable alternatives.
- There is a lot more news with BBC and CNN channels devoted to 24 hours per day news.
- The presenters have become celebrities commanding high salaries for keeping audiences loyal.
- Presentation is more dramatic and showbusiness-like.
- Virtually all stories have accompanying pictures – not just talking heads.
- Politicians use 'sound bites' to get on the news.

2 • Politicians make important speeches early enough to catch the next day's press.
- They agree to early morning radio interviews, which may influence the rest of the day's news.
- They release embarrassing information on days when it can be 'lost' because of more important stories. Government statistics revealing bad news about the persistence of health inequalities released when Diana married Prince Charles went unnoticed.

3 (a) Marxists would see personalization as trivialization that had the intention and effect of distracting attention from real issues. It is one of the ways the mass media keep people falsely conscious.
(b) The market view would be that personalization makes issues more accessible and interesting to the audience who get what they want.

4 They were attacked for neglecting children, being lesbians and for their failure to keep clean. The peace issue itself was not made newsworthy.

Exam question

Use the framework provided in the section. Discuss both technical and cultural factors.

It might help to reverse the order of what you have read as the cultural influences are more obviously sociological and can have different theoretical interpretations, e.g. Marxist and interactionist. There are plenty of arguments you can use. The evidence is best provided by referring to studies.

A good conclusion might point out that selectivity is necessary for practical reasons but what is selected is influenced by cultural factors.

Representation in the mass media

Checkpoints

The most obvious and recurrent moral panic is about immigration. This has prompted a series of stories about:

- being 'swamped'
- illegal immigration
- refugees as scroungers.

Such stories can be related to housing and unemployment issues.

There have been less enduring scare stories about education, health issues, arranged marriages, domestic violence, single mothers, etc. all involving either implicitly or explicitly 'racial' overtones.

2 They were young, first-generation immigrants who were of working age. Many were invited here to work by employers with recruitment problems (NHS, British Rail, London Transport).

Most immigrants went to areas where employment levels were high. Nationally, unemployment was low throughout the 1960s.

3 The mass media produce stories and images which present men and women in stereotypical ways. Women are portrayed as sex objects and/or happy with domestic life. The constant portrayal of such ideas suggests that gender inequalities are normal and natural. This ideology (distortion of reality) helps to maintain patriarchy (male domination of women).

4 • The increased number of women in paid employment is a major change.
- The continued responsibility for childcare and housework suggests some things haven't changed.

Exam question

Arguments for
Feminist theory and concepts such as patriarchy and patriarchal ideology can be explained and illustrated by referring to research on girls' and women's magazines (McRobbie, Ferguson), adverts (Cumberbatch, Goffman) and soaps, etc.

Arguments against
The portrayal of gender is not based on traditional stereotypes. Female presenters and some fiction challenge stereotypes.

The women's movement has received much media attention. New women's magazines are aimed at career women.

Conclusion
Are the media more sexist than real life? Do they reflect real life rather than perpetuate stereotypes?

Things have changed. Men are presented in more caring, i.e. traditionally female roles. *The X-Files* reversed stereotypes. Homosexuality is more openly represented as another set of male roles.

Wealth, poverty and welfare

Many sociologists regard the study of the poor (and the rich) as part of the more general issue of social inequality. However, in the past poverty has been seen as a distinct area for research. This may be because poverty was seen as a social problem and sociologists wished to contribute to its understanding and to a solution. More recently, poverty has been studied separately from social inequality because some sociologists think the poor are not just people with little money but are different in other ways.

The study of the welfare state and poverty are part of the same topic for the AQA syllabus but are treated separately by OCR. As alternative provisions to state welfare have recently developed, there is the possibility of parts of questions focusing on voluntary, private, family and community provision of welfare.

Exam themes

→ Defining and measuring poverty

→ Assessing explanations of poverty

→ Evaluating the welfare state

→ Examining and explaining the distribution of income and wealth

Topic checklist

	AQA Sociology	OCR Sociology	EDEXCEL Social Policy
O AS ● A2			
What is poverty?	O	●	O ●
Explaining poverty	O	●	O ●
The distribution of income and wealth	O	●	O ●
The welfare state	O	●	O ●

What is poverty?

Examiner's secrets

You get marks for evaluation.
Don't take definitions for granted.
Point out that the beliefs (ideology) of
sociologists and politicians influence
the way they define social problems
such as poverty.

Links

Rowntree's work can be used as an
example of the social survey (page 8) in
methods questions. Other sociologists
have used his work as secondary data
(page 12) to make comparisons over time.

Checkpoint 1

Identify periods in the family life cycle
which may lead to changes in living
standards.

Checkpoint 2

Why is it difficult to define basic needs?

Action point

Make notes on the different definitions
of poverty. If you are looking at poverty
research, note what definition was used.

Defining poverty is a political as well as a sociological
problem. A key issue is the distinction between
poverty and social inequality. Social inequality is the
uneven distribution of scarce rewards. It is found in all
societies and is seen by functionalists as a useful way
of motivating people to work hard. However, the poor
have been seen as 'outsiders', and the persistence of
poverty as an undesirable social problem.

Absolute poverty

Rowntree (1899) tried to define and measure poverty in a scientific way
by calculating a poverty line based on the minimum income necessary to maintain a healthy life. He listed '*necessities*' such as housing,
clothing and food, and calculated the family income needed to buy
them. He distinguished **primary poverty**, caused by low income, from
secondary poverty, caused by spending unwisely. He also discovered a
cycle of poverty, where families moved in and out of poverty as their
income and commitments changed.

Evaluation

→ Deciding what is a necessity is problematic. Luxuries tend to become
  necessities. Basic needs change, e.g. as people live longer they need
  to provide for old age.
→ The reduction in job security and the real value of some state
  spending means having to pay for higher education, health care
  and unemployment insurance.
→ The poor may have an income above the poverty line but lack the
  opportunity, knowledge or desire to spend as 'experts' suggest,
  e.g. they may live in a 'food desert' in the inner city or in rural
  areas with no access to cheaper supermarket food.

Relative poverty

The poverty line is calculated by listing what is necessary to take part
in everyday life. This will change as average living standards change
and is thus a measure of **inequality**.

Townsend (1979) saw poverty as **relative deprivation**. He said the
poor, whose income was below 150% of the benefit level, were excluded
from the normal lifestyle of the community.

Mack and Lansley (1985) refined Townsend's method by using
a sample survey to select a list of necessities. They calculated the
number of the poor and their depth of poverty by identifying those
who lacked at least three of the 22 items that had been identified as
necessities.

Other measures of poverty ●●●

Another way to measure relative poverty is to examine changes in the distribution of income and wealth in society. This can produce a variety of indicators of the nature and extent of poverty.

→ **Changes in the real income of the poor** can be calculated over time. Townsend (1991), using the Thatcher government's own figures, claimed that from 1979 to 1989 the income of the poorest 20% fell 4.6% while the income of the richest 20% rose by 40%.

→ *Comparisons with average earnings* Pichaud (1991) calculated that the income of a married claimant of unemployment benefit fell from 35% of average earnings in 1979 to 27% in 1990. J. Williams (1992) showed that the proportion of the population living below half average income had doubled from 10% to 20% between 1979 and 1990. J. Hills (1995) for the Joseph Rowntree Foundation showed a further increase in those living on less than half average wages. In addition there was evidence of falling real incomes.

Evaluation

People may lack 'necessities' by choice rather than being deprived, e.g. people may not eat meat for cultural, moral or health reasons. A weekly joint of meat was on Mack and Lansley's list. Mack and Lansley decided themselves that lacking three items constituted poverty. However, the number of the poor would be fewer if families needed to be deprived of a larger number of items. Lists of necessities would need to be updated regularly as standards change. This would undermine the validity of historical comparisons.

A repeat of Mack and Lansley's work in 1990 showed an increase in the number of the poor from 7.5 million to 11 million. This could show a real increase in poverty or simply changing standards, as the list of necessities had risen from 22 to 32.

Right-wing critics are unhappy with a definition of poverty based on inequality as it implies the failure of the market economy that has, in the long term, produced higher living standards for nearly everyone.

If definitions are linked to levels of social security benefit (e.g. Townsend suggested 150% of benefit), then raising benefit would increase the number said to be in poverty, and vice versa.

Checkpoint 3

Why do some politicians object to defining poverty by comparisons with average earnings?

> *"A family is poor if it cannot afford to eat . . . By any absolute standards there is very little poverty in Britain today."*
>
> K. Joseph, 1976 (former Conservative cabinet minister and a major influence on 'Thatcherism')

Checkpoint 4

List two arguments for and two arguments against Joseph's view in the above quote.

Examiner's secrets

Explaining the difference between inequality and poverty may help you. Make sure you do more than just list studies; point out differences.

Exam question   answer: page 90

Examine some of the different ways researchers have attempted to measure poverty. (20 min)

Explaining poverty

Social problems are issues of public concern – many people think 'something needs to be done'. *Sociological problems* are phenomena which sociologists are trying to explain.

Checkpoint 1

In what ways are the poor different from other members of society?

Action point

Make notes on the similarities and differences between the culture of poverty and the new right explanation.

Checkpoint 2

Give two reasons why people can be blamed for being poor.

Poverty still exists in rich countries such as modern Britain and the USA. Its persistence is seen as a *social problem* and explaining it is a *sociological problem*.

Cultural explanations

Cultural explanations (also called individualistic theories) are favoured by the political right and blame the lifestyle of the poor.

The culture of poverty

The **culture of poverty** is a set of values, norms, attitudes and beliefs that distinguish the poor from the rest of society. Poverty is not just lack of money; the poor are different. This continues Spencer's view that the poor in Victorian Britain were weak or wicked, had large families and spent their money unwisely, particularly on alcohol. Oscar Lewis (1968) described the way of life of the poor in Latin America. They feel helpless and dependent, and they live for today rather than plan for the future. Families are often headed by single mothers and the poor do not participate in organizations such as political parties or trade unions which might improve their position. This view was later applied by Harrington to the poor in the USA, who are disproportionately from black and/or Spanish-speaking ethnic minorities.

The New Right has continued the cultural argument. Murray has claimed the immoral and often criminal lives of the inner-city poor are the causes of their poverty. They choose to be poor. Marlsand in Britain focused on **welfare dependence** as the cause of poverty.

The solution

→ Change the inadequate culture – in Victorian times through the Church and its schools, in the 1960s and 1990s through education.
→ No higher benefits or a minimum wage – the state should use rewards and punishments to reduce welfare dependence.

Evaluation of cultural theories

→ There may not be a distinctive culture; ordinary people move in and out of poverty due to unemployment, ill health, divorce, etc.
→ It is not only 'problem' families who live in poverty – those in full-time but low-paid work are also poor.
→ The different lifestyle may be the result and not the cause, e.g. welfare dependence is the result not the cause of poverty.
→ Those who support inequality can blame the victims of poverty rather than the powerful.
→ The Valentines (1968) said the distinctive culture helped the poor adapt to their deprivation.

Structural explanations of poverty

Structural explanations (favoured by the left) tend to blame class, gender and ethnic inequalities in the job market.

Peter Townsend – a Social Democratic view: the poor are those, usually from the lower social classes, who lack power. They may be unable to work, for various reasons, and may have a weak position in the labour market because they lack skills/experience discrimination.

Marxist views: capitalism is based on the exploitation of the working class and inevitably produces inequalities. The poor are not different, they are the lowest-paid part of the working class. Unemployment and who is unemployed varies as the economy goes through booms and slumps. The poor are a *reserve army of labour* who keep wages low and divide the working class.

Women and poverty: feminists have argued that women are particularly vulnerable to poverty. Women are made dependent on men or the state because of their responsibility for childcare. They have been restricted to 'women's jobs' (often low-paid/casual/part-time).

The solutions

→ Change the unequal structure of society.
→ Marxists advocate revolution and the end of capitalism.
→ The Social Democratic view proposes support for the weak through legal protection, minimum wages and redistribution of income and wealth through taxes and benefits.
→ In the past the poor working class used political parties and trade unions to gain power and improve their position.

Evaluation of structural theories

The New Right, Conservative and Labour politicians try to distinguish between those who should get benefits because they can't work from the undeserving poor who need enabling to work by reducing benefits and increasing training. Inequality is not the same as poverty. Earning less does not mean those at the bottom in rich countries are living in poverty. Marxism doesn't explain the particular disadvantages of women and ethnic minorities.

The jargon

Social Democrats are critical of inequality in capitalist society but see reform rather than a Marxist revolution as the solution.

Checkpoint 3

What is a reserve army of labour? (Refer to the section on family for help page 102.)

Checkpoint 4

Why is the New Right opposed to welfare benefits?

Exam question   answer: page 90

Assess the usefulness of 'individualistic' theories of the causes of poverty. (20 min)

Examiner's secrets

A 'useful' theory would explain poverty effectively and fully.

The distribution of income and wealth

Most sociologists see the distribution of income and wealth as a social inequality issue. It is included in this section to conform to the AQA specification.

Defining income and wealth

Income is the money gained by individuals or families, mainly through wages but also from benefits, pensions, interest, dividends and rent. Income has become more unequally distributed within the population.

Wealth is what people own rather than earn. Marketable wealth excludes houses and rights to pensions which for most individuals are by far their most valuable possessions. Wealth is far more unevenly distributed than income (see the table below).

The growth of income inequality

The distribution of income in Britain corresponds with the political party in power.

1950–1964   There were Conservative governments and income distribution was stable.

1964–1977   Labour was in power for nine of the 13 years and the gap between rich and poor narrowed.

1977–1997   During the last two years of Labour rule and 18 years of Conservative government there was a consistent increase in inequality.

1997–2000   No significant redistribution of income.

The reasons for growing inequality

→ The standard rate of income tax has been reduced and the top rate has left more cash in the pockets of the high-paid.

→ Claiming benefits has been made more difficult, e.g. no unemployment benefit for under-18s or housing benefit for students.

→ The real value of benefits, e.g. child benefit, has fallen.

→ More people have become benefit-dependent owing to higher rates of unemployment, more people living in lone-parent families and longer life expectancy.

→ Unemployment and the weakening of trade unions have allowed employers to pay low wages.

→ The impact of the Labour Government since 1997 is not yet clear. A minimum wage has been introduced and the value of some benefits increased, while others have become more difficult to claim. Party politics is not the whole story. Global unemployment was high during the Thatcher years and has been much lower in most developed countries during the late 1990s.

Example

Official figures omit income from crime and the income of tax dodgers.

Example

The major forms of marketable wealth are cash, land, businesses and shares in businesses.

Checkpoint 1

Why might official figures underestimate household income?

Check the net

www.jrf.org.uk
The Joseph Rowntree Foundation published *Inquiry into Income and Wealth*, 1995.

Links

The growth of poverty is discussed on pages 82–3.

Checkpoint 2

Identify and explain two ways in which governments can increase the extent of inequality in society.

Who are the rich and poor?

Social class   Most of the low paid, unemployed, elderly, sick or disabled poor hold or held unskilled or semi-skilled manual jobs.
Gender   Women are more likely to be poor or benefit-dependent as they head lone-parent families, are not employed and live longer.
Age   The retired tend to rely on benefits. Children of unemployed couples and lone-parent families are more likely to live in poverty.
Ethnicity   Unlike in the USA there is no clear link between ethnicity and poverty, although there is inequality of income.

Links

These issues are examined further in the section on work and leisure, and the section on social stratification.

Exam question
answer: page 91

Item A

Poverty is particularly a problem for older women in all societies. In Britain in 1987 35% of older women were living on an income at or below income support level, compared with 25% of men. Older women living alone are even more likely to be living in poverty – about 50% compared with 40% of single men. In 1988, three times as many older women as men were living in households with below average incomes.

(Adapted from P. Abbott and C. Wallace, *An Introduction to Sociology: Feminist Perspectives* (2nd edition) Routledge 1997)

Item B   Distribution of Wealth, UK

Marketable wealth	1976	1981	1986	1991	1993
Percentage of wealth owned by:					
Most wealthy 1%	21	18	18	17	17
Most wealthy 5%	38	36	36	35	36
Most wealthy 10%	50	50	50	47	48
Most wealthy 25%	71	73	73	71	72
Most wealthy 50%	92	92	90	92	92
Total marketable wealth £ billion	280	565	955	1711	1809

Social Trends 26 (Crown Copyright) 1996.

(a) With reference to Item B
  (i) What proportion of marketable wealth did the most wealthy 1% hold in 1981?
  (ii) How much marketable wealth was there in the UK in 1993?
  (iii) Calculate the percentage of marketable wealth held by the least wealthy 50% in 1993.
(b) According to Item A, what proportion of older men were living at or below the Income Support Benefit level in 1987?
(c) Suggest two ways in which poverty may benefit the non-poor.
(d) Explain the difference between income and wealth.
(e) Identify and explain two reasons why 'older women' are more likely to be in poverty than 'older men' (Item A).
(40 min)

Examiner's secrets

You don't need to memorize the figures but you should be able to interpret tables and explain their findings.

Checkpoint 3

What is 'marketable wealth'? Explain with examples.

Examiner's secrets

You should refer to both age and gender for part (e).

The welfare state

What is the welfare state? Government uses its powers to modify market forces by ensuring a minimum family income, whether people work or not; tackling the effects of social problems such as sickness, unemployment and retirement; and offering social services to all, irrespective of class, ethnicity or gender.

Perspectives on social policy and the welfare state ●●●

Social Democratic reformist approach

The modern welfare state was founded in post-war Britain by the first majority Labour Government. The aim was to battle with the 'five giant evils' identified in the 1942 *Beveridge Report*. These were *poverty*, *disease*, *squalor*, *ignorance* and *idleness*.

Townsend has argued that all citizens have a right to basic levels of welfare provision, including education, health care and pensions, and that these should be *universally* provided. The welfare state was seen as the solution to poverty by providing a safety net for those who are temporarily or permanently unable to support themselves.

The New Right approach

This supports a **market liberal approach** to the economy where state intervention and public spending are minimized. It argues that *redistribution of income and wealth* is not a legitimate role for the state and condemns the state for producing and maintaining a **culture of dependency.** Market forces have been brought into public services:

→ local authorities have 'privatized' some services and use private providers of care
→ schools have been encouraged to compete for pupils and management made more independent of local education authorities
→ market forces were brought into the NHS and private health care encouraged by tax allowances.

Evaluation of the role of the welfare state

→ The New Right is critical of high public spending, the creation of a culture of dependency and the unfairness of supporting 'scroungers'. Their attack on the welfare state remains an influence on the new Labour Government.
→ Increased life expectancy and the rising cost of health care and education means the principle of universal benefits is being abandoned for means-tested benefits, which lack widespread support.

Checkpoint 1

For each of the 'five evils' identify one part of the welfare state which aims to deal with it.

The jargon

Universal benefits are paid to all people who qualify, regardless of income, e.g. old age pension, child benefit. *Selective benefits* are means-tested and depend on income, e.g. income support.

Checkpoint 2

What is meant by 'a culture of dependency'?

Examiner's secrets

The 1997 Labour Government appears to have accepted some market reforms of the welfare state. This means a simple left/right division no longer applies – if it ever did.

- Care in the community has become a cheap and inadequate way to care for the mentally ill.
- Feminists see the existing structure of the welfare state as a means of maintaining the subordination of women. Taxation and benefits support the existing patriarchal family.
- However, some reforms have helped women, e.g. child benefit is paid to mothers and there are now tax allowances for childcare.
- Social Democrats argue that the free market creates inequality and problems for the disadvantaged, and usually fails to deal with them.
- Marxists argue that the welfare state does not redistribute income or wealth. State spending on education and rail subsidies may benefit the middle classes and those in work rather than the poor.

Voluntary organizations

Voluntary organizations are non-profit-making, often charities, and are not controlled by the state. Their main activities are:

- providing services, e.g. housing and care
- acting as *pressure groups* to influence the government and publicize social problems

Advantages
- they speak for the weak
- they can criticize the state
- they can be small, flexible and innovative
- they encourage self-help rather than dependency
- less **stigmatization** for clients
- reduce public spending

Disadvantages
- disguising problems such as poverty and homelessness by dealing with symptoms not causes
- allowing Government to shed universal provision, e.g. care of the old
- staff may be untrained

Private welfare provision

This has been encouraged to reduce public spending, reduce the size of the state sector, and encourage efficiency through competition.

Informal welfare provision

This is mostly provided by women within the family. The financial and other costs to women are disguised. Some state benefits support family carers.

Exam question   answer: page 91

'The provision of universal welfare benefits is responsible for the continued existence of poverty.' Examine the arguments for and against this statement. (45 min)

> *"The richest 20% of the population gained nearly four times as much from the social services as the poorest 20% . . . particularly via education and housing benefits."*
>
> Townsend, 1979

Checkpoint 3

List one argument for and one argument against the view that the voluntary sector undermines the welfare state.

The jargon

Stigmatization is when individuals are given and may accept a negative label, e.g. 'scrounger'.

Checkpoint 4

Identify and explain two ways in which welfare is provided by the private sector.

Examiner's secrets

Extra marks if you can deal specifically with 'universal' benefits.

Answers
Wealth, welfare and poverty

What is poverty?

Checkpoints

1 Living standards depend on income and expenditure. Income is higher when people are in full-time work. Young people may not have begun work, motherhood may interrupt full-time work, and older people may have retired.

   Families may be best off when there are two or more in work and worst off when child-raising leads to women stopping full-time work.

2 • Because different people need and want different things, e.g. manual workers need more food.
   • Standards change over time, e.g. outdoor lavatories are no longer acceptable.

3 • Because rising living standards may have no apparent effect on poverty levels.
   • Rising earnings may increase the number of the poor if benefits are raised in line with incomes – yet a smaller rise could leave the poor better off.
   • Because they think that inequality is functional and benefits the community.

Examiner's secrets

This is probably more of a political/ideological issue than a technical problem in defining poverty.

4 *For*
   • Real pay and real living standards have significantly risen during the 20th century, even for the poorest groups.
   • The welfare state provides a safety net for those unable to work.
   Against
   • Since 1979 the real living standards of the poorest have fallen.
   • Joseph's definition of poverty is inappropriate – relative poverty is real poverty.

Exam question

An obvious framework is to consider absolute then relative definitions of poverty.

   Use relevant studies to support your arguments (Booth, Rowntree, Townsend, Mack and Lansley).

   Discuss the methods used to produce research findings (e.g. social surveys or interpreting secondary data).

   You can also introduce the political/ideological debate by explaining how the New Right, both sociologists and politicians, have rejected the view that inequality necessarily leads to poverty.

   Even where there is agreement on definitions of poverty there are technical issues about measuring it, e.g. who decides what are basic needs – the experts or social consensus?

Examiner's secrets

As always, detailed descriptions of studies are not required. If you only have 20 minutes do not spend it listing Townsend's views on what is a basic need.

Explaining poverty

Checkpoints

1 According to the culture of poverty view, the poor:
   • have different attitudes and values
   • tend to live in lone-parent families
   • accept their position in society.
   The New Right view is more hostile and tends to blame the poor (see Checkpoint 2, below).

2 According to the New Right and often the tabloid press and some politicians:
   • the poor are lazy and choose not to work
   • they have children in order to get state benefits

3 The term 'reserve army of labour' was originally used by Marxists and later by feminists.

   The reserve army of labour is available for work when required by employers but not seen as entitled to work. When not working they may not be visible as registered unemployed. The term has been applied to women, children, the old, ethnic minorities and immigrants.

4 The New Right opposes many benefits because:
   • they favour low taxes; they claim high taxes are a disincentive to work
   • they think benefits encourage a culture of dependency rather than 'standing on your own two feet'
   • they think sections of the poor are undeserving, immoral scroungers who shouldn't be given help.

Exam question

'Assess the usefulness' means you must discuss how successfully such theories explain the existence and persistence of poverty.

   Define and explain 'individualistic' theories. Point out the moral/political judgement they make about the poor. Examine their link with the culture of poverty and the existence of an 'underclass.' Examine the relationship with New Right theories and social policies.

   Evaluate by using structuralist theories to criticize the definition and explanation of poverty.

The distribution of income and wealth

Checkpoints

1 People may not reveal all their earnings. This is because they may be illegal or people wish to avoid tax. Some workers receive benefits in a non-cash form; sometimes these are counted as taxable income, sometimes not.

2 • By reducing the rates of direct taxes on income.
   • By taxing previously untaxed benefits.
   • By not having a minimum wage.
   • By reducing benefits and/or making it more difficult to claim them.

3 Wealth which can be disposed of and spent. You can sell shares but not rights to an occupational pension. Other examples are savings.

Exam question

a) (i) 18%

(ii) £1809 billion

(iii) 8%

b) One-quarter or 25%

c) You would get two marks for each of two ways, e.g. the poor are a source of cheap labour, they are a warning to other workers, they can be blamed for problems of high government spending, they provide work for the middle classes who work in benefit offices and as social workers.

d) Income flows into the household and may be earned or come from rent, dividends on shares, etc. Wealth is owned and may be passed on to others.

e) You would get two marks for identifying an appropriate reason and two for explaining it.

- Longer life expectancy means they are more likely to have the extra expense of living alone.
- Interrupted careers – less chance to save, therefore smaller pension.
- Lower average earnings and earlier retirement age.
- Loss of health in very old age.

The welfare state

Checkpoints

1 *Poverty* – social security benefits, e.g. income support (some benefits have been reduced or eligibility made more difficult).

Disease – the NHS (not all services are free now).

Squalor – subsidized house building (council house building has been phased out and help with rents and mortgages much reduced).

Ignorance – free education (no longer free higher education).

Idleness – training schemes for the unemployed (governments are much less likely to manage unemployment by increasing government spending).

2 The 'culture of dependency', identified and criticized by the New Right, is a set of attitudes, values and behaviour which discourages supporting yourself through working.

The feeling of helplessness was one of the characteristics of the culture of poverty described by Lewis.

3 *For*

Voluntary provision may encourage the reduction in state provision, e.g. care of old people or health research. (The Wellcome Foundation spends more than the NHS on medical research.)

Against

Voluntary organizations have played a major part in persuading the state to tackle social problems by acting as pressure groups and through publicizing problems, e.g. the roles of Shelter and the *Big Issue* in raising awareness and sympathy for the homeless.

4
- Care of old people is provided in various forms by the private sector, which may receive some payment direct from the state.
- Local government must seek competitive bids from the private sector to run some services, e.g. housing maintenance and leisure services.

Exam question

Start by defining and explaining universal benefits. Distinguish them from selective/targeted/means-tested benefits.

Arguments for

New Right view:
- benefits encourage culture of dependency
- universal benefits waste money and lead to high taxes
- real absolute poverty may no longer exist

Evaluation

It should be noted that it is means-tested benefits that discourage people from working, as the benefits are lost if people earn more. Universal benefits can be retained by those working and earning, e.g. child benefit.

Arguments against

- Argue that the welfare state in general and universal benefits in particular have helped the poor, who are seen by Townsend and other social democrats as sometimes lacking the power to help themselves, e.g. the old.
- Point out that poverty existed long before the foundation of the modern welfare state.
- Poverty has structural causes.

Conclusion

Explain briefly Marxist and feminist views of poverty and their rather critical view of the role of the welfare state. The rich may benefit more from the welfare state than the poor.

Examiner's secrets

This is a hybrid question requiring application of knowledge of both theories of poverty and the welfare state. Developing a clear and critical argument is more important than writing down everything you know.

Social stratification

Social stratification is the division of society into layers. These layers are distinguished by unequal rewards and life chances. Social class is arguably the most important form of stratification in modern societies although gender and ethnicity have assumed increasing importance in sociological studies.

Social inequality and difference are examined as the synoptic unit (see page 186) by both AQA and OCR. OCR includes the debates over poverty in its questions. When answering questions in this synoptic unit you should emphasize the ways that sociologists use the study of inequality to debate broader issues, such as the best way to do sociological research and the evaluation of sociological perspectives. You should also show you understand the need to consider social stratification when studying nearly every AS and A2 topic.

Exam themes

→ The major theories of stratification

→ Using these theories to explain changes in the class structure of modern societies

→ The life chances of ethnic and gender groups

→ The relationship between occupation and social class

→ The nature and extent of social mobility

Topic checklist

O AS ● A2	AQA Sociology	OCR Sociology	EDEXCEL Social Policy
Measuring social class and mobility	●	●	O
Theories of inequality	●	●	
Changes in the class structure	●	●	
Life chances: ethnicity	●	●	
Life chances: gender	●	●	

Measuring social class and mobility

Social class has been defined and measured in different ways. This section covers practical rather than theoretical issues. A major use of occupational classifications has been to measure social mobility.

Checkpoint 1

Give one reason for and one reason against classifying non-employed people according to their last job.

"For all its problems, the Goldthorpe Classification is probably the best . . ."

J. Scott, 1998

Action point

Note the different groups used by the Registrar General and Goldthorpe. Point out similarities and differences.
(You don't need to memorize the groups, although they will become increasingly familiar through reading.)

Checkpoint 2

Explain with examples why using male heads of household to classify families may be inappropriate.

Example

When asked to consider replacing the Registrar General's Classification, which has been used since 1911, Lockwood and Rose recommended continuing with an amended version which will be used in the 2001 census.

Measuring social class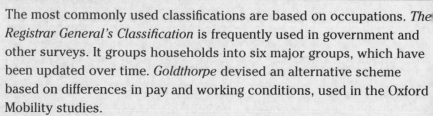

The most commonly used classifications are based on occupations. *The Registrar General's Classification* is frequently used in government and other surveys. It groups households into six major groups, which have been updated over time. *Goldthorpe* devised an alternative scheme based on differences in pay and working conditions, used in the Oxford Mobility studies.

Evaluation of classifications based on occupation

'The trouble with women'

→ Non-employed housewives are excluded as 'non-workers'.
→ Women often appear to be in higher classes than men. However, 'women's jobs' are often in the lower levels of each grouping, e.g. women dominate lower-paid professions like nursing and teaching.
→ Women often earn less than men in the same group (or even lower groups) and their chances of promotion may be less.
→ The division between manual and non-manual workers is less useful when applied to women, as many low-paid, low-status and low-skilled service jobs are classified as non-manual.
→ Wives and children are often classified by male head of household.
→ Feminists claim that all women are proletarianized by their exploitation in the home and possibly in the workplace.

Other problems

→ Ownership is not measured – the rich are not included – and the poor and unemployed are excluded.
→ The ranking of jobs may be based on status and is a source of debate and can change.
→ Classifications attempt to evaluate skills. Critics claim that the evaluation depends on who does the job, e.g. women's skills may be rated lower just because women have them.
→ Self-assigned class may explain behaviour better than objective classifications.

Positive points

Occupation is a good predictor of life expectancy, infant mortality and other measures of health. Parents' occupations predict educational achievement, particularly when the class of both parents is considered.

Social mobility

What is social mobility?

Movement up or down the class structure by individuals or groups. **Intragenerational mobility** is within an individual's working life and **intergenerational mobility** compares classes of parents and children.

What are the causes of social mobility?

→ *Changes in the occupational structure*, e.g. decline of the working class and growth of middle class.
→ *Educational reforms* widen opportunities.
→ *Lower birth rates*, especially in the middle classes, increase the need to recruit working-class children to middle-class jobs.
→ *Equal opportunities* legislation and changing recruitment practices.
→ Women tend to marry men in the same or higher classes.

Action point

Take notes which explain and illustrate each of these five causes of social mobility.

What are the effects of social mobility?

Open societies have higher rates of intergenerational mobilty than *closed societies*. **Class conflict** is reduced. People strive for individual advancement rather than there being collective struggles. Functionalists have pointed out that mobility is necessary to ensure the best people do the most important jobs.

Checkpoint 3

Why is there more social mobility in modern industrial societies?

What are the problems of measuring social mobility?

→ A father's final position is compared with a possibly temporary one for sons, who may move up or down.
→ Records of the father's occupations may be unreliable.
→ The ranking of jobs changes over time.
→ Comparison over time is difficult because different job classifications have been used.
→ Studying only two generations may conceal the sons of downwardly mobile fathers returning to their original position.
→ Classification of women is problematic; they were excluded from major studies (e.g. Glass, Goldthorpe); Heath found women were more often downwardly mobile.
→ Jobs included in Goldthorpe's service class are so varied that really top jobs are included with middle-class jobs with average pay.
→ Studies may ignore the rich and the unemployed.

Checkpoint 4

Explain with examples why ranking of jobs might change.

Example

Jackson and Marsden found working-class grammar school boys often had middle-class mothers.

Exam questions   answers: page 104

1   Identify and explain two reasons why occupation is a useful measure of social class. (10 min)

2   Examine some of the problems involved in using occupation to define and measure social class. (20 min)

Theories of inequality

Checkpoint 1

How do modern Marxists believe employers control workers?

Checkpoint 2

How might a Marxist answer the criticism that workers don't feel exploited?

Links

Inequality of income is discussed on page 86

The jargon

Market situation refers to the ability to earn more or less. It depends on skills, control over entry and other sources of bargaining power.

Example

Parties include unions, professional associations and political parties.

There are three major theories of inequality, which can be distinguished by the way they answer three basic questions:

→ How is social class defined?
→ How many classes are there?
→ How is the class structure likely to develop?

Marx
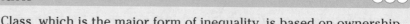

→ Class, which is the major form of inequality, is based on ownership of the means of production.
→ There are only two significant classes: the *bourgeoisie*, who own the means of production (e.g. factories) and the *proletariat*, who are wage labourers (working in factories).
→ The owners exploit and oppress the workers.
→ Owners use force and ideology to control the workers.
→ Marx predicted economic changes would cause class conflict, with *monopolization* of capital (i.e. fewer people own more); *homogenization* of the working class (skill differences disappear); *pauperization* of the workers (they get poorer); and *polarization* of the two classes (more inequality as they move apart).
→ Class conflict will lead to revolution, the triumph of the workers, and the development of a classless equal society.

Evaluation

Class is not the only form of inequality; people are ranked by caste, status, age, ethnicity and gender. And there are competing definitions of class. It can be argued that there are more than two classes. There are also middle classes and working classes. Equally, not all workers feel oppressed and exploited. Force is rare and workers recognize exploitation but need to work.

Some firms have become global and tend to monopoly, but share ownership may be diffuse. Small businesses start up and some remain small. The working class has fragmented, not homogenized. There are divisions between manual and non-manual, more or less skilled, employed and unemployed, men and women, natives and immigrants. Some of the working class have become affluent, not poorer. Inequality has increased since 1979, but there is a growing middle class and a gap between the working class and the poor.

Some modern Marxists have seen the ideological hegemony as inhibiting class consciousness and conflict. Pluralists see higher pay and the welfare state as desirable alternatives to revolution.

Weber

Social inequality is based on differences in power, not just class. The sources of power are: **class** – an objective economic category based on *ownership*, *market situation*, and ease of *mobility*; **status** – a subjective category based on prestige (status groups share lifestyles and patterns of consumption); and **party** – a group who are organized to gain power.

Evaluation

Weber provides a more flexible model that can be used to explain the causes and effects of changes in the class structure. In particular his theories can be applied to *working-class affluence, the growth of the middle classes* and discussion of an *underclass*. Ideas, as well as economic developments, are causes of change.

Functionalist theories

These consensus theories offer a critical view of conflict theories of inequality.

Parsons claims that stratification systems are based on shared values and therefore *integrate* rather than divide societies. The ranking of individuals depends on the consensual view of the importance of their positions. Power is given to those in important positions to enable them to achieve shared goals.

Davis and Moore identify the functions of stratification as *role allocation and performance*. Inequality ensures the best people perform well in the most important jobs.

Evaluation

These explanations and criticisms are largely from Tumin.

→ *Some positions are functionally more important than others.* This is a value judgement. Well-paid jobs may seem important.
→ *Few people have the natural talent needed to perform these tasks.* Inequality inhibits discovery and development of talent. Natural talent is only necessary for a few jobs – sports, arts, etc.
→ *Developing talents into skills, through training, requires sacrifices such as loss of earnings.* Sacrifices are not logically necessary – grants, rich parents, prospective employers could all finance education and training.
→ *Expectation of high pay motivates people to make these sacrifices.* People may be motivated by altruism or posts can be filled by conscription.
→ *Unequal rewards lead to differences in prestige attached to positions which become generally accepted and the basis of stratification.* Davis and Moore are better at explaining inequality in rewards for positions at one moment in time, rather than the inheritance of advantages which results from stratification. They assume equality of opportunity to ensure the best get to the top. Stratification prevents this.

> *". . . [Weber] provides what is missing in Marx."*
>
> Giddens

Checkpoint 3

Identify one similarity and one difference between functionalist and Weberian explanations of inequality.

Checkpoint 4

Give examples of how stratification prevents the most able people filling the most important positions.

Exam question   answer: page 104

'Social stratification is beneficial for both individuals and societies.' Assess the sociological arguments and evidence for this view. (50 min)

Examiner's secrets

Remember to use Marx and Weber in your evaluation.

Changes in the class structure

The issues below should be examined using a critical framework based on the debates between Marx and modern Marxists and Weber and modern Weberian studies.

The working classes ●●●

Marx anticipated an impoverished and increasingly homogenized working class who would become class conscious and revolutionary. This has been challenged in three ways. **Embourgeoisement** – means the working class is becoming middle-class. This was a 1950s argument when rising living standards, full employment, free secondary education and a new welfare state accompanied three consecutive Conservative election victories.

Goldthorpe and Lockwood tested the hypothesis that the affluent workers were becoming middle-class. They concluded that, although they had middle-class incomes they had not developed middle-class attitudes, nor were they accepted by their middle-class neighbours. They were a new working class with an instrumental attitude to work rather than traditional values. Embourgeoisement theory was revived in the 1980s and 1990s when the Conservatives won four elections.

A fragmented working class – is the opposite of the homogenized class predicted by Marx. The divisions may be based on gender, ethnicity, levels of skill, job security, etc. The divided working class is not a new idea. Rose in the 1960s described an 'ideal type' of working class which included only 25% of manual workers.

The underclass are a group of people trapped below the working class. The term has been used by sociologists and the press in a variety of ways: Americans have used it to describe the inner-city poor, often black or Spanish-speaking; some British Weberian sociologists have used it to describe ethnic minorities, but it is now more commonly used to describe the benefit-dependent living on run-down estates with high levels of unemployment. The Left see the underclass trapped in low-paid insecure work with little hope of upward mobility, their condition worsened by increasing inequality, unemployment and benefit cuts. The New Right have defined the underclass in moral terms and see their inferior culture as a cause of poverty.

The middle classes ●●●

Proletarianization of the middle class means that office and other 'white collar' workers are being depressed into the working class. The existence of a middle class represents a challenge to conventional Marxist views and this theory is one way in which modern Marxists have responded. The causes of proletarianization include the worsening pay and conditions of office workers compared to factory workers, the deskilling of office work and the increased proportion of female workers.

Checkpoint 1

Explain why
(a) a fragmented working class and
(b) an affluent working class
represent problems for Marxists.

Checkpoint 2

Outline the Weberian view of an underclass.

Links

See New Right views on poverty and welfare on pages 84 and 88.

Lockwood (1958 and 1989) tested the Marxist hypothesis that routine office workers were falsely conscious proletarians. He used Weber's distinction between class and status to show that the office worker remained superior in terms of market situation, work situation and status. The key difference was the greater security enjoyed by office workers. He concluded the gap was narrowing and clerks were a new middle class.

A fragmented middle class – the gap between middle and working classes is no longer so great or even clear. The middle classes may be growing but so too are the differences within this group of classes. Goldthorpe identified four major groups by examining the origins of parents an'd the life chances of children.

Example

Mills used Marx and Weber to argue that proletarianization extended to managers, sales staff and even professionals who sold themselves on the 'personality market'.

Checkpoint 3

What changes in working conditions can be used to support the proletarianization theory?

The class structure of capitalist societies

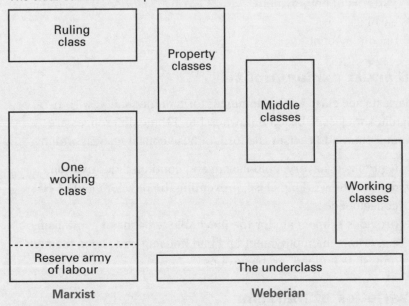

Marxist   **Weberian**

Checkpoint 4

Draw diagrams to illustrate
(a) the functionalist theory of inequality
(b) the result of embourgeoisement.

The Marxist model includes divisions within the working class. Professionals and mangers are at the top and the reserve army of labour in lower strata.

The Weberian model indicates classes of owners based on how much property they have. The non-owning classes are divided on the basis of market situation into a number of middle and working classes. Beneath the working class is an underclass lacking power.

Exam question   answer: page 105

To what extent do sociologists agree that the class structure in modern societies is fragmented? (45 min)

Life chances: ethnicity

Studies of race and ethnicity tend to adopt a conflict perspective and focus on social problems. There are a few exceptions where diversity, not inequality, is considered.

Example

W. Daniel (1969) did a pioneer study of racial discrimination in England. He used a variety of methods to test discrimination in the fields of employment, housing and the provision of services.

Examiner's secrets

You shouldn't generalize too much when looking at patterns of employment. There are differences both *between* ethnic minorities and *within* them (class, gender and disability).

Key terms and the main issues

Ethnicity is defined on page 25 and the question of ethnic identity discussed. *Racial discrimination* is behaviour that treats ethnic minorities worse than other groups. *Racism* was used to describe hostile attitudes towards an ethnic group. The term now tends to include practices and social institutions as well as ideology. Ethnic inequality is discussed throughout this book (deviance, health, media, etc.). The main issues in this section are:

→ patterns of employment
→ earnings
→ unemployment

Marxist explanations

Marxists see class as the dominant form of inequality, with two significant classes based on ownership. Ethnic differences are unimportant and racism is a form of false consciousness which:

→ legitimized slavery, colonialism and continued deprivation
→ divides the working class, preventing the development of class consciousness
→ provides scapegoats for the inevitable tensions of capitalism, e.g. crime, unemployment and bad housing have been blamed on visible and vulnerable groups

Checkpoint 1

How does racism legitimize ethnic inequality?

Varieties of Marxism

Westergaard and Resler identified a **unitary working class** who are exploited by employers.

Castle and Kosack, as Marxists, see a single class, but one that has significant divisions. In all West European societies there is a group of workers, divided by race, nationality or other social characteristics, which does the worst-paid, dirtiest jobs. They use the concept of the reserve army of labour to explain the class position of migrant workers who may be denied citizenship rights, experience discrimination and are confined to low-paid, insecure work.

The jargon

A *unitary working class* is a single class without significant divisions.

Checkpoint 2

Give two reasons why Castle and Kosack's views may not apply to the UK.

Evaluation

→ Weberians reject the view of only two classes.
→ Ethnic minorities may, because of inequalities in power, have different positions in the class structure.
→ *Miles*, criticizing both the Marxist views above, said that there were distinct 'racialized factions' at each level of the working class where minority workers are disadvantaged. The divisions within the working class are not the result of racism but racism influences people's life chances in getting jobs.

Action point

Find up-to-date statistics showing the relationship between ethnicity and employment by referring to census data and government employment statistics.

Weberian explanations: the underclass

Power, rather than just class, is the source of inequality. Ethnic minorities may lack power in a number of spheres.

Rex and Moore and *Rex and Tomlinson* introduced the concept of an **underclass** (used to describe the black minority in the USA) to explain the position of the black and Asian minorities in the UK. Their studies in Birmingham in the 1960s and 1970s describe the limited life chances which result from discrimination and produce a worsened **market situation** in the fields of education, housing, and employment.

These minorities also have:

→ low **status** as a consequence of the racism associated with colonialism
→ little **power** because of their exclusion from working class organization and the absence of influential ethnically based political organizations

Evaluation

Marxists criticize these views on theoretical grounds. They dispute the sources of inequality and the possibility of a class below the working class.

Research into employment and education suggests that ethnic minorities are spread throughout the class structure, not restricted to an underclass or even the working class.

The New Right

The New Right also use the term 'underclass' to describe a group below the working class which is unlikely to be upwardly mobile. They suggest cultural difference (rather than changes in the economic structure and discrimination) encourages the development of the underclass.

Evaluation

People may become poor rather than have a deficient culture that keeps them poor. Old age, job loss and divorce may all lead to low income.

Links

Note how they have used Weber's three sources of power – class, status and party.

Checkpoint 3

Outline changes in the position of ethnic minorities since this 1960s study.

Checkpoint 4

Produce diagrams to demonstrate the different views of the class structure held by
(a) Westergaard and Resler
(b) Castle and Kosack
(c) Miles
(d) Rex and Moore
(the diagrams on page 99 will help).

Exam question   answer: pages 105–6

'The concept of an underclass does not offer an adequate explanation of the social position of ethnic minorities in Britain.' Discuss this statement. (50 min)

Examiner's secrets

There is more than one version of the underclass theory.

Life chances: gender

Links

Inequality within the home is discussed in the section on the family and households.

The jargon

Feminists refer to *paid employment* rather than work to emphasize the fact that housework is real work although it is often unpaid.

Checkpoint 1

Why do more women choose to work?

Example

Ethnicity influences patterns of employment for women. In 1990 the figures for being 'economically active' (i.e. working or seeking work) were:

West Indian women	69%
White women	73%
Asian women	58%

Checkpoint 2

Explain the usefulness to sociologists of the three ethnic categories given in the example above.

Checkpoint 3

How have sociologists criticized the argument that gender inequality is 'natural'?

The rise of women's movements since the 1970s has had a major influence on sociology. Feminism has shifted the emphasis from gender *difference* to gender *inequality*. This section focuses on explaining inequalities in paid employment.

The main issues

The theories on this spread attempt to explain the main issues.

→ *Changes in patterns of employment* More women are working; they work in different jobs from men, are more often in non-manual occupations, and are at lower levels, e.g. fewer managers, more often part-time. However, women are gaining access to men's jobs and higher levels of all jobs.

→ *Earnings* Despite equal pay legislation, women earn less than men. They are in less well-paid jobs, work fewer hours and still experience discrimination.

→ *The relationships between home and work* Whereas marriage enhances men's career prospects and life chances in general (e.g. health), responsibility or anticipated responsibility for home and children inhibits women's prospects.

Functionalism

Gender roles 'fit' the needs of the individual, the family and the social system. These roles are influenced by *nature*, learned through socialization and emphasize women's primary responsibility is in the home. Functionalists generally explain gender *difference* rather than *inequality*.

Evaluation

Conflict theories criticize the failure to consider inequalities in the division of labour and the distribution of power which leads to the exploitation of women within the home and in paid employment.

Marxism

Marxism was the inspiration for many feminists (although the reverse is often true today). It explains gender inequality by referring to class inequalities. Women's confinement to the home is to ensure the physical and **ideological reproduction of labour power**. Women are a *reserve army of labour* who are available for (often low-paid, insecure) work when required but not seen as entitled to work. This can explain high rates of unemployment and the concentration of women in low-paid, part-time work.

Evaluation

Feminists argue that Marxists may underestimate the particular disadvantages of women compared to the male working class. Women can be disadvantaged at all levels of employment and in socialist societies. There is a **gendered labour market** – women are not a reserve army of labour, they do not compete with men for jobs. Women's employment has increased whilst men's unemployment has risen. Women do different jobs from men (see the three Cs below).

Feminism

The housewife-mother role dominates women's lives:

→ it maintains male advantage in the labour market
→ combining it with paid employment may interfere with careers
→ housework is generally unpaid and housewives are seen as economically inactive (like pensioners and children)
→ women's jobs are often extensions of their domestic roles (the **three cs** – cooking, caring, cleaning) and are low-paid, low-status occupations – possibly because women do them.

Evaluation

→ Women may not be or feel exploited at home.
→ They may enjoy motherhood and domestic labour.
→ Marxists claim the cause of any exploitation is capitalism rather than patriarchy.
→ Marxist-feminism combines the insights of the two approaches.

Dual labour market theory

This theory has also been applied to ethnic minorities and immigrants. The labour market is divided into two sectors: the primary sector comprises better-paid jobs with career prospects; and the secondary sector comprises insecure, low-paid jobs with few career opportunities. Access to the primary sector depends on being perceived to have characteristics favoured by employers. Employers may see women as less experienced, lacking training and less reliable.

Evaluation

This is little more than a description of the labour market. It doesn't consider exploitation, class and patriarchy.

The underclass

An underclass is a distinct group below the working class with little opportunity to be upwardly mobile.

The exam question below asks you to see if it is a useful description of women's limited life chances.

Checkpoint 4

Why has women's employment increased whilst men's unemployment has risen?

Links

See page 61 for views on the flexible labour force.

Links

The sections on ethnicity (pages 100–1) and changes in the class structure (pages 98–9) explain different approaches to the underclass.

Exam question   answer: page 106

Assess the usefulness of the concept 'underclass' in describing the position of women in society. (20 min)

Answers
Social stratification

Measuring social class and mobility

Checkpoints

1 *For*
  If unemployment has been short-lived the individual's lifestyle and cultural attitudes are likely to be influenced by the last job rather than unemployment.
  Against
  Retired people may have attitudes, income and lifestyle based on age, dependent status and low income.

2 • There may be no adult male in the household.
  • Woman may have a better job.
  • Cross-class families may behave differently from the way predicted by male head of house classification.

3 In traditional societies few positions require particular skills so people tend to stay in their original positions and follow parents in status and occupation.
  In modern societies functionalists believe mobility is necessary to get the best people into the most important jobs. Marxist more or less agree. They see employers requiring the most efficient workforce to compete and maximize profit. Mass education and the expansion of skilled and middle-class occupations have increased opportunities for upward mobility.

4 Mass education means that previously rare skills such as literacy are now widespread. Therefore office work has lower status.
  Office work has been routinized and deskilled by bureaucratic methods and technology.
  Office work has been feminized, which tends to lower status.
  The status of jobs may change, e.g. clergy are held in less regard.

Exam questions

1 Select two from:
  • predicts life chances/lifestyles/attitudes/behaviour
  • it appears to be objective and can allow comparisons over time
  • in modern society work dominates most peoples' experiences
  • the classifications exist, which is convenient, and are used by other studies.

Examiner's secrets

With this type of question you get one mark for identification and one mark for explanation. A brief explanation is sufficient.

2 You can use a range of the reasons listed on pages 94–5. There should be discussion rather than just description. You should refer to:
  • *methodological issues* (measuring individuals or households, cross-class families)
  • *theoretical issues* (problems for Marxists or feminists)

Theories of inequality

Checkpoints

1 • through the wage contract – workers are aware of exploitation but have no choice if they want to work
  • the ideology of consumerism means workers seek high wages to satisfy what Marcuse called false needs.

2 If they don't feel exploited they are falsely conscious. See second bullet point in Checkpoint 1 above.

3 Both see scarce skills being rewarded if they are saleable in the market.
  However, functionalism does not consider the influence of power on rewards. Occupations that can exclude others from the market are more highly paid – this applies to some professions (barristers, not teachers) and to workers in unions able to exercise some control over recruitment.

4 Functionalism argues that the function of stratification is to ensure the most able people conscientiously fill the most important positions.
  However, inherited advantages which are the consequence of stratification, which is more or less permanent, prevent able people from rising. They can be excluded by discrimination or lack of educational opportunity.

Exam question

Explain functionalist theories which support the view in the question. Parsons sees society benefiting from the integrative and goal attainment functional needs of the social system. Davis and Moore stress role allocation.
  Criticize Parsons, using conflict theories which challenge the alleged integrative effects of stratification. Marxist, Weberian and feminist views can be used here. They will question the benefits for most individuals.
  Use Tumin, Buckley, and conflict theorists to challenge the claim that stratification ensures meritocratic role allocation. It neither benefits society nor most individuals.
  Conclusion: stratification benefits some individuals (men, the ruling class, professions and expert managers, etc. depending on the perspective). Stratification may divide rather than integrate society.

Changes in the class structure

Checkpoints

1 (a) *A fragmented working class* contradicts the Marxist view that homogenization will encourage the development of class-consciousness, which will lead to revolution.
  (b) *An affluent working class* will not be increasingly poor and miserable and have *'nothing to lose but your chains'* (Marx). Marcuse, in 1960s California, faced with economic growth and a rich working class suggested that workers were enslaved by 'false needs' and 'repressive tolerance'.

2 The Weberian view of an underclass sees a separate class below the working class. They are distinctive in terms of market situation, political power and status.

Changes in the economic structure produced a sector without job security and lacking the skills to get better jobs or even work at all. When applied to ethnic minorities, the effects of discrimination were brought into the explanation.

- large open-plan offices like factories
- surveillance by supervisors or using computer systems
- routinization and deskilling of work
- loss of promotion opportunities
- use of technology contributes to routinization

4 (a) Pyramid/triangle/ladder for functionalism – no separation into distinct classes but a continuous ladder of opportunity to the top.
   (b) Onion-shape or diamond for embourgeoisement. The middle class grows as the working class shrinks. For example:

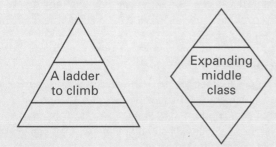

Exam question

Give an introduction stating the framework for the essay.

Weber's theory and studies using Weberian concepts support the fragmentation view. Marx and most modern Marxists tend to reject any argument which suggests real fragmentation of the two-class structure.

Discuss the fragmentation (and even the existence) of a middle class. Particularly consider the proletarianization debate: Lockwood (Weberian) versus Mills/Braverman (Marxists).

Outline debates over the working class. Marxists argue for single working class. Include Marxist views on ethnicity and class, e.g. Castle and Kosack. Weberians see division on the basis of market situation, consciousness, status and party. *Conclusion*: C. Wright Mills in the 1950s and Wright in the 1980s have tried to combine Marxist and Weberian insights

Examiner's secrets

Practise using Marxist and Weberian theories in a range of inequality questions including ethnicity and class questions.

Life chances: ethnicity

Checkpoints

Legitimizing means providing an apparent justification. Racism is an ideology, which proposes that certain ethnic groups are inferior groups and this inferiority explains their lower position in society, e.g. the US Bill of Rights said all men are created equal but slaves were not seen as part of humanity and thus did not have human rights. Racism often claims the intellectual or moral inferiority of minorities and thus blames the victim of discrimination.

2 Castle and Kosack's views are based on migrant workers who enter European countries on fixed-term contracts and have no citizenship rights and/or rights to live in the host country. These workers do not compete with native workers and can be sent home when unemployment rises. In Britain, minorities from the new Commonwealth did have political rights and the permanent right to live here. Exclusion from the labour market is through immigration control, not limiting rights once in the country.

3 Rex, himself, became more optimistic in the light of evidence that ethnic minorities:
- were no longer confined to run-down inner-city areas (if indeed they ever were)
- were increasingly spread through the class structure. Some minorities are over-represented in higher classes (Asians from East Africa, black women) some are over-represented in the working class (Pakistanis, black men). No minority group is confined to an underclass of the unemployed or insecurely employed and low-paid
- have (slowly) assumed positions of power as MPs, union leaders, through pressure groups.

There is still racial discrimination and disadvantage but this does not confirm the existence of an ethnically differentiated underclass.

4

Ruling class	Ruling class
One undivided working class	Main working class
	Reserve army of labour
(a)	(b)

Ruling class	Middle classes
White / Black	
White / Black	Working classes
White / Black	Underclass
(c)	(d)

Exam question

Explain the conventional Weberian structural view of the underclass. More briefly a critical view of Murray's New Right view could be included.

Criticize by using Marxist alternatives. Point out the common ground between the underclass and the reserve army of labour view which both see ethnic inequalities. Point out the variations both *between* ethnic minorities and *within* minorities (class and gender divisions).

The points made in Checkpoint 3 provide empirical evidence against the underclass view whilst still acknowledging racial inequality.

Conclusion: although inequality has increased and poverty persists there is not evidence that, if an underclass existed, it is ethnically distinct. Marxists would deny the existence of an underclass on theoretical grounds and many Weberians would argue that social mobility (up and down) prevents the formation of a permanent underclass.

Life chances: gender

Checkpoints

1 More women choose to work because they are better educated, have careers rather than just jobs, have different expectations from marriage, and marry later or not at all. More marriages break up and families want higher incomes in an increasingly consumerist society.

2 The three categories are widely recognized and thus allow comparison between different research studies. You can make some useful generalizations.

However, Asian is a very broad category which includes different religions, cultural traditions, places of origin, etc. All three categories ignore class differences. They may not coincide with identities.

3 If gender difference/inequality was natural (i.e. biologically determined) gender roles would not vary over time or between different societies. Cross-cultural studies show they do vary.

4 Changes in the occupational structure have reduced traditional male occupations, e.g. mining, dock work, other manual work and also removed layers of management. Service occupations, sometimes low-paid and/or part-time, have attracted women workers. Women are increasingly better educated. It is married women and mothers in families where men work who have joined the workforce in greatest numbers.

Exam question

Explain why (i) functionalism, (ii) Marxism and (iii) feminism would all deny the usefulness of the concept. The latter two would of course agree that women are disadvantaged but offer different explanations and not see women in a distinct class below the working class.

The role of religion in society was debated by the major classical sociologists including Marx, Durkheim and Weber. Nowadays you still have to discuss what they said. In addition, you should be able to apply these approaches to recent events, e.g. the rise of religious fundamentalism. Newer approaches include feminism, which can be applied to familiar issues such as religion as a form of social control or religion and social change.

Exam themes

Questions usually focus on only one of these three areas but sometimes you may have to refer to more than one so you'll need to revise all three.

→ Theoretical approaches to the role of religion in society

→ Is religion in decline?

→ The role of new religious movements

Topic checklist

○ AS ● A2	AQA Sociology	OCR Sociology	EDEXCEL Social Policy
Theories of religion	●	○	
Religion and social change	●	○	
Secularization	●	○	
New religious movements	●	○	

Theories of religion

You will need to know the three classical approaches to the role of religion in society and also the more modern feminist perspective.

Marshist approaches

Religious beliefs and institutions are part of the **superstructure** of society. Religious beliefs are **ideological**; they keep the working class **falsely conscious**.

Changes in the economic substructure produce changes in religion. Religion supports social class inequality.

Religion is the '*opium of the masses*'. It is like a drug in two respects:

→ it eases the pain produced by capitalism
→ it distorts reality so that the real source of the pain is hidden – poverty and suffering may be seen as the will of God and freedom from suffering is promised in the next world.

Thus religion helps the powerful impose **social order** on the weak and inhibits revolutionary **social change**.

Evaluation

→ Weber, see below, argued that religious belief could encourage rather than inhibit economic change.
→ Functionalists, see below, argue that religion **integrates** society rather than maintains social class divisions.
→ Some modern Marxist writers have questioned whether religion is an important source of **ideological control**. The mass media, education and '*consumerism*' may be more influential in maintaining false consciousness.
→ Other Marxists doubt the significance of any ideology, religious or otherwise, for controlling the working class. They say employment provides sufficient control.

Functionalist approaches

The origin, persistence and form of religion can be explained by examining its functions.

The functional needs that religion helps satisfy are:

→ **integration** – shared beliefs, rituals and sacred objects reinforce the consensual norms and values of society, providing a basis for social order. Integration is essential, as societies would otherwise be fractured by class inequality and other differences, e.g. Herberg (1956) described how religions, which cut across ethnic boundaries, integrated immigrants into American society
→ **social control** – religion provides divine backing for important rules and the certainty of justice in the next world.

Durkheim saw moral order as the basis of society, and religion as the worship of society (not the worship of a supernatural God).

Checkpoint 1

Explain the terms '*ideological*' and '*falsely conscious*'.

The jargon

Consumerism is the ideology of a society that values buying, owning and using products above all else.

Links

Remember integrating (i.e. uniting) society is an important function of the family, education and many other ideas and institutions (see pages 32 and 46).

Checkpoint 2

Identify and explain one similarity and one difference between functionalist and Marxist views on the relationship between religion and social control.

Evaluation

Conflict theories, such as Marxism and feminism, deny the existence of a society united by consensual values. Religion is often the cause of conflict and disunity rather than consensus and integration. Both Marx and Durkheim believed that religion could reduce conflict by making social inequalities seem less important.

The Weberian approach ●●●

This provides a clear alternative to Marx. Whereas Marx saw religious belief (and all other beliefs) emerging from the economic organization of society, Weber believed that religious belief (and other ideas) could influence the economy. Marx believed religion inhibited social change but Weber argued it could cause it.

Evaluation

Marxists replied to Weber's argument by reversing his explanation of the link between Protestantism and capitalism. The Marxist view is that capitalism has encouraged Protestant beliefs as they help to *legitimize social class inequalities*.

Other critics have suggested a range of other factors that encourage economic development and particularly the rise of capitalism. These include religious freedom, democracy and the influence of marginal groups such as immigrants.

Feminist approaches ●●●

Religious beliefs can be seen as a patriarchal ideology, where both beliefs and institutions enforce and legitimize gender inequality. Religion supports traditional patriarchal family life and sexual morality, where women and children are seen as needing protection against the sexual desires of other men and also their own sexuality. This encourages limiting women's movements outside the family home. Religious beliefs may legitimize a division of labour based on gender and unequal property and inheritance laws.

Evaluation

C. Butler (1990) questioned the view that religion always oppresses women. In interviews with young Muslim women in Britain she found religion was a source of identity amongst women who saw Britain rather than Bangladesh or Pakistan as home. Their religious identity was strengthened by racism. **Patriarchy** was rejected as man-made – Islam was seen as a defender of equality, not oppression.

Examiner's secrets

Remember there are often similarities as well as differences between Marxist and functionalist approaches. This is a useful point to include when writing conclusions.

Links

Weber argued these two points when describing the importance of Protestant Christian beliefs in the rise of capitalism (see page 111).

Checkpoint 3

Explain 'legitimize social class inequalities'.

Action point

Revise the feminist approach to the family and note similarities with this view of religion.

Checkpoint 4

How does religion support 'traditional patriarchal family life and sexual morality'?

Exam question   answer: page 116

Evaluate the view that religion is an important source of moral values in contemporary societies. (40 min)

Examiner's secrets

Ask the question 'Whose moral values?'

Religion and social change

The relationship between religion and social change is a common theme in exam questions. Put simply, the issue is whether religion encourages or discourages social change.

Religion is a conservative force

Marxists

They argue that religion is part of the **superstructure** of exploitative (i.e. pre-communist) societies and thus helps to maintain the existing social inequalities. These class inequalities are based on ownership of the means of production and the ability of employers to exploit a **falsely conscious** working class.

Religion helps to prevent the development of the class-consciousness necessary for a revolution and therefore inhibits social change.

Feminists

Feminists share the view that religion is conservative and helps to maintain a *patriarchal society*. Women's role is perceived as the **physical and cultural reproduction** of the religious community. The rise of religious fundamentalism has been seen as a major threat to the move towards gender equality.

The term **fundamentalism** describes:

→ **conservative fundamentalism**, which asserts traditional social and religious values
→ **radical fundamentalism**, which rejects corrupt and impure forms of religion and wants to go back to the original roots.

Although the media tend to associate fundamentalism with Islam, Sahgal and Yuval-Davis (1990) see women's position also under threat from Christian, Hindu, Jewish and Sikh fundamentalism.

Functionalists

Functionalists see religion as reinforcing the existing moral values and thus integrating society.

Evaluation

Functionalism is usually seen by critics as a conservative sociological approach. It tends to justify existing social arrangements on the grounds that they are functional for society. They also appear to defend the traditional family, which is part of the existing society. These arguments all suggest that religion discourages social change.

Examiner's secrets

Questions often use the words 'conservative' or 'supports the status quo' to describe resistance to social change.

Links

Turn back to page 108 for an evaluation of the Marxist theory of religion.

Checkpoint 1

Explain what is meant by 'physical and cultural reproduction'.

Action point

List the similarities and differences between Marxist and feminist approaches.

Checkpoint 2

Briefly explain how functionalists explain social change.

Religion is a force for social change ●●●

Weber
Weber argued that Protestant beliefs had encouraged the rise of capitalism in Northern Europe. Other societies such as China, in the Middle East or Roman Catholic Europe may have seemed equally ready for economic take-off but lacked the 'spirit of capitalism'. Weber argued that Protestant beliefs encouraged hard work, thrift and individualism. This led to the investment and rational working methods that were necessary for the rise of capitalism.

Liberation Theology
The Roman Catholic Church in Europe has been associated with traditional values and right-wing political parties, and is seen as opposing socialist and liberal values. In Latin America, however, groups in this church have been involved in the struggle against poverty and oppression. Their beliefs have been called Liberation Theology and have much in common with Marxist ideas. Religious leaders from other denominations have played significant roles in the struggle against existing social inequality and social injustice.

An Islamic revolution?
The 1979 revolution in Iran has encouraged the view that religion can be a vehicle for rapid social change. Left-wing Iranian political parties, who were also involved in the revolution against the Shah, argue that the religious leaders who gained power after the revolution have turned back the clock and resisted progressive change. In other Middle Eastern societies, such as Saudi Arabia, Islam remains a conservative force that is used to legitimize traditional rule. Islam has been a dominant ideology in nationalist struggles in Afghanistan and within the former USSR as well as challenging Western powers in the Middle East and North Africa.

Conclusion ●●●

Some religious institutions and some beliefs are conservative and some are not. The term 'conservative' is interpreted in various ways by sociologists. Generally, it means supporting the status quo. Marxists define conservative as supporting or not challenging capitalism, while feminists define conservatism as supporting patriarchy.

Exam question   answer: page 116

'There are many types of religious movement in modern societies but they all act as an influence against social change.' Assess the sociological arguments and evidence for this view. (45 min)

Example

Martin Luther King in the USA and Archbishop Tutu in South Africa were both leaders of social movements demanding radical change.

Checkpoint 3

Why might Marxists be surprised to read about revolutionary priests?

Checkpoint 4

Using the evidence on these pages explain how Islam can be seen as either a conservative or a revolutionary religious movement.

Examiner's secrets

Remember to mention different types of religious movement.

Secularization

There is no single agreed definition of secularization. However, most sociologists accept that secularization means a decline in the influence of religion in society. There are also problems in *measuring* the extent of secularization in any society. To demonstrate that religion is in decline you must be able to measure the importance of religion in the past as well as its current influence.

The jargon

Religious institutions refer to organizations such as Churches.

Action point

Consider each of these three measures and be able to argue whether there is evidence for or against the view that secularization has occurred.

Examiner's secrets

The main sociological issue here is the social meaning of religious behaviour, not just the extent of the behaviour.

Checkpoint 1

You don't have to be religious to go to church.
   Briefly explain the importance of this view to the secularization debate.

Checkpoint 2

You don't have to go to church to be religious.
   Briefly explain the importance of this view to the secularization debate.

Action point

Find some recent figures on church attendance.

Measuring secularization

The usual measures of secularization are:

→ the decline in religious behaviour
→ the decline in the importance of religious institutions
→ the decline in religious belief.

The decline in religious behaviour?

Religious behaviour includes:

→ *attendance* at religious services for births, marriages, deaths and festivals as well as routine services
→ *observance* of religious ceremonies at home
→ *following religious rules* including prayer, dietary rules and moral rules
→ *identification* with a religion.

Arguments for

Survey evidence shows that, for the population as a whole, all types of religious behaviour are in decline. Even where some types of religious behaviour persist, the motives may not be mainly religious, e.g. non-believers may think religious ceremonies are the most suitable way to mark weddings and funerals; similarly, dietary rules may be followed for reasons of tradition or taste.

Arguments against

Declining church attendance is not conclusive evidence of secularization because the survey evidence is unreliable because different definitions of membership and attendance are used; religious practice has become more individual and private; and some religions such as Islam and Judaism do not require attendance at organized services.

The decline of religious institutions?

Arguments for

Compared to the Middle Ages or even the last century, religious organizations have less influence in society. They have largely withdrawn or been excluded from many secular roles such as education, politics and social welfare, e.g. in 1944 most Church schools were taken over by the state.

Churches have been defeated in political and moral battles over divorce and abortion. Priests have lost influence and doctors and scientists provide moral guidance in place of religious leaders.

Arguments against

Churches today concentrate on purely religious matters, therefore they are less secular. The rigid **differentiation** (i.e. separation) of Church and state is not always a sign of a secular society, e.g. Turkey and USA remain religious societies whereas Britain has a state religion but is a more secular society. Religion can thrive in private whilst churches decline.

The decline of religious belief?

Arguments for

In modern societies religious belief has been replaced by *rational* scientific explanations, and religious values by consumerism. This process is called **disenchantment**.

Arguments against

Many people have non-rational beliefs and many political and moral beliefs are based on tradition and faith rather than reason. Berger claimed that some people have an unquestioning belief that science can explain everything. He calls this '**scientism**'.

Conclusions

→ Both the evidence and the interpretation of evidence are disputed.
→ The importance of religion varies between different societies. Religious fundamentalism thrives in the USA, Israel, Iran and India.
→ Religion itself may be secularized, e.g. by televised religion in the USA. Religious beliefs and practices may be modernized to adapt to a changing society, e.g. allowing women priests.
→ Sects and cults grow in modern societies. They offer stronger and more fundamentalist beliefs, which dominate people's lives.
→ Neither belief nor the social meaning of behaviour can be directly measured.

Exam question   answer: page 117

What problems do sociologists face in trying to define and measure secularization? (50 min)

Checkpoint 3

Identify and explain two ways in which religious institutions influence social life.

The jargon

Rational means based on reason, not tradition or faith.

Checkpoint 4

Give examples of secular beliefs and ideologies which may unite societies.

Action point

Find out which religious groups have declining membership and which have rising membership. (Try *Social Trends*.)

New religious movements

The main issues are:

→ **distinguishing different types of religious groups**
→ **examining their role in society**
→ **explaining their growth and future**

Church, denomination and sect ●●●

Troeltsch distinguished **Church** from **sect**:

Characteristic	Church	Sect
Organization	Hierarchical, bureaucratic	Egalitarian, may be single leader/founder
Membership	Often based on nationality or family	Voluntary – members are recruited
Relationship to society	Supports status quo, e.g. social inequality	Rejects status quo. Doesn't recognize social inequality
Belief (added by Niebhur)	Crucial events in past. Rigid rules but flexible in practice	Crucial events in future, e.g. end of the world. Rigid rules upheld

Niebhur suggested that *denominations* existed as a type between Church and sect and discussed how religious movements changed from one type to another.

Types of new religious movements (NRMs)

B. Wilson (1985) developed the views above but continued to see the relationship with the wider society, which was often either hostile or withdrawn, as a major characteristic of sects. He saw sects as '*Exclusive* bodies which impose some test of merit. . . . faith, knowledge, obedience . . .' He distinguished eight types of sect, based on their attitude to the wider society, which influenced beliefs and organization.

R. Wallis distinguished new religions from new cults. Cults were based on psychology and offered success in this world. He identified three main relationships that new religious movements had with the wider society:

→ **world-rejecting groups** – usually puritanical, fundamentalist sects, demanding obedience from members and hostile to the outside world, although recruiting new members may be a major activity
→ **world-accommodating groups** – members do not form separate communities but live in the wider society. Their religious lives are kept separate from the outside world
→ **world-affirming groups** – seek to improve the world for members. They offer happiness and success.

Evaluation

The sociological value of categorizing new religious movements has been questioned. The media and sometimes Government have

Checkpoint 1

Identify social groups which would be attracted to sects which don't recognize the social differences in society and briefly explain why.

Checkpoint 2

Explain, using examples, how a sect or cult can be 'exclusive'.

Action point

Identify examples of these different types of NRM.

encouraged hostility to groups which have been accused of 'brain washing' or fraud.

E. Barker (1984) did a **participant observation** study to discover why people stayed with the Moonies. This was a group which had received very hostile media reports.

Explaining the origin, growth and future of NRMs

A response to secularization

B. Wilson argued that the growth of sects was a result of secularization, not evidence against the decline of religion. Sects attracted people who were seeking mystery, a stable social order and a sense of belonging and who rejected the impersonal, bureaucratic and wicked world.

The rejection of modern industrial society

R. Wallis identified negative experiences of modern life that pushed people into sects. These included **alienation** at work, restrictions on freedom, secularization and *materialism*.

The political rebels and hippies of the 1960s and 1970s had failed to change the world and instead sought groups which either offered success in the wider society or escape from it.

Wallis also suggested that world-affirming groups would attract people who could not achieve consensual goals (usually financial success). The rejection of *consumerist* values, found in world-rejecting NRMs, tended to be the behaviour of the educated middle classes.

A response to deprivation

Glock and Stark argued that religious groups emerge as a response to deprivation. Responses to deprivation can be religious or secular. (Secular responses would be through political movements or trade unions.)

Responses are more likely to be religious when:

→ the real cause of deprivation isn't recognized
→ the real cause of deprivation can't be eliminated.

Thus religion compensates for the feeling of deprivation rather than eliminates it. If an NRM can eliminate the cause of deprivation it may become a more orthodox religion or become extinct.

The type of deprivation experienced influences the type of group which is formed and the beliefs of the group, e.g. the sick are attracted to faith healers and low-status groups to NRMs which don't recognize social differentiation.

Examiner's secrets

These three explanations share common features. This helps in building a critical argument in answers.

Links

Alienation at work influences life outside work (see page 62).

Checkpoint 3

Explain why the argument concerning the 'real cause of deprivation' is similar to a Marxist view.

Checkpoint 4

Use your own knowledge to give two examples of the links between deprivation and the type of NRM people might join.

Exam question   answer: page 118

Evaluate the contribution made by studies of sects and other religious movements to an understanding of the role of religion. (45 min)

Answers
Religion

Theories of religion

Checkpoints

1 *Ideological* means the beliefs are not complete and true. They serve the interests of a powerful group. For Marxists this means the ruling class.
   Falsely conscious means not aware of the objective (true) nature of an exploitative society. The opposite of falsely conscious is class-conscious.
2 *Similarity* – both Marxists and functionalists see religious belief supporting secular morality, e.g. rules against theft and adultery.
   Difference – Marxists see religion supporting rules which serve the interests of the ruling class, whereas functionalists see religion supporting consensual rules.
3 'Legitimizes' means it appears to justify inequality. People give their consent to legitimate rules. Marxists see this consent as not real consent but based on false consciousness.
4 Religion supports traditional patriarchal family life and sexual morality by supporting beliefs that:
   • the marriage contract is endorsed by God
   • divorce is unacceptable or requires the approval of men only
   • there are 'natural' (divinely ordained) sexual and gender roles for women.

Exam question

Functionalists argue that religion remains an important influence on morality even in a secular society as religious values have been generalized to everyday rules; for example those prohibiting murder and theft.

Marxists argue that religion reinforces rather than is the source of moral values. Also these moral values are bourgeois, not consensual, values. They are imposed on the working class, not shared by all members of society.

Feminists agree with most of the Marxist approach except they condemn patriarchal rather than bourgeois values. They would emphasize the importance of religion in maintaining family values and supporting traditional gender roles and sexual morality
Conclusions
• Question the continued importance of religion in secular society.
• Some Marxists (e.g. Abercrombie) question the continued need for ideological control of the working class.
• Religion is more significant as the source of moral values in contemporary religious, particularly Islamic, societies.
• In others there may be conflict between the religious and secular authorities, e.g. in Israel, India, Turkey, France, Ireland, etc.

Religion and social change

Checkpoints

1 Physical reproduction involves bearing children and meeting their material needs for food and shelter, etc.
   Cultural reproduction means socializing/indoctrinating children to accept religious beliefs and values. This is usually a Marxist or feminist view which is critical of society and sees religious belief as ideological.
2 Functionalists see social change as evolutionary rather than revolutionary. Parts of society adapt to fit the needs of the wider society. Parsons applied this view to the family (see page 34) as well as to religion. He suggested that religious institutions had gradually given up their wider social role to specialize in particularly religious concerns but also that religious beliefs had been absorbed (generalized) into everyday secular life.
3 Because Marxism, in both theory and communist practice, has been seen as anti-religion and sees religion as promoting false consciousness.
4 Islam can be seen as *conservative* because it seems to support traditional values and social arrangements, and it may encourage acceptance of the status quo, including economic inequalities and gender inequalities.
   It can be seen as *revolutionary* for challenging the existing social order in the Shah's westernized, capitalist Iran and for not accepting existing social divisions such as caste in India or race and ethnicity.
   Of course it all depends on what you mean by 'conservative'.

Exam question

Yes, there are many types of religious movement, but they don't all act as an influence against social change.

If you wish to use a basic Marx versus Weber framework remember you must consider different types of religious movement and apply the theories to modern society.

Other perspectives can be included, such as functionalism and feminism.

Marxists would largely agree with both the views in the question, so outline the Marxist view on cultural reproduction.

Weberian approaches suggest that some religion some of the time can be a force for change – outline the argument in the Protestant ethic and illustrate with contemporary references. Develop this view by suggesting that Churches and some sects may be conservative but others are not. Again give examples. Outline and then criticize the feminist view that religion reinforces patriarchy.

Secularization

Checkpoints

1 People go to church for a variety of reasons. Some reasons are more to do with family occasions or conforming to social expectations than they are to do with religious belief. This means that church attendance is not always a valid measure of secularization.

2 People can practise their religion outside formal religious organizations. Private worship or informal gatherings are not included in published attendance figures. The decline in attendance in churches may exaggerate the degree of secularization.

3 Choose two from this list or other acceptable examples.
   - Schools catering for particular religious groups are increasingly popular and provide a religious as well as a secular education. This may lead to separation of ethnic groups.
   - A significant minority of weddings and funerals are conducted as religious ceremonies – this integrates social groups.
   - Religious leaders are sometimes consulted by Government on social and moral issues, e.g. abortion, genetic testing and therapies, crime and punishment, and this may influence legislation.

4 Nationalism and anti-imperialism integrated new African states where integration was threatened by tribal loyalties.
   Communism united the now divided ex-states of USSR and Yugoslavia.
   Consumerism may integrate different social classes.

Exam question

The problems of defining secularization have arisen because:
- sociologists have used the term in so many different ways
- there is disagreement as to what should be included as authentic religion rather than just any magical and supernatural beliefs

These problems may be overcome by using generally accepted criteria, e.g. decline in religious practice, belief and the influence of institutions.
   The problems of measuring secularization can be tackled by focusing on the problems of:
- deciding what behaviour to measure
- attributing meaning to behaviour
- observing and measuring belief
- assessing the influence of religion in the past

New religious movements

Checkpoints

1 Probably disadvantaged groups who have low status. Their self-esteem can be enhanced by recognizing an identity based on religious worth rather than something they have no control over, such as caste or skin colour.

2 Exclusiveness can be maintained by:
   - not seeking converts
   - excommunicating people who break rules
   - insisting members give a full-time commitment to missionary work
   - extending the rules to all areas of social life
   - insisting on physical separation from non-believers

3 If the real cause of deprivation cannot be recognized this is similar to the Marxist concept of false consciousness.

4 If people are 'ethically deprived' they may condemn the secular world as wicked. Some groups campaign to change the world, e.g. the Quakers are committed to peace and decent working conditions for employees.
   Groups experiencing racial discrimination may seek to leave their society, e.g. Rastafarians, or to separate themselves from their oppressors, e.g. the Nation of Islam.
   You could look at other forms of deprivation such as economic deprivation, psychological deprivation, etc.

Exam question

You could discuss the impact of the growth of sects on theories of secularization. Is the growth a result of secularization or evidence against it?
   You could examine the contribution these studies have made towards arriving at a definition of what religion is.
   You could assemble evidence from studies of sects and cults to support or refute arguments about the relationship between religion and social change.

Power and politics

Gramsci said that '. . . *all the essential questions of sociology are nothing other than the questions of political science*'. However, there has been a tendency for the study of political sociology at A-level to be rather isolated from other topics. The main sociological perspectives are not always used and some of the arguments and evidence in this chapter are not much use to you when studying other topics.

The good news is that you can often use mainstream sociological concepts such as social class and ideology. In addition, a confident grasp of Marxism will help in producing critical discussion. Applying feminist and New Right approaches may provide some fresher insights for jaded examiners.

Exam themes

→ What is power and how is it distributed between different groups in society?

→ What is the role of the state in modern society?

→ Political participation, usually with an emphasis on voting

→ The role of political organizations, i.e. parties and pressure groups and new social movements

Topic checklist

	AQA Sociology	OCR Sociology	EDEXCEL Social Policy
O AS ● A2			
Power and authority	●	●	
The role of the state	●	●	O
Political participation	●	●	
Political organizations and new social movements	●	●	

Power and authority

Power is the ability to achieve your aims against opposition. It's useful to remember that power exists in all relationships and discussion need not be limited to the formal political arrangements in society.

The main issues in this section are:

→ what is power?
→ is power concentrated in the hands of just a few people?
→ is consent (accepting others have the right to rule) genuine or based on false consciousness?

The nature of power

Weber defined **power** as the ability to achieve your will against the will of others, and **authority** as **legitimate** power. This means that the people over whom the power is exercised accept the right of the ruler to control them.

He identified three reasons why people accepted the right of rulers (three sources of legitimacy) and thus three **ideal types** of authority.

→ **Charismatic authority** depended on affection and personal devotion to individuals rather than their position in society.
→ **Traditional authority** depended on habit and acceptance of the existing social order.
→ **Rational-legal authority** depended on the idea that rules/laws can be produced and changed by an accepted procedure. Obedience is not to individuals but to the rules.

Parsons introduced a new concept of power based on functionalist theory. This means there is a fixed amount of power in any relationship and thus the more power one person has the less the other(s) can have. Most other writers (Marx, Weber, Dahl) saw power in **zero-sum** terms.

Parsons argued that power was produced by the authority given to leaders by subjects to achieve consensual goals. Thus there is a **variable sum**, not a fixed amount, of power in society.

Giddens criticized Parsons on the following grounds:

→ power is used to oppress and exploit and gives access to scarce resources, thus it is not used to achieve consensual goals
→ apparently consensual goals may be imposed by the ideology of the powerful (see Lukes' third face of power below)
→ unlike Weber, Parsons does not explain the sources of legitimacy
→ if power is exercised covertly it cannot depend on authority granted by the ruled.

Dahl presented a **pluralist** view of power which could be measured by studying who made decisions and who benefited from them.

Links

Feminists emphasized the importance of examining power relationships within the family (see page 33).

The jargon

Ideal type is a term used by Weber to describe a pure example of something which doesn't exist in real life but can be used as a measure to compare real examples, e.g. organizations could be described as more or less bureaucratic depending on the number of characteristics of the ideal type they have.

Checkpoint 1

Identify and briefly describe an example of Weber's three types of authority. These could be individuals or institutions.

Checkpoint 2

Give one argument for and one argument against the view that governments attempt to achieve consensual goals.

The jargon

Pluralism is a theory which argues that power is widely shared in democracies.

Lukes argued that pluralism had a limited view of power. He identified three faces of power:

1 Success in decision-making – winning the arguments.
2 Setting the agenda – deciding what will be argued about.
3 The use of ideology to conceal who really benefits from decisions.

The distribution of power

The Marxist view

→ Power is based on ownership.
→ Apparent consent is false consciousness.
→ **Hegemony** is domination – based on the consent of those who accept the ideology.
→ Power is concentrated in the hands of the ruling class.
→ Power will be used to oppress and exploit the working class until there is a communist revolution.

Elite theories

→ Power may be based on control over economic resources or psychological characteristics (Pareto), control of organizations (Mosca) or military resources (along with economic and political resources – Mills' 'Power Elite').
→ Power will always be concentrated in the hands of a small elite (not a ruling class; this could be applied to communist states).
→ Power will be used to promote minority interests of the elite.

The pluralist view

→ The source of power is authority; leaders rule with consent.
→ Power can be measured by studying decision-making.
→ Power is widely dispersed between competing groups.
→ Power is used to satisfy consensual aims and, sometimes, majority and minority interests.

Conclusion

Each of the three approaches can be used to criticize the others. There are also differences of opinion within each approach. Modern Marxists disagree over the importance of ideological control and the role of the state (see the next page). Different elite theories identify different sources of power. Pluralism has been criticized by elite pluralists who have identified weak social groups who lack organization to promote their interests.

Action point

Make a note of all the social institutions you have studied which Marxists claim maintain false consciousness.

Checkpoint 3

Explain why elite theory might provide a better explanation than Marxism of the concentration of power in communist states.

Checkpoint 4

Identify and explain two ways in which groups can compete in a pluralist system.

Examiner's secrets

To reach higher marks you must go beyond a theoretical debate and apply your knowledge to 'contemporary society'.

Exam question   answer: page 128

Evaluate the contribution Weber made to an understanding of power and authority in contemporary society. (50 min)

The role of the state

> *"A human community that successfully claims the monopoly of the legitimate use of force within a given territory"*
>
> Weber (defining the state)

Many of the theories, arguments and evidence in this section do not come from mainstream sociology. This means you must be able to apply theories borrowed from political science.

Marxist approaches

→ The state is part of the superstructure of capitalist society and therefore it helps to reproduce inequality by maintaining the dominance of the capitalist class.
→ Modern democracy appears to serve the interests of all classes, therefore there is less need to use force to control the falsely conscious working class.
→ The repressive state will wither away after a communist revolution and the workers will govern themselves.
→ Modern Marxists have developed these ideas.

Gramsci distinguished institutions that ruled by force, e.g. police and the army, from institutions that ruled with 'consent', e.g. parties, media and church.

He emphasized the increasing importance of the hegemony maintained by transmitting ruling class ideology.

Miliband argued that the British state was the instrument of the dominant economic class. He gave three reasons:

→ top positions are filled from this class or those socialized into its ideology
→ the dominant class has the resources such as money and time to influence the state
→ big business provides the state with its income, therefore 'the public interest' is defined as what is good for business even by left-wing governments.

Poulantzas disputed that the state was simply an instrument of the ruling class and said it was the structure of capitalist society, not the aims of individuals, which supported capitalism. He argued it was increasingly autonomous (i.e. acted independently) from the ruling class. This autonomy helped the ruling class by balancing the interests of different sections of the ruling class and granting concessions to the working class to maintain ruling class hegemony.

Evaluation

Pluralists deny power is concentrated in the hands of a ruling class. Elite theories see non-economic sources of power and point to elite rule in socialist states.

Elite theories

The state may be the source of power for elite rule, may be part of the elite, and may serve the elite.

Action point

List the arguments and evidence found in the sections on education, religion and media that institutions manufacture 'consent'.

Checkpoint 1

Outline one argument for and one argument against the view that the state acts in the interests of big business.

Checkpoint 2

Identify two different groups within the ruling class who might have conflicting interests.

Links

Different elite theories are identified on page 121.

Elite theories rejected the Marxist view that a communist state would be free from oppression. The need to get the consent of the governed is part of most elite theories. Elite theories see elections as a sham – not really democratic but just the opportunity to choose rulers from within the elite.

Evaluation

Marxists argue that elite theories do not identify the real *source* of power in the economy and instead concentrate on the *instrument* of power (the state) rather than the ruling class.

Pluralist theories

→ The state is part of a political system that exists to help achieve consensual goals.

→ Functionalists also see the state as an integrating force.

→ Pluralism assumes that there are competing interest groups in society and the role of the state is to be a neutral arbiter of the competing aims and interests.

→ Pluralism is a popular theory in the USA, where a number of checks and balances prevent the state becoming too powerful.

→ Pluralism has a favourable view of western liberal democracies, where leaders can be removed by elections.

Evaluation

Marxists argue that participation in decision-making is less important than who benefits from a decision. There is little consideration of the second and third faces of power (see page 121). Weaker social groups do not participate in the political process. The increased participation of women and ethnic minorities may be changing this. Elite pluralism recognizes that some groups are too weak to have influence but may still be represented by the government.

The New Right and the state

Supporters of the free market advocate the minimum of state interference in the lives of citizens. They disapprove of interference in the economy. Privatization of nationalized (state-owned and run) industries was a major policy of the 1980s. The welfare state and any attempt to redistribute income are seen as dysfunctional and inefficient.

Example

The checks and balances include:
(a) the separation of powers between President, Congress and Supreme Court.
(b) division of power between federal government and the 50 states.

Checkpoint 3

What evidence is there of the under-representation of women's interests in the political system?

Checkpoint 4

According to
(a) Marxists and
(b) pluralists
where does the state get its authority?

Links

See the New Right view of poverty and the welfare state on page 88.

Exam question answer: page 128–9

Compare and contrast pluralist and Marxist explanations of the role of the state in an industrial society. (50 min)

Political participation

Questions on this topic have largely been focused on voting. This is also true of sociological research and popular A-level textbooks. However, there are other ways of participating in political processes. Some of these are within the formal political system, such as being a candidate; others are not and may indeed be illegal. Feminism, by declaring that 'the personal is political' has broadened the rather narrow concerns of political sociology.

Voting behaviour ●●●

The main sociological issue is the extent to which social class remains the major influence on voting. In this section we will examine the relationship between class and voting and alternative explanations.

Social class and voting (Butler and Stokes)

Traditional explanations see class as the major correlate with voting and suggest that **political socialization** explains the voters' choice. Explanations of '**deviant voting**' were necessary to explain the defeat of working-class parties such as Labour whilst there was a majority of working-class voters in the electorate. This was an important concept, as it seemed to be deviant voters who decided elections.

Explanations of deviant voting included:

→ the **embourgeoisement** of some of the working class
→ **deferential working-class** voters who voted for their social superiors
→ **instrumental voters** who calculated their individual interests
→ **middle-class radicals** who voted Labour.

Class dealignment and partisan dealignment (Crewe 1983)

After 1974 the link between class and voting appears to have been so weak (this has been referred to as class dealignment) that the concept of deviant voting was no longer useful. The decline in loyalty to the two major parties in terms of membership, support of policy and voting was called **partisan dealignment**.

The reasons given for these changes were:

→ Changes in the occupational structure that led to the shrinking of the *traditional working class*. Analysis of the 1987 and 1992 elections led Crewe to argue that there was a division between the traditional and *new working classes*.
→ There are divisions in the middle classes. Unionized routine clerical workers in the public sector are all less likely to vote Conservative.
→ Most people in all classes had become more affluent, e.g. home-owners, and optimism about the economic future had been associated with voting Conservative.

Checkpoint 1

Identify two ways in which political socialization takes place.

The jargon

Deviant voting means voting for a party which does not seem to represent your class interests, e.g. working class voting Conservative.

The jargon

Embourgeoisement means a more affluent working class develops middle-class attitudes and lifestyles.

Links

See discussion of embourgeoisement on page 98.

Examples

Traditional working class lived in council houses in the North and Scotland, and worked in the public sector.
New working class are owner-occupiers in the South and work in the private sector.

Checkpoint 2

Opinion polls in 1987 and 1992 said Labour had the most popular policies. Why do you think they lost the elections?

Rational choice theories

The voter is seen as a *consumer* who weighs up issues, policies and images of parties and leaders. Political parties have adopted a marketing approach, using opinion research and focus groups to sell themselves.

Back to social class?

Four successive Conservative victories from 1979–1992 led some writers to repeat the **embourgeoisement theory** of the 1950s when the Tories also won three elections. Heath et al argued that social class was still the major factor but new classifications of socio-economic groups were required to reveal the link between class and voting.

Political participation ●●●

Types of political action

→ voting
→ membership of parties and pressure groups
→ holding office
→ decision-making
→ direct action.

Participants in mainstream politics tend to come from more advantaged groups who feel they are 'insiders' (white, middle-aged, higher-class males). There are, however, exceptions to this rule, such as organizations for women and ethnic minorities, and trade unions.

Gender and politics

Women are increasingly participating in parliamentary politics, but there are still fewer women in positions of power in public life because gender inequality in their private life inhibits women's involvement. The important political battles for women need to take place in the family as well as in conventional politics.

Ethnicity and politics

Asian and black minorities remain under-represented in Parliament and local councils. Those in office are more likely to be Asian males and have been mostly Labour supporters, even when this party was performing poorly in elections. Social class explains much but not all of the voting preference for Labour.

Checkpoint 3

Briefly explain the case for new ways of defining social class.

Checkpoint 4

Identify two groups who are less likely to vote and briefly explain this.

"The very division between public and private is a patriarchal idea used to exclude women and women's concerns from politics."

Abbott and Wallace 1990

Examples

The number of women candidates and MPs has increased steadily since 1979. In 1997 there were a record 120 women MPs (101 Labour).

Exam question answer: page 129

'From the early 1970s there have been changes in both voting behaviour and other forms of political participation.' Assess sociological explanations of these changes. (50 min)

Examiner's secrets

Focus on the period after 1970 and remember most, but not all, of your answer can deal with voting.

Political organizations and new social movements

Until recently political sociology has been dominated by the study of political parties and pressure groups. The growing importance of new social movements such as the feminist movement has encouraged a broader view of political movements. However, A level questions may still focus on parties and pressure groups.

Political parties – what are they? ○○○

Political parties are organizations which:

→ seek to get MPs elected to form a government and rule
→ are united by shared *beliefs* (ideology) and *policies* (aims)
→ are relatively new in British politics, yet dominate central and local government.

They are the main link between people and government and *represent* people in two main ways:

1 they *select candidates* for office whom voters can choose
2 they adopt and publicize *policies* for voters to choose from.

What do political parties stand for? ○○○

Labour
In the past, despite internal wrangles, Labour was seen as having a fairly clear socialist ideology. It was committed to public ownership, the welfare state and greater equality of income and wealth. Having lost four elections 1979–1992, unpopular policies were ditched and the party has been repackaged as New Labour with policies that seem to have been market-tested to appeal to voters.

Conservative
Conversely, the Conservatives were seen as a party that wanted to govern and adopted policies which would get it elected. During Mrs Thatcher's leadership, a much clearer ideology emerged, with the party being committed to the free market. This led to selling council houses, lowering direct taxes, privatizing state-run industry and the reduction of trade union power. These policies were criticized by Labour in opposition but not reversed by Labour in power.

Pressure groups – what are they? ○○○

Pressure groups are organizations which:

→ allow citizens to participate in politics and try to influence governments between elections
→ try to get Government to do something, e.g. provide housing
→ try to stop Government from doing something, e.g. build a motorway through a wood.

Checkpoint 1

Do all political parties in the UK seek to form a government?

Links

See the discussion of different attitudes to the welfare state on page 88.

Action point

Note any recent changes in party policies, particularly if an election is approaching.

Examples

Amnesty International is a promotional group which campaigns for human rights. The BMA protects the interests of doctors.

Two types of pressure groups

Promotional pressure groups have a specific cause and are open to anyone who supports the cause. **Protective pressure groups** (or interest groups) try to influence government in favour of the members of a particular sectional interest.

How do pressure groups influence government?

They try to influence public opinion through media campaigns, although this only indirectly influences governments. They bargain behind the scenes with politicians and civil servants in local authorities, parliamentary committees and in Europe, and recruit MPs to pursue their interests. This has caused concern even when the relationship is in the open. The also organize marches, demonstrations and direct action, e.g. sitting in the path of road builders.

New social movements (NSMs) – what are they?

New social movements are movements which present new challenges to capitalism. They may challenge the cultural, economic or political aspects of the existing social order, and they tend not to be based on social class nor try to bring change through the state (unlike the 'old' working social movement which worked through unions and the Labour Party). They often focus on issues of identity and quality of life rather than economic concerns.

Important examples of NSMs are the Black Civil Rights movement in the USA, the women's movements, and the environmental movement. These have all used direct action to further their causes.

The growth of new social movements

The methods of the traditional movements, particularly the political parties and unions, are seen as part of the problem, e.g. oppressing women and ethnic minorities and permitting environmental damage or cruelty to animals. Reforming the state doesn't work, e.g. changes in welfare policy have not eliminated poverty and homelessness.

The traditional working class which produced the causes and the support for old movements is in decline. A new educated middle class has grown without loyalty to existing social movements and has a desire for change. Communist states have collapsed and Marxism has lost its appeal.

The media have publicized, sometimes even favourably, direct action campaigns.

Checkpoint 2

Explain one similarity and one difference between parties and pressure groups.

Checkpoint 3

Explain why feminism may be described as a new social movement.

Checkpoint 4

Explain two ways in which the growth of NSMs can be used to challenge Marxist views.

Examiner's secrets

If you have learned to discuss pluralism and the other approaches to power and the role of the state, you can use this debate as the framework for your answer.

Exam question   answer: page 130

Evaluate the contribution of different sociological approaches to an understanding of the role of political parties and pressure groups in the political system. (50 min)

127

Answers
Politics

Power and authority

Checkpoints

1 One of the best recent examples of *charismatic authority* is the rule of the late Ayatollah Khomeini after the 1979 Islamic revolution in Iran. Hitler could be another example but he did hold formal (bureaucratic) political authority as Chancellor of Germany.

   Traditional authority is exemplified by the monarchy in Britain, where legitimacy depends on habit and respect for the social order based on the family origins of the royal family.

   Rational-legal authority is found in most workplaces where managers exercise power according to rules. Civil servants have bureaucratic authority, as do party politicians but the latter may need a bit of charisma to get elected!

2 *For*
   There may be little overt dissent over issues such as public health, child protection, etc.
   Against
   Governments need to seek periodic re-election but this can be achieved by appealing to majority rather than consensual goals. Those who finance parties and provide government revenue may achieve sectional aims.

3 The power rested with the military, government officials, business mangers, but above all the Communist Party. These groups were all heads of bureaucratic organizations with the resources to coerce people. Power may have brought economic advantages – Mercedes cars and villas on the Black Sea, but did not depend on ownership of the means of production, although they may have exercised control over the means of production. Therefore the rulers of communist states were a series of elites. They were not, in Marxist terms, a ruling class.

4 Parties can seek election to form a government. Pressure groups can conduct campaigns to gain public and government support.

Exam question

Weber's main contributions were:
- to provide a clear definition of power
- to distinguish power from authority
- to explain sources of legitimacy (contemporary or at least recent examples include Nelson Mandela and Ayatollah Khomeini as charismatic leaders, the Gandhi family as having traditional authority but being elected to bureaucratic positions of power)
- to offer a critical alternative to Marxist economic determinism
- to see power as the basis of stratification (see the section on social stratification).

Critical views of Weber come from modern Marxists, pluralism and functionalist views on the nature of power.

   Support for his views can be found in some elite theories and some contemporary views of work organizations.

Conclusion
You could refer to those who combine Marxist and Weberian views, e.g. C.W. Mills on the power elite.

The role of the state

Checkpoints

1 *For*
   - There has been little attempt to redistribute income and wealth.
   - Recent governments have attempted to reduce government regulation of business.
   - The power of trade unions has been reduced by government legislation.
   Against
   - UK and European law controls business, e.g. smoking advertising ban.
   - State provides services from taxing business, e.g. tax on petrol.
   - Legislation, e.g. on health and safety and hours protects workers.

2 *The financial sector's* aim of reducing inflation in the 1980s led to closure of much *manufacturing industry*.

3 - The failure to achieve political objectives which favour women.
   - The continuation of a welfare state that supports a conventional family lifestyle based on exploitation of women in the family and at work.
   - The under-representation of women in Parliament but particularly as ministers.

4 (a) Marxists believe that the working class is falsely conscious and the media, education system, etc. manufacture 'consent'.
   (b) Pluralists believe authority is given to the state to pursue consensual goals. Legitimacy comes from elections and other forms of participation.

Exam question

You should attempt a point-by-point comparison rather than dealing with the two approaches in sequence. If you must do them in sequence you must make explicit the points of similarity and difference – otherwise you will do no better than an E/D grade answer.

Points of comparison include:
- consensus or conflict approach
- the different views on the nature of power
- the distribution of power
- the state as a neutral arbiter of interests (pluralism) or an instrument of class domination (Miliband) or an arbiter of sectional ruling-class interests (Poulantzas)
- the relationship between power and authority – discuss hegemony, false consciousness, and 'consent'; both theories deal with authority and consent
- how are leaders changed?
- both predicted an expanding role for the state although arguably this tendency has been halted and reversed in some fields, particularly the economy and welfare.

Political participation

Checkpoints

1
- Within families (Butler and Stokes noted a strong correlation between parent and child voting habits).
- Through the mass media which define issues as well as take sides.
2 This information comes from opinion surveys compared to election results. Labour may have lost because:
- people didn't tell the truth
- they voted on the basis of self-interest, in particular to avoid feared Labour tax rises
- images are more influential than policies
- voters changed their minds between the survey and polling day.
3 Changes in the occupational structure has meant the disappearance of many traditional working-class occupations and the routinization of much office work. This has blurred divisions between the middle classes and working classes.
More women working has changed the validity of old socio-economic groups.
Consumption plays a more important role in defining class.
4 Young people under 30 may lack interest in the political issues being disputed, e.g. Europe, but be interested in pursuing political aims through NSMs. Those with lower levels of education may be apathetic as they feel their vote makes no difference, particularly in very safe seats.

Exam question

Assess the explanations for changes in voting behaviour since 1970:
- class dealignment
- partisan dealignment
- growth of third parties
- changes in the class structure
- rational choice theory
- non-voting
Explain and discuss other changes in participation since 1970:
- more women in Parliament
- the rise of NSMs
- more direct action
- the decline in union membership and power
- the rise and fall of violence over the Irish issue.

Political organizations and new social movements

Checkpoints

1 Scottish and Welsh nationalist parties have relatively large numbers of seats and few voters because their voters are concentrated in a few constituencies. They seek (some?) independence from the UK but not to govern it.
- Northern Irish parties also have local agendas.
- Some parties are more like pressure groups and focus on specific issues, e.g. green issues or opposition to the EC. They tend not to survive in this form.
- The Liberal Democrats may seek to form a government in the long term. In the short term they hope to influence governments by entering pacts but not yet coalitions.
2 Both parties and pressure groups represent individuals so that their voices can be heard.
Parties seek to form governments and are generally interested in a wide range of issues.
Pressure groups try to influence governments. They are interested in a smaller range of issues and/or represent a limited section of the population.
3 Feminism has many of the characteristics associated with NSMs:
- it challenges the existing social order, which is patriarchal
- it wishes to change the cultural and the political order as well as economic relationships
- it is not class-based
- it is concerned with identity issues as well as, or instead of, just economic and formal political ones.
4
- NSMs indicate that there are divisions and issues in society that people perceive as being more important than social class.
- Working class organizations such as the trade unions and Labour party may be seen as part of the problem rather than the solution to inequality of, e.g. women and ethnic minorities.

Exam question

Marxism, pluralism and functionalism provide distinct views of the political system in society. You may wish to gain higher marks by discussing varieties of Marxism and pluralism.

Generally, pluralism sees both types of organization successfully representing individuals in a Liberal Democratic state. Power is dispersed between competing interest groups and parties must satisfy a wide selection of society to get elected.

Elite pluralism recognizes that more powerful interest groups can get their way at the expense of the weaker groups and even the majority in society. Nevertheless, parties will seek votes from less organized and articulate groups.

Marxism sees parliamentary democracy as a sham. It shares with elite theories the view that the majority is not represented. They only have the illusion of participating in decisions.

Some modern Marxists, though critical of political parties, see NSMs as being at least part of an effective opposition to capitalism along with working-class movements. Other Marxists see them as irrelevant diversions from real issues, i.e. social class inequality.

Examiner's secrets

You must go beyond describing parties and pressure groups and consider their role in the political system according to different approaches.

World sociology

In the past the sociology of development was rooted in the classical theories of social change. It was updated when Marxist criticism of global capitalism was used to explain the problems of Third World poverty.

World sociology has become a more popular topic in A-level Sociology with the growing interest in the effects of globalization and fears about the effects of economic growth and tourism on the environment.

Exam themes

→ Evaluating different explanations of development and underdevelopment

→ The impact of aid, trade, transnational corporations and international agencies on development

→ The inter-relationships between societies, world systems and globalization

→ Education and health as aspects of development

Topic checklist

○ AS ● A2	AQA Sociology	OCR Sociology	EDEXCEL Social Policy
Development and underdevelopment	●		
Strategies for development	●		
Globalisation	●		
Aspects of development	●		

Development and underdevelopment

The New Internationalist has a subject
index where you can identify past articles
at www.oneworld.org/ni/

Check the net

There is an ideological as well as an academic debate
about the meaning of development, the factors which
encourage development and the effects of relationships between rich and poor countries.

Development and underdevelopment

A western point of view from *Bendix* is that development is
industrialization and modernization. **Industrialization** is economic
change brought about by new technology utilized in a rational way.
Modernization is social and political change.

A Marxist point of view from *Frank* is that *underdeveloped* has a
different meaning from *undeveloped*, *non-developed*, *developing* or *not
yet developed*. Rich countries have developed by underdeveloping
(exploiting and making dependent) poor countries.

Checkpoint 1

Give two reasons why developed and
undeveloped societies could not be simply
referred to as rich and poor.

Modernization theory and development

Western industrialized countries are seen as the most advanced, that
is, the most economically developed societies with the best political
systems. Non-developed countries are those which have not yet
industrialized. In order to develop they must acquire Western
(capitalist) economic and social institutions and values. Thus,
aid, trade, investment and the spread of Western culture are all
potentially beneficial.

W. W. Rostow
Rostow states all countries developed in an evolutionary way through
five stages of economic growth, brought about by high investment,
which are accompanied by changes in social structures and values.

Parsons
His functionalist view of social systems places less emphasis on purely
economic stages than Rostow. Traditional culture inhibits economic
development, whereas modern culture (nuclear families, rational
thinking, individualism, emphasis on achievement and mass education)
'fits' industrialization.

Links

Parsons associated industrialization
with the development of the nuclear
family (see page 34).

Marxist and dependency theories

Marx examined development within one society. His model of progress
applies to nearly all societies. They go through fixed stages based on
a different mode of production. Economic change leads to changes in
the superstructure. Change is revolutionary, not evolutionary.

Lenin wrote about **imperialism** as well as development in one
country. Metropolitan capitalist countries exploit satellites using state
force, not market forces. The working class in the colonies are doubly
exploited by the ruling class of capitalist countries and the ruling class
in the colonies.

Checkpoint 2

Identify one similarity and one difference
between Marx and Rostow.

Frank revived interest in the sociology of development by using Marxist-Leninist ideas to challenge the pro-Western evolutionary optimism of Rostow's modernization theory. He argued that **neo-colonialism** has replaced imperialism and the development of the rich world depends on exploitation of the poor world by multinational companies and global institutions.

Exploitation occurs through profits from imperial trade being invested in rich nations, unequal trade (import cheap raw materials, export to captive markets), the replacement of subsistence farming with single cash crop economies, and migration of skilled labour from satellite to metropolis.

Evaluation

Criticism of modernization theories

→ Dependency theories have challenged all the main assumptions of modernization from a left-wing critical view of international capitalism.
→ The neo-liberal approach shares the pro-capitalist and anti-communist views of modernization theory but supports the use of these three free-market solutions:
  1 private investment, not aid and loans from international organizations
  2 international free trade
  3 minimize state involvement in the economies of Third World countries.

However, free-market solutions have led to increased debt and inequalities within the Third World, which has inhibited development. The success of the 'Asian Tigers' and other NICs may have involved state planning as well as successful exporting based on free trade.

Criticism of dependency theories

→ The collapse of communism and the success of some previously undeveloped countries.
→ Most trade takes place between rich countries.
→ The wealth of rich countries is based on capital, know-how and Productivity, not international exploitation.
→ Non-colonized countries remain poor.
→ Development can be helped or hindered by relationships with other nations or transnational organizations.
→ Dependency theories ignore internal obstacles to development.

Exam question answer: page 140

Assess the view that Marxist theories are becoming less relevant to an understanding of development and underdevelopment. (50 min)

The jargon

Imperialism was the process of empire building where usually European powers took political and economic control of colonies. *Neo-colonialism* is the continuation of imperialist relationships with independent nations through economic and cultural domination.

Checkpoint 3

Explain why two groups of skilled workers came to Briatin from ex-colonies.

Examiner's secrets

There has been no single pattern of development. Today's rich countries were never underdeveloped like today's poor countries. Britain, as the first industrialized nation, had little or no competition and had an empire.

Checkpoint 4

Explain with examples two distinct ways in which rich countries developed.

Strategies for development

This section deals with the impact on developing countries of aid, trade and transnational corporations (TNCs). Once again there are two main sociological perspectives, distinguished by their ideological assumptions. The consensus theories assume that contact with rich countries is potentially helpful to economic development. The conflict theories see relationships that maintain global inequalities rather than strategies for development.

Aid?

The term 'aid' suggests a helpful contribution. The reality that results from 'aid' is frequently debt and poverty.

Aid comes largely from governments, although charitable contributions are significant and serve to gain public support for government overseas aid. Rich countries have supported a UN agreement to give a certain percentage of their GNP. This target has been rarely met as cuts in public spending are unpopular at home and recipients of aid don't vote.

The jargon

GNP stands for Gross National Product, which is a measure of the total national income.

The case for aid

→ Modernization theory supports the view that diffusion of economic, political and cultural ideas from rich countries will help the development of poor countries, which lack what is essential for development
→ Charities support aid on the basis that it can reduce poverty. Clearly, the targeting of aid to reach those in need is essential. There has been a tendency for charities to move from famine relief to also support small-scale projects with longer-term outcomes, which will encourage economic independence.

Checkpoint 1

Identify two ways in which ideas are 'diffused' from the West to the Third World.

Action point

Using advertisements, identify the type of projects in the Third World which are supported by charities.

The case against aid – from the left

Hayter shared Frank's dependency theory approach, which saw underdevelopment as the result of exploitation. She saw aid as a cause of underdevelopment as it maintains the dependency of the satellite on the metropolis.

Aid is profitable for rich countries. Debt repayment exceeds the value of aid. It has strings attached to it. Food aid destroys local markets and creates a demand for Western types of food. It supports the elite, not the poor masses, in the receiving country.

Third World debt created a crisis in the West for banks facing falling profits, and for the poor in the Third World who had to carry the burden of higher interest rates.

Checkpoint 2

Explain one reason why aid is not always profitable for the receiving nation.

The case against aid – from the right

The New Right also criticize aid for maintaining dependency. Aid is seen as a waste of money if it encourages the rich to consume more, rather than save for the investment which is necessary for economic take-off. If aid is to be given it should be tied to 'good behaviour', e.g. the

Links

The New Right argument against aid is similar to their critical view of the welfare state (see page 88).

privatization of state-owned resources, cuts in public spending and moves to democratic government.

Trade

The case for

→ Competition should provide the incentive for more efficient production.
→ Encouraging exports from poor countries allows them to pay the interest on the loans, which can provide investment.
→ Exporting was the basis of successful development in the Far East.

The case against

The terms of trade for Third World countries have worsened. This means that the prices they receive for exports (often raw materials and cash crops) have fallen compared to the price to be paid for imports from rich countries.

Illich added the concept of **cultural imperialism** to economic exploitation through unequal terms of trade. He used the term '**coca-colonization**' to describe the selling of a harmful Western lifestyle. Coca-Cola is the symbol of such trade, which includes also arms, Western drugs, pesticides and baby formula milk. These create dependency and may threaten, rather than help, health. Illich argued that schemes to produce pure water and teach low-technology agricultural skills would be economically and ecologically superior.

Transnational corporations

The case for

TNCs bring capital investment, training and higher incomes which stimulate the local economy. They may be better employers than local employers owing to pressure from Western consumers.

The case against

The profits are not reinvested in the poor country but taken by shareholders in rich countries. TNCs encourage dependency and there is no local control.

Checkpoint 3

Apart from its harmful effects on the recipient nation, why might the right oppose government aid to the Third World?

Example

Is it still the case that poorer nations export mainly raw materials? Rich nations export oil. Poorer nations export manufactured goods (e.g. trainers and clothes) and services (data input for British student loans).

Checkpoint 4

What term might a functionalist use to describe coca-colonization? What distinguishes the functionalist approach from Illich's view?

Links

The role of TNCs in creating a global economy and social system is discussed on pages 136–7.

Exam question answer: page 140

Discuss the role of aid in the development of Third World countries. (50 min)

Globalization

Globalization means societies are becoming interconnected and interdependent on a world-wide scale. The limits imposed by space and time are shrinking. International travel has become faster and cheaper. However, the real technological revolution has been in communications, where advances in information technology have allowed production and consumption of economic and cultural products to be almost freed of the constraints of location.

Action point

Try to apply the concept of globalization to other topics you are studying, e.g. it's useful when studying culture, media and politics.

World systems theory ●●●

Wallerstein (1974) developed a Marxist approach to globalization. He stressed the importance of international economic relations in explaining development. He saw economic exploitation as the major influence on political and cultural factors. He described a new international division of labour (NIDL) with three levels, where the core nations (1) exploited the nations of the semi-periphery (2) and periphery (3). There was the possibility of changing a nation's economic status.

Evaluation

→ Giddens argued that international political relations were separate from, though influenced by, the economic system.
→ There are different social systems at each level.
→ World systems theory is about international economic relations rather than globalization. It describes nations exploiting each other rather than global capitalism, which is not always limited by national boundaries.

Sociology of the global system ●●●

Checkpoint 1

Identify transnational organizations that are
(a) economic
(b) political
(c) cultural

Sklair (1993) argued that there is a global system structured by a global capitalist class. This system is based on:

→ relationships between nation states (Wallerstein's view)
→ transnational practices which originate with non-state actors (e.g. TNCs) and cross national boundaries.

Sklair's global system is based on three kinds of transnational practices:

Checkpoint 2

What is the difference between international and transnational organizations?

1 *economic*: these are dominated by TNCs; relations include trade, investment and the NIDL
2 *political*: dominated by the transnational capitalist class, including TNC executives, politicians and media producers
3 *cultural*: dominated by the culture-ideology of consumerism; other aspects of culture are seen as far less important.

The globalization of culture ●●●

Many sociologists have identified the globalization of culture as an alternative model of globalization to the economic theories of

Wallerstein and Sklair. A global culture is seen as a present or future possibility. The mass media, which are increasingly dominated by TNCs, may transmit a global culture. Global TV programming was pioneered in the 1980s by CNN (news) and MTV (promotional videos for popular music).

Despite the spread of the use of English there is not yet a global language. Culture which exists independently of language, in particular sport, has been promoted by TNCs. Celebrities from Hollywood, pop music and computer games have become global brands.

Global tourism

In addition to the mass media and consumerism, tourism has become a major feature of the sociology of the global system. Most tourism is between rich countries. Tourism is the major export of many poorer countries. The impact of tourism is open to debate.

The case for
→ it generates employment and investment

→ it may encourage the liberalization of oppressive political regimes
→ it may preserve traditional sites and customs

The case against
→ it undermines subsistence agriculture and raises property prices

→ it may destabilize the political system
→ it may commercialize and destroy authentic culture

Conclusions ●●●

→ Globalization has challenged the authority of the nation state.
→ Global communication has made control of national borders more difficult.
→ TNCs have become increasingly powerful.
→ Class inequalities exist within societies as well as on a global scale.
→ Globalization is a political and cultural phenomenon, not just an economic development.
→ Globalization may be a consequence of modernity (Giddens) or has helped to produce a postmodern era.
→ Marxism emphasizes economic development.
→ Postmodernism emphasizes the global culture based on media representation.
→ Cultural images are sold as products, and used to sell other products.

Links

Illich predicted the globalization of culture in the form of cultural imperialism. He called it 'coca-colonization' (see page 135).

Example

The modern Olympics, which began in 1896, is an early example of a global sporting event. Soccer, and to a lesser extent cricket, are heavily sponsored and promoted by media and other TNCs (cars, Cola etc.).

"Global tourism results from globalization but also promotes it."

Fulcher and Scott (1999)

Checkpoint 3

Explain two effects of nation states losing control of borders.

Checkpoint 4

'There is no absolute distinction between economics and culture.'
Briefly explain this view.

Exam question answer: page 141

'Globalization will help the development of Third World countries.'
To what extent do sociologists agree with this view? (50 min)

Aspects of development

The development of the Third World is inhibited by poorer health and the absence of free mass education. Improving the health and education of the population of poor countries requires investment. Increasingly, aid has targeted health and education projects. However, spending on weapons remains a high priority for both Third World leaders and their suppliers.

Development and health

The study of the relationship between development and health inevitably tends to focus on:

→ economic explanations of ill health
→ inequalities in the social distribution of health.

There is a correlation between the distribution of GNP and levels of health measured by **life expectancy**, **infant mortality** and **death rates**.

The impact of development and underdevelopment on health

Development in the First World led to a decline in mortality, particularly for higher social classes, because of:

→ improved living standards and better nutrition from improved home agricultural production and cheap imported food from colonies
→ environmental improvements, including pure water and sewage works
→ medical advances; these were important after World War II, e.g. antibiotics and immunization.

Imperialism and colonization led to the spread of infectious disease from Europe to colonies and between colonies, e.g. STDs.

The cash crop economies imposed by capitalist nations worsen nutrition in the Third World by dispossessing tenant farmers and lowering production of subsistence crops, damaging the environment – destroying trees caused drought and dams created swamps – and encouraging exports to pay debts.

Trained doctors and nurses were lost to the rich world.

Global capitalism has been blamed for unsafe working conditions and endangering local populations. Manufacturers seek to produce where costs are low and this may be due to low health and safety standards. TNCs sell dangerous products in the Third World including:

→ cigarettes, which are heavily marketed as demand falls in the rich countries
→ banned pesticides such as DDT, which are still used in the Third World, as the risk is less than failing to control the mosquito population
→ long-acting contraceptive injections which were widely used in poor countries (and on women with learning difficulties living in institutions in the UK)

Checkpoint 1

Explain in your own words *life expectancy, infant mortality* and *death rates.*

Checkpoint 2

Explain with examples how economic development has threatened the health of people in rich countries.

The jargon

STD = sexually transmitted disease.

Example

Jamaica lost 80% of nurses trained in 1978 to the UK and Canada.

→ baby formula milk, widely sold in countries without pure water supplies to mothers capable of breast-feeding.

Drug companies sell inappropriate products to Third World countries which spend a higher proportion of their health budgets on drugs than rich countries. Preventive healthcare would be more cost-effective. Only the rich in the cities may have access to complex and expensive health care.

Education and development

There are massive inequalities in the provision of education between rich and poor countries. There are also inequalities within both rich and poor nations. Overall, in the Third World women are far more likely to be illiterate than men are. Mass education was not available in Britain, then the richest country in the world, until 1870 when the Industrial Revolution was well established.

Education and modernization

Functionalists argue the benefits of the diffusion of technology, skills, knowledge and values from developed countries to the Third World. They share the Weberian view that economic development depends on the acceptance of modern values.

Balogh (1961) proposed two principles for supporting development in Africa:

→ agricultural development was necessary before industrialization
→ aid should invest in human capital, especially technical education for agriculture.

Balogh may have been right but the expansion of education did not take the form he suggested. Foster, writing about the expansion of education in Ghana after independence, noted that education was seen as a means of upward mobility rather than a form of technical training. The highly educated minority competed for government jobs, emigrated or remained underemployed.

Conclusion

The education system does not respond directly to the needs of the economy for skilled labour but is relatively independent. Education expanded more quickly than modern jobs were created.

Checkpoint 3

Explain two types of preventive health care that would be useful in Third World countries.

Action point

List points which compare and contrast functionalist and Marxist views on the relationship between education and economic development (see the section on education).

Checkpoint 4

Explain two reasons why there is a strong correlation between a mother's education and lower infant mortality rates.

Action point

List the beliefs and values that Weber argued encouraged the rise of capitalism in the West. If necessary refer to the section on religion. (page 111)

Example

Indian doctors came to Britain.
Indian engineers went to oil states.

Exam question   answer: pages 141–2

Critically examine the view that 'education is the major means of achieving modernization'. (50 min)

Answers
World sociology

Development and underdevelopment

Checkpoints

1 • Development is usually defined in terms of industrialization and modernization. Some rich countries are non-industrialized and have traditional cultures, e.g. the oil-rich states of the Middle East.
   • Industrialization can be associated with poverty, e.g. where there is a high level of inequality or rapid population growth, e.g. Indonesia, India or Britain in the 19th century.

2 • Both theories see development as mainly the consequence of economic change.
   • Marxists see communism as the peak of progress whereas Rostow described communism as a 'disease of transition', meaning an unfortunate and unnecessary stage on the way to mass consumption.

3 *'Push' factors*: Asians, many of whom were well-educated, fled oppression in East Africa.
   'Pull' factors: Indian-trained doctors and Jamaican nurses have been actively recruited overseas by a short-staffed NHS which provided better opportunities and pay than their country of origin.

4 Britain and other early-industrialized nations raised capital through the slave trade and imperialism. Denmark and New Zealand became rich through agricultural exports.

Exam question

Outline classical Marxist theory (Marx and Lenin).
Case for
• Provides a clear explanation of change based on changes in the mode of production.
• Identifies slavery and imperialism as sources of capital.
• Explains both development and underdevelopment.
Case against
• Modernization theory – Rostow's attack on communism; Parsons' alternative to purely economic accounts.
• End of communism.
• Weberian 'voluntarist' criticism of economic determinism.

Outline dependency theory
Case for
• Identifies weaknesses of modernization theories.
• Explains underdevelopment.
Case against
Postmodern view of globalization rejects grand metanarratives of both functionalism and Marxism.

Strategies for development

Checkpoints

1 • Through the mass media, e.g. Hollywood films or global TV programmes such as CNN and MTV
   • Through education, e.g. provided in the West for Third World students or in the developing country funded by aid

2 The major reason is probably the burden of debt if aid is in the form of a loan. You can also mention creating dependency, destroying local agriculture, environmental damage, etc.

3 The right might resent spending (or, as they would see it, wasting) tax payers' money in this way.

4 This spreading of Western values might be described using Parsons' term 'cultural diffusion'.
   Functionalists see this as beneficial as developing nations take on the rational competitive values, which encourage modernization.
   Illich saw it as destructive of indigenous culture as well as damaging the economy and perhaps the environment.

Exam question

This question can be answered using a fairly straightforward framework applying modernization and dependency theories to the issue of aid.
   Modernization theory argues that aid, particularly where it involves education and training, is investment in human capital and will encourage economic take-off.
   Dependency theory is critical of the provision of aid because of its negative effects. You can explain Hayter's critique of the Brandt Report (which advocated more aid from rich countries), mentioning debt, exploitation, damage to subsistence farming, etc.
   You can include other critical views of aid from the New Right, environmentalists and feminists who argue aid goes largely to male elites in Third World countries.

Globalization

Checkpoints

1 (a) IMF, World Bank or any TNC
   (b) EU but not the UN (see Checkpoint 2)
   (c) FIFA, IOC – these sporting bodies have authority over national organizations

2 International organizations are collections of nations who maintain their individual independence. New nations join the UN to demonstrate their independence.
   Membership of the EU requires some surrender of national sovereignty.

Transnational organizations operate independently of national boundaries. Some TNCs are richer and in many respects more powerful than many nations.

3 Chose two of these or a reasonable alternative.
- Social problems such as crime, ill health and threats to the environment become international.
- Immigration control becomes more difficult. Britain has had strict immigration policies since the early 1960s, mostly aimed at excluding immigrants from the New Commonwealth. EU membership gives right of entry to hundreds of millions of European citizens. Freedom of movement within the EU and expansion of air travel have enabled and encouraged movement of refugees and asylum seekers.
- Electronic media, such as the internet and satellite TV, make it difficult for totalitarian governments to control information within a country.

4 Postmodernism has emphasized the importance of media images in creating social reality. Media images, such as Hollywood films, are sold, often on a global scale. They are also used to sell other goods, e.g. Sky TV can sell transmissions of Premiership football matches. These matches are used to sell the sports equipment worn by players and the lager and cars produced by match sponsors. Soft drinks can be sold globally with brands that sell a glamorous image of the USA.

Exam question

The arguments for globalization aiding development
These are based on modernization theories. Globalization is seen as encouraging the diffusion of competitive values and technology as well as investment and movement of labour. These all are seen as helping development.

Global awareness encouraged by tourism and media images may provide support for aid programmes.

The arguments against globalization aiding development
These are largely based on various versions of Marxist and dependency theories.

The model of international economic exploitation begins with Marx and Lenin's views on imperialism and is developed through Frank's dependency theory and Wallerstein's world systems theory with its emphasis on the international division of Labour.

Sklair has added the adverse effects of the globalization of politics and culture to the political dimension.

Environmentalism has also identified adverse effects of globalization including industrial pollution, the damaging effects of agri-business (e.g. destroying forests for beef ranches for burgers) and tourism.

Aspects of development

Checkpoints

1 Life expectancy, infant mortality and death rates are all measures of the social distribution of health.
   Life expectancy is the average number of years a group of people will survive. It varies between social classes, gender and ethnic groups.
   Infant mortality is the death of children within the first year of life.
   Death rates are the number of deaths in a population per year. They are usually expressed per 1 000. Death rates can be calculated for different age groups, occupational groups, smokers and non-smokers, etc.

2 There are diseases of affluence associated with an unhealthy lifestyle where physical exercise for non-manual workers is minimal and diet is unhealthy. Development can also damage the environment, e.g. smog is produced by the combination of climate and carbon monoxide produced by cars.

3 *Immunization* has been very successful in eliminating smallpox. It could be extended to other infectious diseases.
   Sex education, which changed values as well as providing information, could help slow the global Aids epidemic.

4 Education is often associated with social class, which is in turn directly related to IMRs.
   More directly, education may encourage lower birth rates and better hygiene, both of which can reduce IMRs.

Exam question

Evidence supporting the view that education is 'the major means' can be explained.

Education can promote modern values (rationality, individualism, competitiveness, etc.). This can be linked to Parsons and functionalist views of education.

Education is an investment in human capital. You can explain functionalist views on education and the economy and training for jobs.

Education can integrate societies where social solidarity is threatened by rapid industrialization and urbanization.

Specific education programmes for health and birth control can be mentioned.

Evidence against the view
You can accept the functionalist/modernization view in general but question whether education is 'the major means'. Alternatives might be investment, birth control, aid, etc.

Specific criticism of the success of education programmes in meeting the needs for economic growth can be explained using Balogh and Foster, who describe the failure of vocational education in some Third World countries.

The modernization approach has been criticized by dependency theory, world systems theory and some approaches to globalization.

Conclusion
- Education could possibly, but doesn't necessarily, encourage modernization.
- Globalization of economic, culture and political transnational practices may spread the know-how and values which encourage modernization.
- Modernization may not be beneficial to all the population of Third World countries.

Crime and deviance

In common with the Sunday newspapers, Sociology exams are more concerned with deviance and crime than they are with social order. Studying deviance is a useful way to identify social rules, which we may otherwise take for granted. Garfunkel helped his students to learn how 'common sense assumptions' guided family life. He told them to go home and treat their homes like hotels and their parents with formality.

This is a synoptic unit for AQA, so you should emphasize the ways that sociologists use the study of crime and deviance to debate broader issues such as the best way to do research. Knowledge of sociological studies of suicide and crime statistics can often be used in theory and methods questions.

Exam themes

➜ Sociological explanations of crime, deviance, social order and social control

➜ Different explanations of the social distribution of crime and deviance

➜ The social construction of deviance and the amplification of deviance

➜ The sociological issues arising from the study of suicide

➜ An understanding of methodological and theoretical debates

Topic checklist

○ AS ● A2	AQA Sociology	OCR Sociology	EDEXCEL Social Policy
Theories of deviance and crime	●	●○	○
The social distribution of crime	●	●○	
The amplification of deviance	●	●	
Suicide	●	●	

Theories of deviance and crime

There are so many different theories of deviance that you may find learning all of them an overwhelming task and reproducing them in an exam question impossible. The best way to organize learning and answers is to use a simplified grouping of theories and studies under three main headings: *Durkheimian*, *Marxist* and *Interactionist*.

Durkheimian theories ●●●

Deviance is defined as *breaking consensual rules* and deviants are defined as rule-breakers. Crime and other forms of deviance are studied. The main question asked is 'Why do some people break the rules?' The popular explanations are **functionalism** and some **sub-cultural theories**. These theories use a **positivist approach** to explaining deviance. A common method is to compare the *biographies* of known deviants with those of normal people, and see the differences as the causes of deviance. *Crime statistics* are seen as a useful resource that can be used in *comparative studies* of different social groups. The role of police and courts is to enforce consensual rules.

Evaluation

Marxist and other conflict theories deny the existence of genuinely consensual values. If rules are accepted it is because people are falsely conscious. Interactionists challenge the definition of deviance, the positivist approach and related methods (see below).

Marxist theories ●●●

Marxism is a conflict theory, which rejects the existence of consensual values. Deviants are seen as the real or alleged breakers of ruling class rules. The main questions asked are 'Who makes the rules?' and 'How does their enforcement serve ruling class interests?' Research on both deviants and those who make and enforce the rules is interpreted in a Marxist light as evidence of class conflict. Marxists often study 'crimes of the powerful' which may be conventional crimes or acts that threaten the working class, e.g. dangerous working conditions.

Evaluation

→ The possibility of genuinely consensual norms and values is avoided.
→ Studies may appear to excuse or even glorify offenders and ignore victims.
→ Interactionists claim that Marxists overemphasize economic explanations of crime.

Interactionist theories ●●●

A deviant is not a rule-breaker but someone who has been *labelled* deviant. Labelling theory focuses on the ways in which agents of social control such as the police and courts attach negative stereotypes to 'offenders'. This labelling may change their behaviour. The main question asked is 'Why are some people more likely to be labelled?' Favoured methods, such as participant observation, try to examine the interaction between 'offenders' and the authorities, often from the viewpoint of the 'offender'. Crime statistics are not seen as a useful resource that describes real patterns of crime. They are seen as a social construction and tell us more about police and judicial processes than they do about offenders. Interactionists often study non-criminal forms of deviance such as suicide, stuttering and mental illness.

Evaluation

Interactionists do not even attempt to explain why some people commit crimes. Marxists share the views on unequal law enforcement and the social construction of crime but criticize interactionists for failing to see underlying economic causes of patterns of crime and law enforcement.

The 'new' theories of deviance

These explanations are only new in the sense that they are developments from the three dominant approaches discussed above.

The new criminology

Combined interactionist and Marxist views   Taylor, Walton and Young felt that the labelling theories they had previously supported failed to relate policing to wider issues of power and class inequality.

New Left realism

Young and Lea became dissatisfied with the new criminology because of its dismissal of crime as a real problem and its sympathy with the offender rather than the victim. They identified three causes of crime:

→ **marginalization** – groups such as the unemployed and some ethnic minorities are excluded from the mainstream society
→ **relative deprivation** – the feeling of being denied rewards
→ **criminal subcultures** – are adaptations to economic conditions; they tend to promote individualism, aggression and masculinity.

Evaluation

→ It's an old-fashioned view that focuses on working-class street crime rather than white-collar crime.
→ It has been used to support racist views of black criminality.
→ It overemphasizes the experience of victims – better explanations come from looking from the offender's viewpoint.

Links

Labelling theory has been applied to educational achievement (see page 48).

Checkpoint 3

Explain why some acts are labelled deviant.

Examiner's secrets

These new theories can be usefully applied to exam questions which link crime with race, class and gender.

Checkpoint 4

New Left realism was inspired by surveys of victims. Why are victim studies a useful source of data?

Exam question   answer: page 152

Evaluate sociological explanations of the relationship between deviance and social control. (50 min)

The social distribution of crime

> *"Women appear to be remarkably non-criminal."*
>
> P. Abbott and C. Wallace 1990

You need to be able to apply the theories on the previous page and some newer ones to explain the higher rates of *recorded crime* for some social groups.

Social class and crime

Why is working-class crime more common than white-collar crime or crimes of the powerful?

Anomic theory

Merton explained deviance using Durkheim's concept of **anomie**. He saw deviance as caused by individuals being unable to achieve society's goals using legitimate means. He argued that lower social classes had limited access to legitimate means so were more likely to be deviant.

Subcultural theories

These identify a different set of values within the subculture, which may be rebellion against middle-class values (A. Cohen) or an exaggerated form of mainstream working-class values (W. Miller).

Interactionist theory

This focuses on the stereotyping and labelling of the working class. As a result, their activities are more likely to be defined as crime and the police spend more time in contact with them.

Marxist theories

These explain how the ruling class define crime and ensure that law enforcement acts against the working class. *Crimes of the powerful*, in politics and big business, tend to go unpunished or undetected. Studies of '**white-collar crime**' emphasize the difficulty of detecting and proving crime at work, particularly crimes such as fraud.

Gender and crime

Why are women offenders so under-represented in crime statistics? There are two possible explanations for this and both could be valid:

→ women commit fewer crimes than men
→ women are less likely to be caught than men.

You should be able to apply the theories outlined earlier in this section, to women and assess how useful they are in explaining the gender differences. Here are three useful examples:

→ *Merton's theory* seems to suggest women, with fewer opportunities, should be more, not less, criminal. Perhaps they have more limited goals than men.
→ Many **subcultural theories** studied working-class gangs of boys. Some of these have linked masculinity with deviance, e.g. Miller wrote of the importance of toughness and masculinity, as did the studies of football hooligans by J. Williams and racist skinheads by P. Cohen.

→ Heidensohn's **social control theory** is specifically concerned with the low rates of female criminality. She argued that women were less deviant because their lives are more constrained. Women are controlled *within the family* – their domestic responsibilities and subordinate roles limit opportunities to commit crime outside the home; and *within society* – women learn not to be aggressive or violent. The ideology of femininity sees crime as doubly deviant because it is unfeminine as well as breaking a particular law.

Ethnicity and crime

●●●

Why are some ethnic minorities over-represented in some crime statistics? Once again the two logical answers are:

→ because they offend more
→ because they are more likely to be arrested and processed as deviant.

Some minority groups are over-represented in other groups where rates of offending seem high, such as the working class, the unemployed, inner-city dwellers and, perhaps most significantly, the young. A 'bulge' in the proportion of young men in a group is likely to produce a higher crime rate. Immigration and then different patterns of fertility can produce a younger black population.

The new criminology (NC) versus New Left realism (NLR)

→ The **NC** has accused the public, media, police and government of labelling the black population as criminal.
→ Both S. Hall and P. Gilroy offered explanations, based on class inequality and racial discrimination, for higher rates of black offending.
→ Gilroy saw crime as resistance against racial oppression. He felt the colonial past still existed on the streets of Britain and this encouraged conflict with the police, demonstrations and riots.
→ **NLR** challenges the NC view that unequal policing is the main cause of a higher rate of recorded crime amongst blacks than whites. They point out that recorded crime is largely reported by the public and is not the result of policing.
→ NLR does accept that policing can be racially biased and also acknowledges that if street robbery in some cities is largely a black crime, burglary is largely a white crime.

Checkpoint 3

Explain briefly how gender might influence law enforcement.

Examiner's secrets

Discussing victims as well as offenders is a useful source of evaluation when answering questions on gender and ethnicity.

Links

S. Hall's *Policing the Crisis* (1978) focused on the moral panic, encouraged by the media, about mugging in the 1970s. He applied a mix of interactionist and Marxist views (see pages 76 and 149).

Links

Turn over the page for a discussion of moral panics.

Checkpoint 4

Explain how the three causes of crime identified by NLR can be applied to ethnic minorities.

Exam question   answer: pages 152–3

Assess the evidence and arguments that suggest that female crime and delinquency are significantly under-represented in official statistics.
(50 min)

The amplification of deviance

This section will help you answer questions that deal with the amplification of deviance and the relationship between the mass media and *crime waves*. It provides evidence and arguments that you can use to evaluate interactionist theories and for questions on crime statistics.

What is deviance amplification? ●●●

Deviance amplification can be approached from a number of sociological perspectives, although it is particularly associated with the **interactionist perspective**. It can mean one or more of the following:

→ more deviant acts are being committed
→ more serious acts are being committed
→ people think there is more crime
→ people have an increased fear of crime.

The first two explanations refer more to deviance and the second two refer more to the social reaction to deviance, which can cause more deviance and/or more social reaction. A combination of these can produce a real or perceived **crime wave**.

The interactionist approach ●●●

S. Cohen described how '*Folk Devils and Moral Panics*' could be created and amplified by the mass media. Press reports described a minor disorder involving 'mods', 'rockers' and unattached youths at the seaside as a riot. Worse disorder between mods and rockers was predicted and became a **self-fulfilling prophecy** as youth polarized into the two groups, and more extensive policing produced more arrests, e.g. for obstructing the police.

J. Young used the interactionist perspective to explain '*the role of the police as amplifiers of deviancy, negotiators of reality and translators of fantasy*'. He explained the special role of the police and courts in amplifying deviance associated with drug abuse.

The following diagram, based on Young's work, can be used to illustrate the role of the media or the role of the police in amplifying deviance.

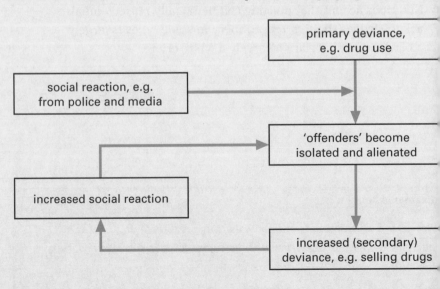

> **Checkpoint 1**
>
> What method have sociologists used to study fear of crime?

> **The jargon**
>
> *Crime waves* are real or imagined increases in the rate of a particular crime. They may cause a moral panic.

> **The jargon**
>
> A *moral panic* exists when people or events become defined as a threat to society .

> **Checkpoint 2**
>
> Explain the term *self-fulfilling prophecy*.

E. Lemert distinguished **primary deviance**, which nearly everyone committed and usually went unnoticed or had no consequence, om **secondary deviance**, which resulted in labelling the person s a deviant. He argued that social reaction could be a cause of econdary deviance rather than a response to it. He applied this pproach to show how social reaction amplified mental illness nd stuttering.

The conflict approach

Hall provided a Marxist context for the moral panic about mugging the 1970s. He supports the interactionist approach described above ut adds that the moral panic, which falsely identified street crime as lack crime with white victims, distracted the public from the economic risis. It divided the working class on ethnic lines and legitimized the troduction of more repressive policing.

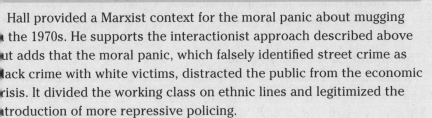

Checkpoint 3

Identify and briefly describe a more recent moral panic about deviance.

The functionalist approach

unctionalism does discuss moral panics and the effects of social eaction. However, the approach is **structuralist** (rather than teractionist) and there is, as expected, an emphasis on how onsensus can be maintained (rather than on underlying conflict etween groups).

Durkheim saw the function of social reaction against crime and riminals as a way of *reinforcing the collective consciousness*.

K. Erikson followed Durkheim and argued that the witch hunts onducted by the authorities in Puritan New England helped to larify and reinforce norms of behaviour. The moral panic was n invention as the Puritan society was very conformist and isplayed little real deviance which could be transformed into a oral panic.

Checkpoint 4

What are the similarities between the works of Hall and Erikson?

M. Douglas described the persecution, in pre-World War II USA, f Jehovah's Witnesses. They refused on religious grounds to salute he US flag and this was seen as unpatriotic in a society which as already unsettled and divided by economic depression. The ersecution of scapegoats may reinforce the unity of the majority; stopped after the bombing of Pearl Harbour by the Japanese, hich provided a new enemy both within and abroad.

Exam question answer: page 153

With reference to the diagram on page 148 and using your own knowledge, explain the interactionist explanation of deviance amplification. (15 min)

Suicide

The main issues here are:

→ How can we explain the social distribution of suicide
→ Are suicide statistics reliable and valid?
→ What is the best way to do sociology?

Durkheim's study of suicide ●●●

His two main aims were:

→ to identify the social causes of suicide
→ to encourage the use of scientific methods in sociology.

The social causes of suicide

Durkheim, as a functionalist, identified social rather than individual causes of suicide. He argued that any given society or social group within a society had a stable suicide rate over time. Thus it was the social characteristics of the society, rather than individual factors, which explained the variation in suicide rates between different groups and societies. The two social causes he identified were:

→ *The extent to which individuals are integrated into society*. Integration is the result of shared values. In traditional societies integration is based on the sameness of the population. In modern societies integration is based on the interdependence resulting from the division of labour.
→ *The extent to which individual desires are morally regulated*. This means society provides a framework of goals and the means to achieve them.

Where these two factors are in balance suicide rates are low. If they are too high or too low then the risk of suicide increases. This produces four types of suicide. The first two are characteristic of *modern societies* where the individual is freed from social constraints. The second two are characteristic of *traditional societies*, or *close-knit groups within modern society* where the individual is dominated by the social group.

1 **Egoistic** suicide is caused by too little integration and is higher among the unmarried, the childless and Protestants than among Catholics.
2 **Anomic** suicide is caused by too little moral regulation, which occurs when there is too large a gap between aspiration and achievement.
3 **Fatalistic** suicide is caused by too much moral regulation, where individuals feel they have no control over their lives. This might apply to young offenders in custody.
4 **Altruistic** suicide is caused by too much integration, where the individual may give up his life for the group. This might explain the behaviour of martyrs who die for a cause, e.g. the IRA hunger strikers of the 1970s.

Checkpoint 1

Explain briefly what you understand by 'the use of scientific methods to do sociology'.

Examiner's secrets

Many A-level textbooks see Durkheim as the clearest example of the positivist approach. This is perfectly acceptable in exam answers. However, S. Taylor (1990) wrote that Durkheim, unlike many of his followers, was not a *positivist* but instead took a *realist* view of science.

The jargon

Positivists study only observable facts. *Realists* look for hidden causes, e.g. being unmarried or living alone do not cause suicide. They are both examples of the low level of integration that does cause high suicide rates.

Action point

You can find up-to-date suicide figures from the Office of Population and Census Statistics (OPCS).

Checkpoint 2

Explain why anomic suicide might be more common in modern societies than simple societies.

An evaluation of Durkheim's work

Criticism of Durkheim's functionalist approach comes from:

→ The **internal critics**. These have followed Durkheim's model for researching suicide but come to different conclusions, e.g. Iga (1986) identified the main causes of suicide in modern Japan as fatalistic and altruistic.

→ The **psychiatric critics**. Although using a positivist approach to establish a relationship between suicide and other characteristics, the psychiatric view tends to focus on *individual* rather than *social* causes. Pritchard linked suicide with mental illness – a cause rejected by Durkheim.

Criticism of Durkheim's scientific approach comes from:

→ Those who study the individual and social meanings of suicide. Interactionists reject the use of scientific methods and deny that there are social factors which cause individuals to commit suicide. Instead they explain suicide by examining the social meanings given to behaviour which leads to the behaviour being labelled as suicide. It is the motive for the act which defines it as suicide, not the outcome. An act is only a suicide if this is the meaning given to it. Stengl wrote about suicide and attempted suicide. All but the first type in the table below might be called attempted suicide.

Act	Motive	'Successful' outcome	'Unsuccessful' outcome
suicide	death	dead	alive
faked suicide	cry for help	alive	dead
failed suicide	death	dead	alive
trial by ordeal	risk taking	unsure	unsure

→ Those who see suicide statistics as a social construction. Suicide is not an objective fact, it is not a real world event. An act becomes a suicide when coroners decide it is a suicide. Thus suicide statistics are a list of coroners' decisions, not objective acts. Coroners, juries, witnesses, the media, researchers, even the victims themselves share common-sense assumptions about what is and isn't suicide. These assumptions and thus the coroners' decisions are based on:

→ *the biography of the 'suicide'* – did the victim have the characteristics of a typical suicide, such as age, job, and medical history?

→ *the circumstances of the death* – e.g. how many pills were taken? If death was by shooting was it while hunting or at home?

Exam question   answer: pages 153–4

Assess the influence of Durkheim's study of suicide on later studies of crime and deviance. (50 min)

The jargon

They are called *internal critics* because they accept the scientific approach but question Durkheim's findings.

Checkpoint 3

Does Iga criticize or provide support for Durkheim?

Checkpoint 4

What methods do interactionists use to study suicide and suicide statistics?

The jargon

Interactionists write 'suicide', 'deviant' and 'offender' in quotes to indicate that these are not objective facts but the result of labelling.

Examiner's secrets

Durkheim will have influenced both supporters and critics.

Answers
Crime and deviance

Theories of deviance and crime

Checkpoints

> **Examiner's secrets**
>
> You can choose any social characteristic but not a biological one (e.g. sex) or a psychological one (e.g. maternal deprivation). You can choose ethnicity, class or the two below.

1. • *Gender* is associated with deviance in two ways. Firstly, males are more criminal than females. Secondly, what is considered deviant depends on gender, e.g. promiscuity is considered deviant for women, not men.
   • *Age* is related to deviance, with much higher rates of crime for youths, particularly males, than older people.
2. • Laws which protect property serve the interests of those that own the means of production. These include laws of inheritance, favourable tax laws and laws against trespass.
   • Laws which restrict the interests of employees, such as curbs on trade union powers, strengthen the bargaining power of employers.
3. According to H. Becker, labelling depends on:
   • the consequences of an act, not the act itself, e.g. getting pregnant rather than underage sex
   • the characteristics of the victim, e.g. it is claimed that the Metropolitan Police has failed to pay sufficient attention to crimes against black and Asian people
   • the characteristics of the offender, e.g. young men are more likely to be stopped and searched than women or older men.
4. They are based on a representative sample of the whole population so can indicate the extent of crime in society. They reveal unreported crimes. They can measure fear of crime. They are independent of police figures, which may be incomplete or biased.

Exam question

Functionalists argue social control is necessary for society to contain deviance. The forces of law and order are seen as enforcing shared norms. Social control can help to reinforce the collective consciousness by drawing attention to consensual norms and values and punishing the rule breakers.

Evaluation comes from the other three approaches. You can, for example, question the existence of consensual values and lead into conflict approaches such as those of Marxists and feminists.

Marxists see agents of social control serving the interests of the ruling class. They enforce ruling class ideology and norms (see answer to Checkpoint 2). Law enforcement can be used as a distraction from the underlying problems of capitalism (see S. Hall on deviance amplification, page 149).

Evaluation can come from consensus or interactionist theories. The latter would identify a range of deviant activities, which are unrelated to economic inequalities.

Interactionists argue that social control is not a response to deviance but creates and amplifies it. See Becker in the answer to Checkpoint 3 and Lemert on the role of social reaction in the creation of secondary deviance.

Evaluation might point to the overemphasis on social reaction at the expense of explaining rule breaking.

Feminists argue that both formal and informal agents of social control define deviance on the basis of gender and enforce patriarchy. If Heidensohn's social control theory is discussed you can point to its failure to explain those women who do commit crimes.

> **Examiner's secrets**
>
> You don't need to cover all these theories to get full marks. You must ensure your answer focuses on the issue of social control; don't just discuss the theories in general or describe studies fully just because you know them.

The social distribution of crime

Checkpoints

1. This question can be answered by referring to the different types of deviance identified by Merton.
   • *Innovators* try to achieve consensual goals by illegitimate means.
   • *Retreatists* reject both the goals and the legitimate means of achieving them.
   • *Rebels* try to substitute new goals.
   • *Ritualists* overconform to rules but no longer try to achieve the goals.
2. Women may be socialized to expect less than men, e.g. in pursuing careers. Feminists would explain this process as reproducing patriarchal ideology.
3. The police and courts may be more lenient towards women who accept traditional gender roles. They may be more severe towards women who behave in unfeminine ways, e.g. women who have killed abusive partners have had the defence of provocation rejected.

   Women victims of domestic violence may be disregarded. Judges have defined nagging as provocation, which partially excuses murder of wives. Women victims of rape are often accused of provoking attack.
4. *Marginalization* – black and Asian youth may be excluded by racism and their higher risk of unemployment.

   Relative deprivation – economic inequality which results from disadvantage in the job market creates a feeling of deprivation, particularly as ethnic minorities are more likely to live alongside the rich in inner-city areas.

   Criminal subcultures – ethnicity can be the basis of a subculture, though not necessarily a criminal one. Religious subcultures provide another response to deprivation.

Exam question

Describe the theoretical and methodological issues associated with the reliability and validity of crime statistics

nd apply the discussion to gender differences. Consider
hether women commit fewer crimes and/or are less likely
o get caught.

You could critically apply the traditional explanations of
ariations in crime rates to women. You can include anomic
heory, subcultural theory, interactionist theory, etc.

Evaluate specifically feminist explanations of the amount
nd type of crime committed by women. These include
eidensohn's social control theory and critics such as
, Carlen.

Finally, you could introduce the idea that women are more
kely to be victims of some crimes related to patriarchy, such
s domestic violence and rape.

Examiner's secrets

You don't have to cover all these arguments. The more general
debates on crime statistics are useful if you lack detailed
knowledge of feminist studies.

The amplification of deviance

Checkpoints

Sample social surveys of potential victims, e.g. the British
Crime Survey.

Dobash and Dobash conducted interviews with victims
of domestic violence.

A self-fulfilling prophecy is a prediction that happens partly
because it has been predicted. Labelling theory argues
that this explains crime and educational failure.

There are several you can choose from. It depends what
you regard as recent! Often old moral panics are revived.
There are lots of studies of football hooligans – Pearson
traced these fears back to the last century.

The race for the first elected mayor of London led to a
revival in the press of the idea of the 'loony left' from the
1980s.

Moral panics about (new) drugs are revived periodically.

- Both identify a functional role for scapegoats – black
youth in Hall's study and women witches in Erikson's.
- Both identify imaginary crime waves, i.e. there can be
social reaction to a perceived problem which has not
objectively occurred – witches don't exist, and there
was no mugging crime wave.

Exam question

he interactionist approach to deviance amplification
escribes how social reaction to real or imagined deviance
an increase the extent or seriousness of deviance. You can
se Cohen, Young or Lemert to illustrate this argument.

The diagram is based on Young's work on drug takers.
e argues that social reaction from the police is based on
n ill-informed stereotype of the often unfamiliar middle-
lass users.

This reaction encourages the development of a more
solated drug subculture where the police are feared and
rug use becomes more central to users' lives. The informal

drug economy where buyers and suppliers were often the
same people changes. Drug selling is treated as a serious
crime and becomes an activity dominated by professional
criminals.

Examiner's secrets

Sources don't just provide you with knowledge, they also allow
you to demonstrate your understanding of the issues in the
question.

Don't be tempted to go into positivist or other approaches
in a short answer. If the question asked you to assess rather
than explain you would have to refer to critics.

Suicide

Checkpoints

1 Scientific methods involve the use of quantitative
approaches, such as the comparative social survey, to
test a hypothesis.

2 In simple societies peoples' aspirations (the goals they
wish to achieve) are more likely to match the means
available to gain them, e.g. there may be a rigid caste-
like stratification system where lower-status groups
don't expect very much – in this world anyway. Moral
regulation is reinforced by shared traditional religious
beliefs.

Modern societies are more open so that people share
the same, usually materialistic, aspirations. Consumerist
values are encouraged by advertising and an ideology
which encourages people to believe in equal opportunities
means increasing numbers of people have limited
opportunities to achieve goals by legitimate means.

3 Iga appears to criticize Durkheim because he associated
altruistic and fatalistic suicide with simple societies. But it
is not a rejection of Durkheim because Japan has the high
degree of integration and moral regulation usually
associated with traditional simple societies.

4 Interactionists might study suicides by seeking to identify
the individual and social meanings attached to 'suicidal'
behaviour. Douglas advocated the study of suicide notes
which look at suicide from the point of view of the
suicidal actor.

Suicide statistics, which are seen as socially
constructed, can be studied by observation in coroners'
courts to discover the reasons why suicide verdicts are
reached in some cases.

Exam question

There are two simple ways to structure this answer:

- Examine the impact of Durkheim (both his functionalist
explanations and scientific approach) on later work. Then
see if later studies of suicide influenced and/or were
influenced by later studies of deviance.
- Discuss methodological approaches and explanations
separately.

Explain Durkheim's aim to provide a model of sociological research in his study of suicide. You could refer to:

- scientific methods
- positivism
- the comparative method
- quantitative methods
- social surveys
- official statistics

Explain, with examples, later research into crime, deviance, suicide, which follows this model. You can choose from a wide variety of studies such as those that link suicide with single-person households, unemployment or gender with the nature and extent of crime.

Explain, with examples, later research into crime, deviance, and suicide, which rejects this model. The interactionist approaches to suicide, deviance and crime could all be mentioned.

The studies of suicide which challenge the positivist approach were influenced by earlier interactionist work on deviance, such as Becker's writing on labelling. These studies (e.g. those by Douglas and Atkinson) in turn influenced later work. Atkinson's critical views on the limited usefulness of official statistics may have encouraged the use of victim surveys as an alternative to police figures.

Durkheim's functionalist explanations were continued by Merton's anomic theory and a variety of subcultural theories. They were challenged by Marxist, feminist and interactionist alternatives. Depending on dates, later interactionist research may have been influenced by the 1960s work on suicide.

Examiner's secrets

You will probably have prepared thoroughly for a more conventional question on suicide. Don't just reproduce it here. It is important to know Durkheim and his critics, but you need to apply this knowledge to the issues in the question and also be able to trace the impact of this work on later studies of deviance.

The sociology of health is an increasingly popular sociological topic. It can be used in debates about methods and theories and has much in common with the sociology of deviance, so you can refer to common studies and arguments. You can use the study of health to debate broader issues such as the best way to do sociological research and the evaluation of sociological perspectives. Knowledge of sociological studies of health and health statistics can be used in theory and methods questions.

Exam themes

Exam questions frequently require discussion of the social distribution of health by class, gender, ethnicity and age.
   This involves consideration of:

→ why some groups have unequal chances of getting sick

→ inequalities in health care

   The social definition and construction of health and illness is a major theme and this involves discussion of the relationship between doctors and patients.

Topic checklist

	AQA Sociology	OCR Sociology	EDEXCEL Social Policy
O AS ● A2			
Perspectives on health	O	●	O
Inequalities in health	O	●	
Health care	O	●	
Gender and health	O	●	

Perspectives on health

Check the net

For health statistics,
check www.phls.co.uk
To find studies in medical journals,
check medline and medline plus at
www.nim.nih.gov
The NHS site is at www.nhsdirect.nhs.uk

Example

Good health is falsely assumed to be
normal. Surveys indicate that the majority
of people feel unhealthy.

Checkpoint 1

Use examples to explain how someone
can have a disease without feeling ill
and be ill without having a disease.

Example

Contemporary medicine has been
revolutionized by increased understanding
of genes.

Checkpoint 2

Give one argument for and one argument
against the view that improvements in
health have been the result of scientific
discoveries.

Examiner's secrets

This debate between positivist and
interactionist approaches is more or
less the same set of arguments found
in the sociology of suicide and crime.

Action point

Make notes on studies of mental illness
which use the interactionist approach.
If you have studied deviance you may
be able to use the same examples.

The main issues that divide sociologists are:

→ the definition of health
→ explanations of the social distribution of health
→ the role of doctors and others who care for the sick.

This part concentrates on definitions: the following
parts deal more thoroughly with the other issues.

Key terms

→ **Disease** is a pathological abnormality with an objective biological
  cause (you have a disease).
→ **Illness** is a patient's subjective response to a real or imagined
  disease. It involves the experience of pain, discomfort or
  abnormality (you feel ill).
→ **Health** can be defined as absence of sickness (either disease or
  illness), or in a more positive way as a sense of well-being.

The biomedical model

This is not a sociological perspective. It is usually the basis of the
public's common-sense view of health. Good health is seen as normal.

It is now challenged by some experts, including doctors, and the
public.

Disease is seen as the cause of ill health. Modern medicine has often
explained disease as external attacks on the body from bacteria and
viruses.

Doctors use scientific knowledge to treat individuals in a rational,
professional way. Scientific discoveries of cures are the way to improve
health.

Positivist approaches

These share the scientific approach with the medical model but focus
on social rather than individual biological causes. Definitions of health
and sickness tend to be taken for granted.

Positivists use the comparative method to identify social and
economic causes of disease. Health statistics, which record variations
in mortality and morbidity between different social groups, are seen as
a useful resource for research. Both consensus and conflict theories
may use positivist research methods.

Interactionist approaches

Health statistics are seen as a social construction. They tell us more
about the processes of doctors' diagnoses and recording than they do
about patterns of illness.

Studies of sickness, particularly mental illness, may adopt the
labelling approach. Some interactionists believe there are no real
rates of illness to be discovered, as illness and even death may be
socially defined. All the following approaches share the interactionist

view that defining health depends on negotiations between doctors, patients and others. The conflict approaches tend to stress the importance of power in these relationships.

Functionalists ⚫⚫⚫

Parsons wrote about how doctors legitimize patients taking on the 'sick role'. This is functional for society as the patient is allowed to drop out from responsibility without challenging consensual norms.

Marxist approaches ⚫⚫⚫

→ Disease is caused by capitalism.
→ Health care institutions and definitions and explanations of ill health are part of the superstructure of capitalist society, e.g. individuals are blamed for ill health when the fault lies with capitalism.
→ Medicine is a form of social control (see Foucault and feminism below).
→ Improving health depends on medical advance, e.g. better drugs rather than reducing poverty and inequality.

Feminists ⚫⚫⚫

→ Disease results from inequalities in patriarchal society.
→ Women experience disadvantages in both providing and using health care.

Foucault ⚫⚫⚫

Foucault saw medicine as a new way, associated with capitalist society, of disciplining the body. Medicine applied scientific knowledge to replace torture and prison as a major form of social control of the body and later the mind.

Foucault's view of the biomedical model saw doctors as 'experts' – the possessors of scientific knowledge which allowed them to control patients. This replaced the traditional views, where the rich regarded doctors as servants and the poor relied on folk remedies.

Postmodern approaches ⚫⚫⚫

These share with Foucault and the interactionist approach a mistrust of scientific medicine. The biomedical approach is seen as a metanarrative which claims a monopoly of truth when it is no more than a story which serves the interests of doctors.

Example

Death is socially defined in the sense that doctors pronounce a patient dead by interpreting physical signs. Deciding whether to resuscitate or not may be influenced by patient's age and wishes and negotiations with relatives.

Checkpoint 3

How might capitalism cause disease?

Links

See gender and health on page 162.

Checkpoint 4

Explain how medicine can be seen as a form of social control.

Exam question   answer: page 164

Illness and disability are socially constructed rather than medically defined. Assess sociological arguments and evidence for this statement. (50 min)

Inequalities in health

The social distribution of health refers to the fact that different social groups have distinctive patterns of health and illness. Sociological research often focuses on inequalities in both health chances and health care. This part concentrates on chances, the next focuses on care.

Example

There is a close correlation between infant mortality rates and social class.

Measuring health inequalities ○○○

Mortality (death) rates can be calculated for different age groups and expressed as life expectancy or deaths per thousand.

Morbidity rates are the frequency with which diseases occur in different social groups.

The Black Report (1980) linked occupational classes and health. It examined four possible explanations for health inequalities and concluded that low income was the major cause of shorter life and higher risk of illness.

Checkpoint 1

Outline two reasons, apart from low income, why unemployment is linked to ill health.

Material deprivation and health ○○○

Townsend, in the Black Report, argued that material deprivation was the most influential cause of health inequalities. Later he argued that inequality itself, rather than just absolute deprivation, may adversely affect health.

Bad housing has been linked to stress, respiratory problems and contagious diseases. Unsurprisingly, sleeping on the streets is associated with short life expectancy.

Unemployment correlates with stress-related disease, suicide, and drinking, smoking and poor diet. Civil servants on lower incomes or those who lost their jobs had worse diets than those in higher-paid jobs. Working conditions can also increase risks to health through accident, dangerous substances and stress.

Examiner's secrets

The distinction between material and cultural factors can also be used to answer questions on poverty and educational success.

Checkpoint 2

Explain how you could assess whether low income or culture causes worse health in lower social classes.

Cultural deprivation and health ○○○

This is similar to the culture of poverty argument. It may seem to blame ill health on the 'victim'. Disease can be blamed on the poor who choose an unhealthy lifestyle involving drinking, smoking and high-fat diets.

Critics of this view tend to support the material deprivation argument. Critics may question the evaluation of culture, which depends on time, place and power. What is seen as an unhealthy diet may depend on who eats it.

Example

When potatoes were the food of the poor, the rich ate meat. Meat was seen as healthy. Expert opinion on nutrition changes.

The artefact explanation ○○○

There are critics of the view that there is a correlation between social class and health. They suggest that the apparent inequalities are a result of the way in which class is defined and also of the way health is measured. In particular, changes in the occupational structure have led to the shrinking of the number of unskilled manual workers. These were the class with the worst health in the Black Report. They were older than other classes, which could explain worse health.

Critics of the artefact view have demonstrated that using other definitions of social class produces a consistent pattern of health inequalities.

The selection explanation ●●●

This agrees that social class and health are related. However, the causation is reversed. Ill health is seen as the cause of lower social class and low income rather than the reverse, e.g. unhealthy people may be disadvantaged at school, more likely to be unemployed, and more likely to be downwardly socially mobile.

Criticism of this view based on longitudinal surveys suggests that ill health is rarely the cause of downward mobility.

Ethnicity and health ●●●

Both materialist and cultural explanations could be applied to the issue of ethnicity and health.

Some ethnic minorities may be over-represented in lower social classes and amongst the unemployed. Health inequalities may be reduced or disappear when research controls class differences.

There are problems comparing different studies because of the inconsistency in defining ethnic groups. Different ethnic groups have distinctive patterns of health and ill health. Generally, ethnic minorities have lower rates of lung disease than the native population but higher rates of heart disease and of accident and injury through violence. Immigrants from Ireland have higher death rates than those from the New Commonwealth.

Conclusion ●●●

Inequalities have persisted despite nearly half a century of the NHS. Political views influence the choice of explanations and remedies for the inequalities. Materialist theories are favoured by the left. The recommended remedy is to reduce inequality – the cost would be enormous and would be borne by the rich. Cultural theories are favoured by the right. The cure is to change the lifestyle of the working class and poor.

Checkpoint 3

Explain why some ethnic minorities might have higher rates of heart disease than the national average.

Checkpoint 4

Why might rates of mental illness be related to ethnicity?

Action point

Take notes on health inequalities and differences between ethnic groups. Use the headings materialist and cultural explanations.

Examiner's secrets

This question *requires* consideration of both the social definition and the social distribution of health. You can mention ethnicity and gender as well as social class when discussing distribution.

Exam question   answer: pages 164–5

'Health and illness are not chance occurrences but are socially defined and produced by the societies in which people live'.
Explain and evaluate this view. (50 min)

Health care

The social distribution of health depends on access to care as well as inequalities in health chances. Rich countries spend more on health care than poor countries. In the UK there is an ideological commitment to equality of treatment and to free care. The extent to which the NHS achieves this and who is to blame for health inequalities are party political issues. The main concerns are *the provision of health care*, which depends on allocation of limited resources, and *the effective use of health care*, which may be influenced by material and cultural factors.

Example

Britain spends less on health care than other rich countries – about 6% of GNP compared to 8% in other European countries.

Provision of health care

Private health care

Private health care is available for individuals who can and wish to pay. Generally, private health care is used by people who are insured against the cost. Employers may provide health insurance for workers and perhaps their families. In the UK there is no private accident and emergency service so even the rich and those with insurance use the NHS.

Action point

List different forms of health care. Use subheadings, including hospital care.

Allocation of NHS resources

Spending decisions depend on social policy, political considerations and market forces. Spending tends to be on: curative rather than preventive medicine, hospital rather than community care, acute beds in hospitals rather than geriatric and psychiatric beds.

Checkpoint 1

How might a Marxist explain greater spending on curative medicine?

Geographic inequalities

The quality of care affects survival rates of patients and varies between different regions of the country. There are local and regional inequalities in health. Separate studies in East London by Harrison (Hackney) and Skrimshire (Newham) blamed, respectively, poor access to care and industrial pollution.

Links

Bourdieu's concept of cultural capital which he applied to education (see page 53) could be applied to using health care.

The use of health care

Even when services are open to all, the middle classes use them more effectively than the working classes. The working classes use the NHS more, but they are less healthy so have a greater need.

The middle classes use preventive care more, including family planning, antenatal care, cancer screening and immunization. The middle classes seek earlier treatment, get longer consultations, and are more able to communicate effectively with doctors.

Ethnic minorities may experience disadvantage in using health care if providers fail to recognize cultural difference, e.g. language. Evidence is not consistent: a high proportion of Asian patients have doctors from a similar ethnic background. Gender and class will also influence relationships between doctors and patients.

Example

In a study of prostate disease, Howlett and Ashley found middle-class men were more likely to seek early treatment and be admitted to teaching hospitals than working-class men. (Prostate disease effects men of all classes more or less equally.)

Checkpoint 2

Explain the methodological reason why Howlett and Ashley chose to study prostate disease to study the effects of social class on using health care.

Illich

Illich has criticized health care providers, particularly doctors and drug corporations for the '**medicalization of life**'.

He uses the term **iatrogenic** illness to describe illness caused by medical care. He distinguished three types of iatrogenic illness:

→ **Clinical iatrogenesis** is the result of harmful medical intervention in the form of incompetent or unnecessary surgery, side effects of or addiction to drugs, and accidents in hospital

→ **Social iatrogenesis** describes the 'medicalization of life'. Moral and social issues such as abortion or 'mercy-killing' become technical problems to be left to doctors rather than politicians and priests.

→ **Cultural iatrogenesis** involves individuals giving up their independence and relying on experts to control their lives.

Health care and mental illness

Interactionists have suggested that social reaction to real or imagined behaviour leads to people being defined as mentally ill. Doctors and others who deliver care play a major role in this labelling process.

Lemert distinguished primary and secondary mental illness, the latter resulting from labelling. He argued against the medical view that paranoia was the result of delusions, perhaps with a biological cause. Instead he said that social misfits really were excluded from normal society and this produced increasingly deviant behaviour.

Goffman's *Asylums* describes the 'career' of the mental patient. Total institutions, such as psychiatric hospitals, exert control over the patient, who may respond rationally by wishing to leave or by hoarding food. These behaviours are seen as evidence of madness.

Szasz dismissed mental illness as a myth and psychiatry as a form of social control. He pointed out that madness is often defined legally rather than medically. Deviance may be seen as illness rather than resistance.

A critical view

Positivists use the approach found in Durkheim's *Suicide* to identify the social causes of mental illness. They accept the traditional biomedical model except they emphasize social rather than physiological causes. Taylor used Durkheim's concept of integration to explain higher rates of mental illness amongst the unemployed and divorced.

Checkpoint 3

Explain how unhappiness and appearance have been medicalized.

Links

Lemert made the same observation about primary and secondary deviance (page 149).

Checkpoint 4

Szasz attacks the therapeutic state from a conservative viewpoint. Explain how a Marxist might criticize psychiatric care.

Exam question   answer: page 165

How might sociologists contribute to our understanding of the relationship between doctors and patients? (50 min)

Gender and health

This section is largely about women. It is often the case that when we consider gender differences we end up writing largely about women. You should be able to discuss how gender influences the social distribution of health, considering both health chances and health care. Women provide health care, as well as use it, and this is discussed here.

Gender and health chances

Despite their longer life expectancy, women use the health care services more than men do. This is not, however, the reason why they live longer. Nor do they use health care most in their old age. Their most intensive use is while they are fertile, between the ages of 15 and 44.

Mental illness rates are much higher than those of men and the type of illness diagnosed is different. Women have higher rates of depression and lower rates of psychosis.

Feminism has embraced other approaches to explain the influence of gender on health.

Biological explanations

Women are biologically more at risk than men, particularly while of child-bearing age. However, female infants are stronger and have better survival rates. This difference is reducing as medical care is improving.

Positivist explanations

→ Women are socially more at risk, because of their roles within the home and family.
→ Married men live longer than single men do but never-married women live longer than married women do.
→ Marriage reduces women's access to resources, i.e. has the effect of reducing social class, e.g. married women eat less than single women do, even single mothers living on lower household incomes (H. Graham 1986). Rowntree recorded similar findings in his poverty study in 1901.
→ Higher divorce rates have created large numbers of female-led single-parent families which often become benefit-dependent. This is a threat to health.
→ The more confined lives of women means they are less at risk of death or injury from accident or violence. However, they are more likely than men to be victims of domestic violence.

"Women get sick but men die."

Nathanson

". . . four times as dangerous to bear a child as to work in a mine"

D. Russell (campaigning for access to birth control in the 1920s)

Checkpoint 1

Explain two social reasons why patterns of women's health are becoming similar to those of men.

"In truth, being a housewife makes women sick. Never-married women are 'the cream of the crop'. Never-married men are 'the bottom of the barrel'."

J. Bernard 1976

Checkpoint 2

Give two reasons why domestic violence is rarely seen as a health problem.

Women as users of health care

Interactionist approaches

- Women are (seen as) different from men.
- Biological and socially constructed differences have been 'medicalized'. This applies particularly to differences related to reproduction.
- (Usually male) doctors attempt to control women; fertility, infertility, contraception and pregnancy are all managed as 'health problems'.
- Women are diagnosed differently from men. They are more likely to be seen as mentally ill and are more likely to accept diagnoses and treatments which allow temporary respite from household responsibilities, e.g. hospital in-patient care and mood-changing drugs.
- Men can avoid stress by being absent from work. They avoid being labelled mentally ill as it may threaten their employment and sense of identity.
- Women's illness behaviour is different.
- Women are more likely to go to the doctor: this may have been because they were less likely to have been in full-time paid employment.
- Women are also more likely to be encouraged to seek medical solutions to problems associated with housing, poverty, marriage, sex, unhappiness, etc.

Women as providers of health care

Most paid NHS workers are women. They are under-represented in higher-paid, higher-status jobs.

Women as mothers, wives and daughters provide unpaid health care in the home. As well as caring for children, women care for the elderly and those with disabilities. They maintain health in the family through domestic labour and providing emotional support (**the 3 Cs**). Government financial aid only recognizes this to a limited extent. Men are provided with support to employ care when wives are not available. Married women have in the recent past been excluded from some benefits because it was said that they should be doing the caring. The responsibility for informal health care contributes to the perception of mothers as less reliable employees.

Men with disabilities are more likely to do paid work than their wives or women with disabilities.

> **Checkpoint 3**
>
> Briefly explain how pregnancy is 'medicalized'.

> **Checkpoint 4**
>
> How are women encouraged to seek medical solutions to social problems?

> **The jargon**
>
> *The 3 Cs* means cooking, cleaning and caring. These, along with clerical work, are also amongst the major sources of women's paid employment.

> **Example**
>
> The expectation that women will care for family members has been called *'compulsory altruism'* (Land and Rose).

Exam question   answer: page 166

Compare and contrast the contributions of Marxist and feminist approaches to an understanding of health inequalities. (50 min)

Answers
Health

Perspectives on health

Checkpoints

1 You may have a disease such as tooth decay, HIV, cancer but not be aware of it, have no obvious symptoms and experience no discomfort: therefore you don't feel ill.

   In addition, some mental illnesses have no biological basis (or at least none we know at the moment).

   You may experience pain, discomfort and feel ill or imagine you have a disease without having any biological abnormality. Old age, menstruation and pregnancy may all produce the experience of feeling ill without the subject having a disease.

2 Scientific discoveries have produced:
   - curative drugs such as antibiotics
   - vaccines for immunisation
   - the ability to predict genetic disease.

   The reduction in the incidence of diseases such as TB were the result of improved living standards (housing, nutrition, etc.) before the discoveries of drugs used for immunization and treatment.

3 - By maintaining poverty and inequality.
   - By tolerating unhealthy or even dangerous working conditions to maintain profits.
   - By producing dangerous products (cigarettes, guns, etc.).

4 Psychiatric patients are incarcerated and controlled using drugs which affect mood and behaviour. Foucault, Goffman and Szasz have explained this from different perspectives.

   Functionalists see the need for doctors to legitimize absence from work as a form of social control.

   Feminists see male doctors exercising control over women, e.g. by medicalizing pregnancy.

Exam question

Define illness as a subjective experience perhaps based on disease. Explain the difference between them.

Define disability and related concepts such as impairment and handicap. Explain the difference between:

(a) the biomedical definition of disability – restriction in capacity to do things because of impairment (physical or mental dysfunction)

(b) social model of disability – the relationship of a person with impairment (incapacity or difference) to society. (This implies discrimination so that disability becomes a dimension of inequality, not a medical problem.)

   Outline biomedical explanation of illness and disability, which emphasizes objective organic causes.

   Use interactionist theory to explain how illness is socially constructed (e.g. Lemert, Goffman). Substantiate arguments supporting view by referring to conflict theories such as feminism (medicalizing of pregnancy), Foucault. The social construction of disability has been argued by T. Shakespeare, F. Davis on blindness.

   Criticize by referring to positivist explanations of disease which have been used by followers of Marx as well as Durkheim.

Inequalities in health

Checkpoints

1 Unemployment may be seen as a direct or indirect *cause* of ill health. Apart from low income, unemployment may cause stress-related disease because of loss of identity, anxiety, depression, and suicide resulting from loss of integration.

   Unemployment might be an *effect* of ill health. People with chronic sickness or disability may find it harder to get jobs as they may have had an interrupted education or are seen as unreliable workers.

2 This is a methods question.

   The way to assess the effect of one variable is to control other variables. Culture can be controlled by studying the changing health of middle-class people who have experienced loss of income. This reduction of income might follow divorce or job loss. This of course raises the problem that such events may in themselves be detrimental to health. *The Health Divide* was a survey that included data on health differences between civil servants in different income bands. Culturally they would have similar backgrounds.

   Similarly, families within the same income band could be studied and the effects of cultural change, e.g. through health education programmes, could be measured.

3 More stressful lives as a result of racism.

   More likely to be in lower social classes and thus in more stressful jobs. The typical diet may contribute to heart disease.

   Language and other cultural barriers may limit benefits of health education and medical advice.

4 The same arguments about stress are discussed in Checkpoint 3.

   Social definition of mental illness may make it more likely that social behaviour is interpreted as mental illness by doctors from other cultures. Police and doctors may treat minorities differently.

Exam question

No sociological perspective would argue that health and illness were chance occurrences. The common-sense view of health based on the traditional biomedical approach might suggest that infection and accident are chance occurrences.

   You can write critically about how the major perspectives:
   - define health and illness (objectively or social definitions)
   - explain the social causes of the social distribution of health, particularly health inequalities

explain the impact of socially produced inequalities in care (consider both provision and use)

You don't have to cover all the perspectives and you could try to group some together.

To bring about the major arguments over definition, you should discuss interactionists (including Illich) on the one hand and positivists on the other.

For the discussion of social distribution of health, Marxism provides a clear explanation of inequalities with consensus theories suggesting an alternative.

Health care

Checkpoints

Marxists would see this emphasis on scientific cure rather than prevention as encouraging false consciousness, because it suggests that ill health is not the inevitable result of the working conditions and inequality produced by capitalism. Also profits can be made from drugs. Health education is more difficult to sell. (In contrast *Illich* sees the emphasis on cures as part of the medicalization of life and argues it provides an opportunity for doctors to exercise control over patients.)

This is a methods question.

By choosing a disease which affects men of different social classes equally they are able to control this variable. If patients have different outcomes it is likely to be a consequence of *health care* inequalities.

Most other disease affects the working class more, therefore they may use more health care because of greater need.

The medicalization of life suggests that more aspects of life are seen as health problems to be dealt with by doctors.

Unhappiness has been medicalized by suggesting that unhappiness is an abnormal condition, that doctors can advise on treatment and that mood-changing drugs are a suitable solution.

Appearance has been medicalized by the offering of cosmetic surgery as the solution to disfigurement and other perceived problems with the body. This depends on socially defined views of what is acceptable appearance. The ideas about what mental illness is and the social institutions which deal with mental illness are seen by Marxists as part of the superstructure of capitalist society.

Psychiatric care is seen as a form of social control (a point suggested by Szasz).

Exam question

You should offer a selection of the following approaches with evaluation of the contribution of each.

Interactionist theory pioneered a critical approach to the relationship between doctors and patients. You can discuss the role of doctors in defining health and illness and the possibility that social reaction is what defines illness rather than objective biological factors.

Marxists offer similar insights but emphasize the role of medicine as a form of social control. This view is shared by other conflict approaches, including feminism and Szasz.

You can evaluate these by pointing out differences between them, e.g. defining people as ill is in whose interest?

Illich's work on iatrogenic illness provides an excellent contrast with more favourable views of medicine offered by *functionalists* who see doctors as providing a vital social function.

Your conclusion might mention the common ground between sociological theories in their critical view of biomedical approaches. Also Parsons' functionalist theory uses interactionist arguments in the social definition of the sick role.

Gender and health

Checkpoints

1 Women are taking up full-time employment. Consumption of alcohol and cigarettes are increasingly similar to those among men. Arguably, gender roles within the family are converging.
2 It may be kept hidden and not reported. If visible, it may be tolerated, or seen as a legal problem.
3 • Medical diagnosis of pregnancy may be required to claim benefits.
   • Women are discouraged from having babies outside hospital.
   • Birth may involve use of drugs, surgery, etc.

   In Canada, doctors, rather than midwives, deliver babies and they have a much higher rate of Caesarean sections. In Holland, most births are at home and there is not a higher rate of complications.
4 Women's magazines, doctors, and housing officials may all suggest that the solution to poverty, bad housing, marital breakdown, etc. may be found with doctors. In a rational, scientific society, medicine may have replaced the functions of religion.

   If problems are seen as individual medical problems, then there is no pressure to change the circumstances which produce the problem. Recently, stress at work has been legally recognized as a problem which employers may be responsible for, rather than an individual illness.

Exam question

Compare and contrast Marxist and feminist explanations of differences in health chances

- Both identify social causes.
- Both see inequality itself as a cause of ill health.
- Marxists focus on inequalities in employment.
- Feminists focus on inequalities in the family.

Compare and contrast Marxist and feminist explanations of differences in health care

- Both are critical of medical profession.
- Both see medicine as a form of social control.
- Marxists explain emphasis on curative rather than preventive care as evidence that health care is run for profit.

- Feminists such as Oakley have developed Illich's arguments about medicalization of life and adapted them to explain how men use health care to subordinate women.

Conclusion

- Feminist analysis is based on the existence of a patriarchal society, whereas Marxists blame capitalism; therefore feminists fear the persistence of inequalities in socialist societies.
- Marxist-feminists combine the two perspectives.

Whereas most of this book has been based on sociological debates about the nature of society, this section involves discussions about the nature of sociology. It is worth revising the section on sociological methods and referring to other topics which illustrate theoretical debates. Remember, a theory is an explanation and sociologists explain social phenomena in different ways.

Exam themes

→ The evaluation of sociological theories

→ Postmodernism and sociological theory

→ The relationship between theory and methods

→ Is sociology a science?

Topic checklist

	AQA Sociology	OCR Sociology	EDEXCEL Social Policy
O AS ● A2			
Structuralist theories	O●	O●	
Feminism and the New Right	O●	O●	
Action theories	O●	O●	
Postmodernism	O●	O●	

Structuralist theories

Functionalism dominated sociology after World War II. During the 1960s Marxism became a popular way to challenge the consensus perspective on society. Both have been criticized by action and postmodernist approaches.

Functionalist theory ●●●

Main assumptions

→ Structuralist theory – external social forces limit individual behaviour.

→ Consensus theory – social order is based on shared values.

→ Society is seen as a system of interrelated parts – like a biological organism or a machine.

→ The system has needs that must be met if it is to survive and remain stable.

→ Functions are the ways that social arrangements meet the needs of the system.

→ Social arrangements (e.g. the family) adapt to fit the needs of the system; this change is gradual and evolutionary.

→ Inequality is seen as functional for society.

→ Functionalism is associated with the positivist approach and scientific quantitative methods.

Evaluation

Arguments for: It explains predictable patterns of behaviour within social groups, i.e. **social facts**, and it explains the influence of culture and society on individuals, in contrast to biology and psychology.

Arguments against: Conflict theories challenge the consensual view of society, e.g. on inequality. Action theories challenge the oversocialized view of individuals. This is seen as justifying the status quo.

Main applications

Functionalism can be applied to nearly all the topics. For example, Durkheim's *Suicide* used functionalism to explain the stable and distinctive suicide rates in particular groups and societies.

Main writers

Durkheim saw society as based on moral consensus – the 'collective conscience'. He distinguished the ways in which simple societies and modern industrial societies were integrated.

Parsons identified four functional needs of social systems:

→ *adaption* to the environment through economic activity
→ *pattern maintenance* – the need to motivate individuals to conform
→ *integration* – the need for social solidarity

Checkpoint 1

How did industrialization change the family?

Links

See Davis and Moore, page 97.

Checkpoint 2

Why is functionalism often linked with scientific methods?

Examiner's secrets

Answers on family, education, religion and deviance can often be based on a debate with the functionalist approach.

Links

See suicide, page 150, and secondary data, page 12.

The jargon

Pattern maintenance is usually called social control by Durkheim and most others.

→ *goal attainment* – achieved by allocation of resources by those given authority, e.g. politicians.

The mnemonic A PIG will help you remember Parsons.

Marxism ⬤⬤⬤

Main assumptions

→ Structuralist theory.
→ Conflict theory: order is imposed by the dominant social class.
→ Marxist explanations are based on the relationship between the economy (the substructure) and all other social arrangements and ideas (the superstructure).
→ Social change is the result of the class struggle.

Evaluation

Arguments for: The important role of the economy and social class in explaining social arrangements and change is accepted by many sociologists. The concepts of cultural reproduction, **ideology** and **false consciousness** have been adopted and/or amended by other theories – notably feminism.

Arguments against: Consensus theories challenge the Marxist view that conflict is normal and will lead to change. Action theory since Weber has attacked the structuralism of Marxism and particularly the emphasis on economic explanations. Other conflict theories claim the Marxist focus on social class does not adequately explain gender or ethnic inequality. Note the oppressive nature of communist states and their failure.

Main applications

Questions on social class are often debates with Marxist views. For most other topics you can argue institutions and ideas are part of the superstructure of capitalist society.

Main writers

Althusser argued that the ideas and institutions of the superstructure were largely independent of the economic substructure yet supported it through **ISAs** and **RSAs**. These terms can be used to describe the police, education system and the media.

Marcuse emphasized the role of the illusion of democratic freedom, e.g. voting and civil rights, and the 'false' consumer needs encouraged by advertising, these are both created by capitalism and maintain false consciousness.

Exam question   answer: page 176

Compare and contrast Marxist and functionalist theories of social change. (50 min)

The jargon

The *substructure* shapes the superstructure and comprises the technology used to produce goods and the roles of different classes in production.

The *superstructure* reproduces the substructure and comprises social institutions such as the family, and ideas, beliefs and values such as religious beliefs.

Checkpoint 3

Explain two differences between Marxist and feminist approaches to cultural reproduction in schools.

Checkpoint 4

How do Marxists explain the absence of overt class conflict in capitalist societies?

The jargon

An *ISA* is an ideological state apparatus which controls people's minds. An *RSA* is a repressive state apparatus which uses force.

Examiner's secrets

Remember to examine similarities as well as differences.

Feminism and the New Right

There is no natural link between the two perspectives discussed in this section. Frequently, they can be used to present opposite political points of view, e.g. when doing family or poverty and welfare questions. They are similar in the sense that both are closely linked to social and political ideas and movements, which expressed discontent with the post-war consumer society in liberal democracies.

Feminism

Main assumptions

→ Gender relationships are based on inequality of power.
→ Gender inequality is the result of **patriarchy** – it's not natural or functional.
→ Power is exercised publicly (e.g. in the law and/or at work) and privately in the family.
→ Women may be economically exploited, victims of violence, dominated by cultural beliefs (ideology) and social structures.

Feminism and sociology

→ Sociology has operated within a patriarchal framework; men have been the subject of research and women either ignored or seen as an unusual variant of men.
→ 'Malestream' sociology has been seen as ideologically neutral (i.e. value-free).
→ Sociology needs to emphasize the importance of gender relationships in all topic areas.
→ Feminist sociology has its own principles for doing research.

Types of feminism
Radical feminism – emphasizes the oppression of women within families. The mother-role and men's greater physical strength are sources of patriarchy. Sexuality and violence are forms of oppression.

Marxist-feminism – emphasizes economic exploitation of women at work and at home. Capitalism and patriarchy work together to produce culture and structure which subordinate women.

Liberal feminism – inequality is the result of prejudice and ignorance and can be tackled through legal and political reform.

Evaluation
Arguments for: Feminism has successfully highlighted and challenged inequality, which was previously ignored or seen as reflecting natural differences, and has demonstrated that uncritical sociology is not value-free – it supports the (patriarchal) status quo. It has inspired social movements which have improved some women's position in society.

Examiner's secrets

As far as sociology students are concerned, feminism is a much more important theory than New Right theory.

Checkpoint 1

How do functionalists explain relationships between men and women?

The jargon

Patriarchy is the domination of women in a society ruled by men.

Action point

List the topics you are preparing for the exam. Have you studied a feminist perspective? If not, check past questions to see if it is needed.

Links

See 'Doing feminist research' on page 15.

Examiner's secrets

There are even more varieties of feminism. For exams you don't need to know all the subtle differences, just show a broad awareness and understanding of some basic types.

Example

Some feminist writers: *Millet, Finestone* on Radical feminism *Barret, Delphy* on Marxist feminism. Many important writers such as *Oakley* combine a number of perspectives.

Checkpoint 2

Explain how women are economically exploited
(a) at work
(b) in the home

Arguments against: Marxists claim that the importance of class has been obscured by the focus on gender. In the past, feminism has focused on the experience of white middle-class women and neglected to study women in the Third World, and other forms of inequality, such as race, disability and sexuality. Masculinity and men tend to have been ignored (modern feminism does now cover these issues). They claim feminism is biased and sociology should be value-free.

Main applications

→ Increasing numbers of topics
→ Feminism now dominates the sociology of the family
→ Methodological debates

New Right theories

The New Right perspective has two main strands:

→ **The market liberal view** that the free market produces affluence and political freedom whereas planned socialist economies produce poverty and political tyranny.
→ **The conservative view** that traditional values are threatened by trends and beliefs in modern society undermining the conventional family, traditional education, nationalism and ethnocentrism.

Evaluation

Arguments for: The case for a free market provides a useful criticism of the Marxist analysis of capitalism and the failure of communist states. It encourages the study of enterprise, affluence and consumerism which are now important to Marxists and postmodernists.
Arguments against: The economic and political benefits of capitalism are limited to some people in some societies. The free market does not inevitably bring political freedom and human rights.

There may be some contradiction between the two strands – global capitalism threatens national identity and traditional values.

Main applications

Particularly useful in the debates over poverty and welfare and provides a good opposition in family questions to feminist views. Market reforms in education were inspired by New Right thinking.

Examiner's secrets

Some of these criticisms apply to some feminist writers but not others, e.g. Marxist-feminists do consider class.

Example

H. Graham has shown how class and race interact with gender in her study of domestic servants.

Example

The New Right has attacked sociology, including A-level, for being biased against business. We study inequality and poverty more than prosperity.

Checkpoint 3

Give two examples of attempts by New Right politicians to promote traditional values.

Examiner's secrets

The New Right has been more important in influencing government policies than in sociological debates, but is useful in providing 'the other side' in some answers on family and welfare.

Example

Main New Right writers:
Marsland on poverty, family and learning sociology
Murray on poverty, family, education and deviance
Hayek advocated the market to ensure political freedom

Checkpoint 4

How did Murray link family, welfare and crime?

Exam question   answer: page 176

Examine the contribution of New Right perspectives to an understanding of contemporary society. (50 min)

Action theories

Weber wrote that sociologists should seek

"the interpretive understanding of social action"

Checkpoint 1

Read these two pages and explain with examples what followers of Weber believe
(a) sociologists should study
(b) how they should study it

"If men define situations as real, they are real in their consequences."

Thomas

Checkpoint 2

Explain the statement above with reference to health or disability or deviance.

Example

Goldthorpe and Lockwood explained the behaviour of the 'affluent worker' by referring to their instrumental attitude to work. Work is seen as a means to an end. The end is money to provide for a home-centred family lifestyle.

Links

This is a good time to refer back to the culture and identity section.

This section deals with a variety of different theories, which share certain basic assumptions. The two major concerns of these theories are explaining social behaviour and doing sociological research.

The conclusion refers to Giddens' structuration theory and combines the action approaches discussed here with the structuralist approaches discussed on the previous pages.

Social action theories

Main assumptions

→ Individuals or small groups are studied, not whole societies.
→ Roles and identities are negotiated by individuals, not imposed by society.
→ Sociologists should study the meanings actors give to their own and others' behaviour (not external causes of behaviour).
→ Interaction is possible because we can take the role of others.
→ The social world does not exist separately from the minds of individual actors.
→ Social order emerges from shared meanings (it's not imposed from outside).
→ The methodological approach is interpretivist (interactionist) and anti-scientific.
→ Research methods seek insight into the actors' experience of the social world.

Types of action theory

Social action theory has its roots in the work of Weber. People are seen as actors who carry out actions to achieve goals. Choices of goals and the means of achieving them are influenced by the actor's perception of the social situation rather than the objective nature of a situation.

Symbolic interactionism has its roots in the work of Mead and Cooley. The key concept is 'the self'. This is how we see ourselves as objects in the social world. We see ourselves as we think others see us. Cooley called this the 'looking-glass self'.

Evaluation

Arguments in favour: Studying behaviour from the actor's point of view may help to explain apparently 'mindless' behaviour, such as vandalism and football hooliganism. Individual motives and choices are seen as significant. Humans are social beings, they do not just respond to external stimuli as if they were plants or rocks.

Arguments against: Structuralist writers are critical of the unwillingness to recognize the influences of social structure on individual behaviour. Conflict theories argue that the unequal distribution of power is not given sufficient consideration. Structural constraints are imposed on individuals whether they like or recognize it or not.

The subject matter of interactionist studies has been criticized for being trivial. It tends to deal with small-scale studies of ordinary or deviant behaviour rather than social problems.

Main applications

Interactionism has had a major influence on sociological research methods. It has provided the major theoretical criticism of Durkheim's study of suicide. Labelling theory and the concept of the self-fulfilling prophecy have had a major impact on the sociology of deviance, health and education.

Main writers

Becker is known for the application of labelling theory and explaining the social construction of deviance.

Lemert used the concepts of primary and secondary deviance/illness to show how social reaction created and amplified deviance.

Goffman developed Mead's concept of the self, describing the presentation of self as being like a dramatic production.

Goldthorpe and Lockwood used a social action approach to explain a range of behaviour in their large-scale studies based on survey research (unusual for an interactionist study) of affluent workers in Luton.

Conclusion

Weber combined the theories of structure and social action theories in his work, and criticized Marx for economic determinism and Durkheim for not considering social action along with social facts. Weber's views were echoed in the work of Parsons, Goldthorpe and Lockwood and many others who saw social action helping to create and modify social structure.

Marx refers to different types of social action as well as stressing the importance of consciousness for social action. More recently, *Willis* used interactionist methods, within a Marxist theoretical framework, to study the ways that working-class boys made sense of the worlds of school and work.

Giddens introduced the theory of structuration in an attempt to combine the insights of both structuralist and action theories.

Checkpoint 3

What methods were used by
(a) Durkheim
(b) interactionists
to study suicide?

Links

The work of these writers can be found in several sections, notably culture and identity, crime and deviance, and work and leisure.

Checkpoint 4

What is economic determinism? Why do interactionists criticize it?

Examiner's secrets

Refer to the methods section to refresh your knowledge of participant observation and the links between theory and methods.

Exam question   answer: page 177

Outline and evaluate the reasons why participant observation is frequently used by interactionist sociologists. (50 min)

Postmodernism

Postmodernist ideas have been around for some time. Their use is increasingly popular in AS/A Sociology, particularly in media and culture and identity questions.

Main concepts

Postmodernity refers to the current period of history which is succeeding modernity.

Postmodernism is the cultural movements which are characteristic of postmodernity, e.g. there are postmodern movements in architecture and film.

Postmodern social theory is the new set of sociological ideas which have challenged the classical modernist theories of Marx, Durkheim, Weber and their followers. The main concerns include culture and identity.

Main assumptions

The world has changed, modern society has been discredited and there is no more progress. Modern society, which followed medieval/pre-modern society has been succeeded by postmodern society.

Modern society has been discredited – modern architecture doesn't work, assembly line work is alienating, the modern state is capable of mass murder.

The main features of a *modern society* according to postmodern writers are:

→ *Economic*: a capitalist industrial economy characterized by specialised workers, technological developments, mass production and mass consumption.
→ *Political*: an increasingly centralized and bureaucratic nation-state is the dominant form of political organization.
→ *Cultural*: the traditional and often religious thinking of the premodern society has been replaced by rational scientific thinking.

The main features of a *postmodern society*, in contrast, are:

→ *Economic*: some reversal of the trend towards a deskilled mass of unionized workers. The new flexible labour force includes more (often female) part-time workers and new forms of employment and self-employment. Secure jobs for life are becoming rare. The economy is no longer dominated by mass-produced goods. There are more services and cultural products distributed through new media. Images are sold as well as goods. Niche markets for specialized products have been developed.
→ *Political*: centralized nation-states are less important. The New Right movement has encouraged a reduction in state activity. Globalization has weakened some nation-states.
→ *Cultural*: postmodern society is concerned with image rather than objects. Cultural phenomena are increasingly important. Culture rather than social structure is a major concern of postmodern sociologists.

Examiner's secrets

It is quite common to see *postmodern social theory* described as *postmodernism*.

Checkpoint 1

Why might some sociologists share the view that modern architecture doesn't work?

Link

Postmodern culture is explained on page 27.

Example

G. Ritzer in *The McDonaldization of Society* agrees with postmodernists that the globalization of consumption is occurring and images have become important. However, the modernist processes of rationalization and use of new technology are also continuing.

Checkpoint 2

Explain how the New Right has encouraged a reduction in state activity.

Sociology must change

The ways that sociology and other social sciences describe and explain social life are no longer useful. Postmodernism rejects the truth of so-called **metanarratives**. It dismisses these theories as 'big stories' which are no different from any other story we use to make sense of our lives.

Postmodernism also rejects the belief that societies will progress and that rational scientific thinking will help this progress.

Postmodernism: an evaluation ●●●

Do we live in a postmodern society?
Critics argue that there has been no distinct break with modernity. Capitalism has always encouraged technological developments and needed new products and markets.

Lash and Urry (1987) have shown how Marxism can incorporate some postmodernist ideas. Capitalism has developed though various stages, including mass production and mass consumption, to the production and consumption of information and other cultural forms. The motive remains profit and exploitation is seen as continuing.

Defenders of modernity have pointed out:

- modern methods of production allowed mass consumption
- modern political systems may be liberal, pluralist democracies
- the mass production of computers, VCRs, and editing equipment allows the creation of images and other cultural products; this enhances rather than limits freedom.

Conclusion ●●●

Bauman suggested three ways that sociology could respond to the challenge presented by postmodernism:

- Accept the postmodernist arguments that society cannot be explained rationally, and give up doing sociology.
- Ignore the claims and criticisms of postmodernism and carry on doing scientific sociology.
- Take a middle way and study the new social relations identified by postmodernism and accept some of the criticisms of scientific methods.

The jargon

Metanarrative is the term given to grand sociological theories, such as Marxism, which attempt to explain many or all aspects of social life.

Checkpoint 3

Briefly state the views on rational thinking and progress held by
(a) Marx
(b) Durkheim
(c) Weber

Checkpoint 4

Explain how other sociological theories have challenged the scientific approach.

Exam question   answer: page 178

Assess the view that modern society has changed but not yet been replaced by a postmodern society. (50 min)

Answers
Theory and methods

Structuralist theories

Checkpoints

1 Functionalists have argued for a number of possible relationships between the family and economic change. Parsons talked of a fit between the nuclear family and industrialization. Willmott and Young argued that industrialization and urbanization led to changes in family structure. Laslett and Anderson both questioned this link between nuclear families and industrialization. See the section on the family.

2 Functionalism explains social behaviour by looking at the influence of external forces on individuals, i.e. they are interested in outside *causes* of behaviour (rather than looking into their minds for *reasons* and *motives*, which is the action approach).

   Scientific methods involve testing the relationship between independent variables (causes) and dependent variables (effects).

3 1 Marxists – schools reproduce ruling class ideology.
     Feminists – schools reproduce patriarchal ideology.
   2 Marxists – emphasize preparation for work.
     Feminists – emphasize reproduction gender roles in a wider sense, not just work but also family and sexuality.

4 Generally, Marxists point to the role of the superstructure in reproducing the ideology which keeps the working class falsely conscious. This maintains the hegemony of the ruling class. This ideology is transmitted by religion, education, media, etc.

Exam question

Functionalism presents an *evolutionary* model of social change. It is a *consensus* theory.
- Social institutions adapt to fit the needs of the social system. (Explain some examples of change from family, education, religion, etc.)
- There is need to maintain the integration of society, which social change can threaten.
- You can explain Durkheim's account of the shift from mechanical solidarity in simple societies to organic solidarity in modern societies.
- Parsons can be used to explain the change from traditional to modern society.

Marxism presents a *revolutionary* model of social change, which results from class conflict.
- Explain the development of class conflict resulting from contradictions of capitalism, e.g. competition for profit produces the need to depress wages, which encourages class consciousness.
- You can explain how false consciousness inhibits change and the role of ideology in keeping the working class falsely conscious.
- Marxism has inspired theories of *underdevelopment*, unlike modernization theory, which is a theory of *development*.

Both theories are *structuralist* theories. Both theories have been criticized by *interactionists* although both have writers who include a consideration of social action. Both theories have attempted to *explain global change*. There are internal debates within each theory, e.g. the Marxist debate over *economic determinism*.

Feminism and the New Right

Checkpoints

1 Functionalists have been accused of supporting the status quo of gender inequality and even accepting biological explanation of gender differences. They tend to emphasize difference rather than inequality and see the gender division of labour as being functional for the family and society.

2 (a) Exploitation as defined and explained by Marxists and feminists involves workers not keeping the value of what they produce. Women are paid less than men (80% of men's wages in 1999) and there is evidence of a 'glass ceiling' limiting women's promotion chances. In the workplace an employer keeps what workers produce in the form of profit.
   (b) At home, men are seen as benefiting from women's work. Delphy suggested that just as employers own the means of production so men own the home and the tools in it and can thus exploit women.

3 • 'Clause 28' prohibited Local Authorities from promoting homosexual lifestyles. This had an intimidating effect on those in schools, health education and other services.
   • Attacks on benefits for single mothers expressed disapproval as well as attempting to save money. The limiting of benefits was continued by the Labour Government after 1997.

4 Single mothers were encouraged to live on welfare; unattached single men were seen as more likely to be criminal and to celebrate living off crime rather than working. In the USA, Murray's work is generally seen as focusing on the black population. He has been criticized for encouraging racist views.

Exam question

Outline the main characteristics of New Right theories:
- commitment to free market
- commitment to traditional values

Explain links to political movements particularly in the USA and UK (Reaganomics and Thatcherism).

Explain, using examples, links to social policy: family, education, poverty and welfare, crime, etc. and how these differ from other sociological perspectives.

Conclusion: Point out that New Right theories are clearly ideological – defending certain interests in capitalist society and condemning various socialist alternatives.

Their critics are also ideological.

Action theories

Checkpoints

(a) Weber believed that sociologists should study social action, that is, the meanings given to behaviour rather than just objective behaviour.

(b) Weber said sociologists should seek 'the interpretative understanding of social action' that is, understanding behaviour from the point of view of the actor. He called this 'verstehen'.

A simple interpretation is to say that if people are labelled as criminal, disabled, mad, etc. then they will be treated differently – perhaps as an outsider.

In each case, what is seen as ill health, disability and crime is socially constructed. Defining behaviour as mental illness means both the subject and others will see behaviour from this perspective. Rosenhan et al. acted insane in order to be admitted to a psychiatric hospital and were only able to 'prove' themselves sane with the aid of a lawyer rather than a doctor. In psychiatric hospitals and prisons you may have to publicly accept you are insane or guilty in order to be cured or rehabilitated and thus allowed to leave.

(a) Durkheim conducted a comparative survey using secondary data (official suicide statistics).

(b) Interactionists have studied suicide notes (J. Douglas) and observed in coroner's courts (Atkinson).

Determinism suggests that a single factor can explain behaviour. Sociologists have criticized economic determinism for suggesting that all human behaviour can be explained by looking at this aspect of social life. Marx has been criticized for overemphasizing the importance of the economic substructure.

Interactionists reject any determinist explanation for denying the importance of the meanings individuals give to their actions and the motives for their behaviour.

Exam question

To gain insights into subjective experience of actors. But only objective data can be directly observed and measured.

To discover how actors make sense of social situations, giving meaning to the behaviour of self and others (underestimates the importance of structural limitations on action).

To share the experience of actors. Explain examples of 'real' PO.

But is it possible to take the role of others? Assess any practical and ethical problems, which might limit the choice of PO by interactionists.

Conclusion:

- Theory does influence choice of method but it is not the only influence.
- Other methods may achieve interactionist aims, even those which are associated with scientific approach, e.g. experiments (Atkinson on suicide), surveys (Goldthorpe and Lockwood in affluent worker studies).
- PO is used by other theorists, e.g. by functionalists doing anthropological studies.

Postmodernism

Checkpoints

1 Because of the social problems associated with tower blocks and 'streets in the sky.' These include crime, social isolation, breakdown of the extended family, etc.

2 • By advocating tax cuts
  • By encouraging privatization of state-run industry such as gas, telecommunications, water, schools and health
  • By arguing that the state is a threat to freedom

3 (a) Marx saw social change moving through a series of historical stages based on economic factors. He saw progress towards a non-exploitative communist society. Scientific rational thinking required the shedding of false consciousness.

(b) Durkheim also believed in progress from traditional to modern society. He saw rational scientific thinking as an important characteristic of modern society.

(c) Weber saw the development of rational thought associated with the rise of capitalism (see the section on religion). He was pessimistic about the prospects of life in a society characterized by rational thought, as it would become increasingly bureaucratized.

4 *Interactionists* have challenged the view that social behaviour can be explained by identifying external social forces which determine individual action. They prefer the use of subjective methods to discover the meanings people give to the behaviour of self and others.

Feminists have on occasions challenged the value-freedom associated with the scientific approach. They claim that by not challenging the status quo the scientific approach legitimizes patriarchy.

Exam question

Outline the main features of modern society and for each discuss the changes that supporters of postmodernism have identified.

These are, with the main changes:

- *economic* – changes in technology, employment, products and patterns of consumption
- *political* – globalization, decline of nation-state, new ethnic identities, new social movements
- *cultural* – increased importance of mass media, globalization, and concern with images rather than objects

Outline and discuss Marxist arguments that we are still in late capitalist stage of history.

Conclusion:

- Modern and postmodern characteristics could coexist in the same society. Indeed, so too could characteristics of traditional society.
- Use Ritzer on McDonaldization of society.
- The claim that a new postmodern society exists could be seen as ideological. Such views may be seen as defending consumerism and global capitalism and assuming that socialist alternatives have failed both as academic theories and as alternative blueprints for society.

This section is intended to help you develop the essential study skills for examination success. You will benefit if you try to develop skills from the beginning of your course. Modern AS and A-level exams are not tests of your recall of text books or teachers' notes. Examiners who set and mark the papers are guided by assessment objectives which include skills as well as knowledge. You will be given advice on revising and answering questions. Remember to practise the skills.

Exam boards

In order to organize your notes and revision you will need a copy of your exam board's syllabus specification. You can obtain a copy by writing to the board or by downloading the syllabus from the board's website.

AQA (*Assessment and Qualification Alliance*)
Publications Department, Stag Hill House, Guildford, Surrey
GU2 5XJ – **www.aqa.org.uk**
EDEXCEL
Stewart House, 32 Russell Square, London WC1B 5DN –
www.edexcel.org.uk
OCR (*Oxford, Cambridge and Royal Society of Arts*)
1 Hills Road, Cambridge CB2 1GG – **www.ocr.org.uk**

Topic checklist

	AQA Sociology	OCR Sociology	EDEXCEL Social Policy
○ AS ● A2			
Effective revision	○●	○●	○●
Doing data response questions	○●	○●	○●
Writing essays	○●	○●	○●
Exam words	○●	○●	○●

Effective revision

This section gives advice on how 'active' reading, note taking and revising can help your preparation for exams. Everyone has their favourite ways of learning and you'll find some tried and tested methods here, which you can try to see if they work for you.

Examiner's secrets

Teachers recommend using more than one of your senses to aid learning. That's why they often combine 'talk and chalk' or talk with other visual material such as work sheets, TV, etc. Think about using graphic representations of knowledge.

Active revision: write a plan

Start revising in good time; it will allow you to practise and develop the necessary skills to use in the exam.

If you are doing other subjects, devise a plan where you use set times to study each subject. Be clear about what you need to learn in terms of skills, as well as topics. You will probably only prepare for one topic for each unit so you will need to make sure you cover it thoroughly. Plan revision on a week-by-week basis.

Review your plan regularly and adapt it as necessary. Some topics and activities will take more or less time than you anticipated. Build opportunities for relaxation and fun into your schedule; breaks for fresh air and exercise will help your concentration.

Active revision: use your eyes

Use tables
Tables can help you organize information so it can be used in different ways. Uses of tables include:

Summaries of types
For example: research methods can be organized into categories.

	Primary	Secondary
Quantitative	questionnaire, e.g. the census	official statistics, e.g. suicide
Qualitative	participant observation	diaries

Action point

Complete a table showing different methods with examples.

Comparisons
For example, compare two theories of the role of education in society.

	Marxism	Functionalism
Relationship with the economy	education is part of the superstructure	education meets the need for skilled labour
Cultural reproduction	reproduces ruling class ideology	secondary socialization

Action point

Choose another topic and produce a comparative table. Identify similarities and differences.

Diagrams
For example, to show:

→ Marxist and Weberian views of the class structure
→ the relationship between ownership, control and output of the media

Links

Diagrams of the class structure are shown on page 99 and of the mass media on page 70.

Active revision: use your ears

→ Discuss issues in class.
→ Have question-and-answer sessions with fellow students.
→ Ask a family member to test you.
→ Use audio tapes – either commercially produced ones or make your own.

Active revision: use examination questions

After you have revised a topic area it is vital that you are able to apply your knowledge and understanding in a critical way to an examination question. Whole questions may appear daunting at first. Try answering the shorter sub-questions from the data response questions or writing plans for essay questions.

The benefits of using real questions include:

→ you become familiar with the style and language used in questions
→ there will be popular questions which examine similar areas, even if the precise wording changes
→ it provides a check on your understanding as well as your recall of knowledge
→ it may reveal gaps in your knowledge and weaknesses in one or more of the sociological skills; use this feedback to review your revision plan
→ you can practise doing 'difficult' questions (once you have practised the more common questions you can build your confidence by attempting less predictable ones and developing strategies for coping with the unfamiliar).

Examiner's secrets

Tackle an unfamiliar question by applying your knowledge of relevant theories and/or using information in the items.

Active revision: applying key points

You can save precious time and effort if you learn to use the same sociological material to answer a variety of questions. This will also help you make the links between different points you have learned, which encourages a better understanding of sociology as a whole and is essential for success on the synoptic unit.

Key points to learn and use

Sociological theories: Major theories such as functionalism and feminism can be applied to virtually every topic.

Sociological concepts: Some concepts can be widely used such as consensus, ideology, false consciousness, patriarchy, and inequality in all its forms.

Sociological arguments: The debates between structure and action, culture and structure, consensus and conflict can be used in many questions.

Sociological evidence: Try to use important studies in different contexts.

Action point

List major theories, concepts, arguments and studies and match them with topics and familiar questions.

Doing data response questions

Particular skills are necessary to achieve high marks on the variety of data response questions found in sociology exams.

What is a data response question?

A question that provides you with one or more items of information and a series of sub-questions which are designed to test a number of sociological skills is a data response question. Generally, the questions become increasingly difficult.

The first questions may ask you to interpret the data provided, giving a short answer. This might be a number, word, short phrase or sentence, e.g.

> *With reference to item A: what was the approximate percentage in 1976 of all families with dependent children in the 'All lone-parents' category? (1 mark)*

The middle questions, worth, say, 4–8 marks, will ask you to use the items and provide specific answers to instructions such as:

> *Identify and explain . . .*
> *Suggest two reasons why . . .*

Finally, *mini essays* which will instruct you to:

> *Refer to item A and use your knowledge to . . .*
> *Using material from item B and elsewhere, discuss . . .*
> *Assess the view in item C that . . .*

The emphasis in these higher tariff questions is likely to be on more difficult skills such as analysis and evaluation rather than just presenting your sociological knowledge. These questions carry from 10–20 marks on the AQA papers.

What does the examiner want?

The command words explained on pages 186–7 make it clear:

1   What the examiner wants you to do. This will be the basis of the mark scheme which instructs examiners what to give you marks for.
2   How to do it. You will be told to refer to one or more items and in some questions to use your own knowledge.

What kind of items are used?

→ *Text*: from sociology textbooks, from sociological research, newspapers and magazines
→ *Statistics*: in tables
→ *Graphic items*: usually presenting statistics as bar charts, pie charts or line graphs, they may show sociological ideas in graphic form, e.g. representing Blauner's theory of alienation as an inverted 'U' shape

Action point

Review past papers to identify popular questions, e.g. methods questions frequently ask you to assess the strengths and weaknesses of particular research methods.

Examiner's secrets

Buy one or more 'highlighter' pens. You can use different colours to indicate different ways you may want to use material, e.g. one colour for answers to specific questions and another for arguments and evidence which can be used in longer answers.

Links

See page 58 for Blauner's theory.

How to answer data response questions

Read the questions first. This might seem strange advice! However, reading the question before the items may help you to identify relevant points in the item. The mark allocation will indicate what you should focus your attention on.

Highlight key words. These are the command words and the key issues in the question, e.g.

*Drawing on material from **the items** and **elsewhere**, **assess** the **advantages** and **disadvantages** of using **quantitative methods** of data collection.*
(20 marks) AEB specimen Unit 5

Read the items all the way through to get the overall sense of them.

Read and highlight key words. These are the concepts, arguments and evidence you will use in your answer. Often items will provide contrasting theoretical perspectives although these may not be identified as Marxist or feminist as you are expected to recognize the perspective.

Answer the short questions. These will usually involve interpreting and applying information from items rather than treating the item as a comprehension test. It is unlikely to be worth copying out sections from items except for key words or brief phrases.

Plan and write the longer questions. These have been described above as mini-essays, therefore a plan will help ensure a balanced and relevant answer.

You will need to follow instructions carefully and you will probably need to use your own knowledge of the topic as well as using information provided in the items.

Mark schemes frequently indicate that a reasoned conclusion will be rewarded. This can be briefer than a full essay conclusion but should follow the same principles. For the question above you might find it easier to separate the sections on advantages and disadvantages and use the conclusion for much of the assessment. This is less sophisticated than evaluating as you consider advantages and disadvantages but is a simpler structure.

How much should you write?

This should be determined by the allocation of marks and the total time available. This depends on which specification and which unit you are doing, e.g. AQA Unit 5 has 80 marks available for a 90-minute exam. Spend about one minute on each mark and this will leave 10 minutes for reading.

There is an essay question worth 40 marks. The remaining 40 are allocated to data response questions. The highest scoring is worth 20 marks. This allows 20 minutes' thinking and writing time. An average student can write about one and a half sides of an exam answer book in this time.

Writing essays

Writing good sociology essays is one of the more difficult examination skills to be mastered. This section gives some practical advice. You will be taken through each step from the planning stage to conclusion and review.

What is a sociology essay?

Sociology essays are extended pieces of writing which answer a question on a sociological issue or debate. Examiners expect a formal structure of:

1 introduction
2 separate paragraphs for main points
3 reasoned conclusion

AS and A-level sociology examinations are no longer dominated by essays, but they are compulsory and are still a major part of assessment if you go on to university.

How much should you write?

Examinations impose time limits. The new AS and A-level exams are shorter than the old three-hour papers because there are now six instead of two papers. Typically, you have to do one or two questions. This means you must pay careful attention to time limits.

The clearest indication of how much time you should spend on a question and thus how much to write is the number of marks allocated to the question. Remember that you must allow time for planning as well as writing.

When is a data response question an essay?

When it carries a large number of marks and you are answering a single question for perhaps 20 minutes. What distinguishes it from an essay is the requirement to interpret and apply knowledge from sources which have been provided.

Planning an essay

Firstly you must interpret the question. (Advice on 'command' or 'activity' words is given on pages 186–7.) You should expect to present a critical discussion of some sort.

Decide what the examiner wants and what opportunities there are for demonstrating what you know and what you can do. Make a firm decision about how you will organize your answer.

Typical frameworks for essays include:

→ assessing different sociological approaches to an issue, e.g. *feminist, functionalist and Marxist approaches to family roles*
→ presenting arguments for and against a view expressed in the question, e.g. *'The main function of religion is the control of weaker social groups by the more powerful.' Evaluate sociological arguments for and against this view*

→ identifying an issue and seeing what each perspective says about it, e.g. *Compare and contrast Marxist and New Right perspectives on the role of the state in society.*

Writing an essay

Establish a clear framework, which will provide a full answer. A full answer doesn't mean you have to write everything you know about the topic; it means you must provide a balanced response to the main issue or issues in the question.

The introduction

Keep it short. Use the introduction to make clear to the examiner (and yourself) what you intend to do in the answer. This may involve explaining the question.

The main points

You must develop a series of arguments and link these together so that the whole essay is coherent (this means that the arguments develop in a logical way). Good essays are not just lists of potentially relevant points, or even worse, irrelevant points.

Follow through your plan. You will gain marks for providing *sociological arguments* and, where possible, supporting them with *sociological evidence*.

Conclusion

Don't spend too much time repeating arguments from the main part of the essay. Refer back to the question and state a final reasoned position on the main issue(s). You may raise new issues such as what you might predict will change or not change in the future.

Quality of language

You will be assessed on the *quality* of written communication in your essay. This does not refer solely to *spelling, punctuation and grammar*. You must write in an appropriate formal *style* and make sure your answers are *relevant*, *coherent* and *well* organized.

Getting good marks and getting better marks

1 *Revise.*
2 *Learn arguments* rather than whole essays.
3 *Practise the real thing* – practise applying knowledge to different questions.
4 Check you are making critical points to get *evaluation* marks; you can think about making a critical comment at the end of every paragraph or whenever you mention a study.

Example

For this question you could take a point such as 'How is consent gained?' and see what each perspective says about it. Then say if the views are similar or different.

Examiner's secrets

Listing the main arguments to include in an essay is a good way to do a plan. If you can't do a plan don't choose the question.

When revising, trying to list main points will show you gaps in your knowledge.

Examiner's secrets

Make your meaning clear!

Watch out!

Avoid common mistakes
→ Don't learn a complete answer and reproduce it in the exam when there is a different question set on the topic.
→ Don't write in too much detail about studies you have learned and then run out of time to put down your main arguments.

Exam words

Action point

All this information can be found in the specification published by Awarding Bodies. These complex documents are not designed for students and should only be used with guidance from teachers.

What does the examiner want you to do?
In this section the assessment objectives, including synoptic assessment, and the command words used in questions are explained and linked to the mark schemes used by examiners.

Assessment objectives

These are statements of what exams must test and thus what candidates must do.

AO1 is knowledge and understanding. You must demonstrate knowledge and understanding of sociological theories, methods, evidence and concepts, and the links between them. When writing, you must be able to organize and present your arguments and supporting evidence clearly and logically.

AO2 involves the skills of identification, analysis, interpretation and evaluation. There is more emphasis on AO2 in the A2 exams.

Synoptic assessment

Synoptic assessment is intended to ensure that you have an understanding of the subjects as a whole rather than just knowing isolated fragments of sociology.

In the AQA specification this is done in Unit 6. The topics used are stratification and differentiation, and crime and deviance. In the OCR syllabus it is done in Unit 8: Social inequality and difference.

In all cases you will need to demonstrate you understand the links between the topic being examined and:

→ sociological theories
→ sociological research methods
→ other topics

Ensure that your answers to *all* the questions on the synoptic exam do demonstrate one or more of these links. You can do this in a fairly straightforward fashion by:

→ using different theories if asked to explain something such as inequality or different rates of crime
→ discussing methodological issues such as the difficulties of measuring social class or the problems with the reliability and validity of crime statistics
→ demonstrating links between different topics such as the similarities between the social construction of deviance and the social construction of ill health.

Command words

The command words in questions are used to direct you towards an answer which will gain marks. They are linked to the assessment objectives. Some of these instructions are aimed mostly at knowledge; others mostly at the AO2 skills of identification, analysis, interpretation and evaluation.

Action point

Identify questions from past papers and this book which use these command words.

→ **According to item** A is asking you to interpret evidence from an item in a data response question.

→ **Assess** means 'come to a judgement by weighing up evidence, examining different arguments and considering strengths and weaknesses'. You should come to a conclusion based on your judgement.

→ **Critically discuss** means you should present different sides of an argument or issue and come to a conclusion.

→ **Define** or **What is meant by . . . ?** are used in short answer questions and require a description of the major features of a concept or term.

→ **Describe** is usually restricted to AS questions and is often used in conjunction with another command such as 'explain'. It means 'show your knowledge and understanding of, e.g. an issue or event'.

→ **Discuss** means the same as 'critically discuss'.

→ **Evaluate** is more or less the same as 'assess'. A judgement of evidence and/or arguments is required.

→ **Examine** means 'study in detail'.

→ **Examine sociological contributions to** means looking at different sociological approaches to an issue and assessing their usefulness.

→ **Examine the view** usually means evaluate as well.

→ **Explain** or **What do you understand by . . . ?** means you must explain rather than just describe your knowledge of a concept or an issue.

→ **How useful is . . . ?** is usually a command to assess the usefulness of a theory in explaining events and issues.

→ **How far . . . ?** used with 'do sociologists agree'? or 'do you agree?' In both cases an assessment of arguments is required.

→ **How successful . . . ?** asks whether a concept is useful or a theory helps to explain events.

→ **Identify** requires a word, phrase or brief statement. Show you recognize a concept or a theory in an item.

→ **Identify and explain** requires you to provide the example and a (brief, depending on marks) explanation.

→ **Outline** means you should briefly explain the main points of a theory or argument.

→ **Suggest two reasons why . . .** means you should make sure reasons are explained and are distinct.

→ **To what extent . . . ?** is used as a command to evaluate by measuring the extent or degree that something is reliable, valid or useful.

→ **Using information from item A** or **with reference to . . .** is an instruction to interpret and apply information from an item.

→ **Using your own knowledge** is an instruction to interpret and apply information that is not in the items.

→ **What do you understand by . . . ?** requires an explanation of your knowledge of a term or concept used in an item.

Examples

These variations on the term *assess* all require a critical judgement:
Assess the advantages . . .
Assess the view . . .
Assess the claim . . .
Assess the usefulness . . .

Examiner's secrets

Assess and *evaluate* are common commands for essays as they make it clear that you will be rewarded for showing evaluation skills.

Examiner's secrets

If a question uses 'sociologists' it usually means talk about different sociological views, e.g. 'How far do sociologists agree that . . . ?'

Glossary

Alienation

The feeling of loss of humanity resulting from working conditions and exploitation.

Autority

Power which is seen as legitimate, i.e. the right of the ruler is accepted by the ruled.

Bourgeoisie

According to Marxists, the ruling class who own the means of production in capitalist societies.

Conflict perspectives

These see society as divided into competing interests. Social order is imposed by the more powerful on the weak.

Consensus perspectives

These see society as normally harmonious, with order being based on shared values.

Covert research

Research where the subjects are unaware they are being studied.

Crime

A form of deviant behaviour which breaks the law.

Culture

The whole way of life of a society.

Culture of poverty

This includes the attitudes and behaviour of the poor which are claimed to explain poverty.

Development

The change to a more modern and industrialized society.

Domestic labour

Housework and childcare.

Ethnicity

This refers to a distinctive cultural identity accepted by a group and/or attributed to them by others.

Ethnic groups

These share a common culture and identity.

Ethnic minorities

Groups with a different ethnic identity from the majority of the population.

False consciousness

A Marxist term to describe the inability of the working class to see the true nature of their exploitation by the ruling class, who use ideological control to prevent revolution.

Functionalism

A consensus theory which explains the existence of patterns of behaviour through the role they perform for society as a whole.

Gender

The socially defined differences between men and women.

Globalization

The process whereby societies are becoming increasingly interconnected and interdependent.

Hawthorne effect

The unintended effects of researchers on the subjects of research.

Health

This be defined as the absence of disease or as a sense of well-being. Sociologists see health as socially rather than biologically defined.

Ideology

A set of ideas that serve the interests of a particular social group. Marxists and feminists use the term to describe how the powerful impose their false ideas on the weak.

Interactionist perspectives

These emphasize the role of individuals in creating society, whereas structural perspectives emphasize how society shapes the behaviour of individuals.

Patriarchy

A system of social inequality where men dominate women.

Proletariat

The Marxist term for the working class.

Roles

Expected patterns of behaviour.

Secularization

The decline in the influence of religion.

Sex

The biological differences between men and women.

Social class

A type of social stratification where society is divided into economic groups.

Social mobility

Movement up or down the class structure.

Socialization

The process of learning culture.

Status

Social position. *Social status* is a Weberian term for the way society ranks groups in terms of honour and respect rather than social class.

Underclass

A class beneath the working class. There are differences between New Right and Weberian uses of the term.

Underdevelopment

The process of exploitation whereby rich countries make other countries poorer.

Index

→ Sociological explanations based on feminism, functionalism, interactionism and Marxism are to be found in nearly all the sections and are usually identified by clear headings. They are not listed here.
→ The different types of social inequality are discussed in most sections. They are listed here under age, class, ethnicity and gender. The list is not exhaustive.
→ Use your sociological knowledge and understanding to make links between related terms and concepts. For example you could follow up references to ideology by looking at false consciousness, ideological state apparatuses, legitimation, patriarchy, etc. You can also look at relevant names.

action theories   see interactionist theories; social action theories
age 24   see childhood; old age; youth
aid   134–5
alienation   58–9, 61, 115
Althusser, L.   169
amplification of deviance   148–9
anomic   146, 150
Atkinson, J. M.   151
audience   70–1, 72–3, 77
authority   120–1

Ball, S.   53
Barker, E.   115
Becker, H.   152, 173
Bell, C. and Newby, H.   14
benefits   86
Bernard, J.   39
Bernstein, B.   49
Black Report   158
Blauner, R.   58, 60
bourgeoisie   96
Bowles, S. and Gintis, H.   46
Bourdieu, P.   53, 160

Castle, F. and Cosack, G.   100
child abuse   32
childhood   36, 37
children   32, 33, 34–5, 36
cities   see inner city
Clarke, J. and Critcher, C.   63, 65
class   see social class
class structure   98–9
Cohen, S.   148, 153
Cohen, S. and Young, J.   70, 74, 75
colonialism   133
comprehensive schools   52
conflict perspectives   5
conflict at work   59
conjugal roles   see family roles
coroners   151
consensus perspectives   5
consumerism   108
covert research   10, 11, 14
   (see observation)
crime
   distribution   146–7
   explanations   144–5
   statistics   13, 144

criminal subculture   145
cults   114–5
cultural deprivation   49, 57, 158–9
   see also culture of poverty
culture   20, 24
   folk culture   26
   globalization of   136–7
   high culture   26
   mass culture   26–7
   of poverty   84
cultural theories of poverty   84–5
curriculum   53
   see also hidden curriculum

Dahl, R.   120
Daniel, W.   16
Davis, K. and Moore, W.   97
dependent old   35
dependency theory   132–3
dependent variable   6
deskilling   47, 98
development   131–42
development strategies   134–5
deviance   143–54
deviance amplification   148–9
deviant voting   124
disability   157, 164
divorce   38–9, 162
Dobash, R. and Dobash, R.   37, 39, 162
domestic labour   see housework
domestic violence   37–9, 162
Douglas, J.   154
dual labour market   103
Durkheim   6, 13, 108, 109, 144, 149, 150, 151, 168

education   45–56
   and development   139
   and the economy   46–7, 52
   functions of education   46–7
educational achievement   48–51
   and class   48–9
   and ethnicity   50–1
   and gender   50–1
educational policy   52
elites   121, 122, 123
embourgeoisement   98, 124–5
environmental movement   127
ethnicity   21, 25, 100–1

and education   50–1
and employment   100–1
and family   41
and health   159
and housing   101
and inequality   100–1
and the law   76, 147
and the media   76
and politics   125
and unemployment   65
ethics   11, 14
experimental method   6, 14
   see also scientific method

false consciousness   47, 70, 100, 110, 121
   see also ideology and Marxism
family   31–44
   definition   40
   disorganization   38–9
   and ethnic diversity   41
   extended family   34, 40, 41
   functions   32, 34–5
   nuclear family   32, 34, 40
   family roles   36–7, 41
      see also gender and childhood
   structure of family   34–5
   symmetrical family   37
feminism   15, 25, 124, 170
feminist perspectives   14, 15, 25, 103, 130, 170–1
feminist methodology   15
flexible workforce   61
Fordism   60–1
fragmented classes   98–9
Frank, A. G.   132–3
free market   33, 53, 171
functionalism   5, 27, 102, 110, 168–9
fundamentalism   110, 114
Fuller, M.   25, 49, 50

gender   24
   and crime   146–7
   and education   50–1
   and employment   94, 102
   and health   162–3
   and media   76
   and politics   125

and poverty 85
and religion 109, 110
gender roles 36, 37
gendered labour market 103
Giddens, A. 23, 120, 136, 172, 173
Glasgow University Media Group 73, 75
globalization 23, 136–7, 174
Glock, C. and Stark, R. 115
Goffman, E. 23, 161, 173
Goldthorpe, J. 95, 99
Goldthorpe, J. and Lockwood, D. 58, 98, 173
Graham, H. 33, 162, 171
Gramsci 22, 119
Griffin, C. 25, 50

Hall, S. 76, 147, 149
Hawthorne effect 7
  see also Mayo
Hayter, T. 134
health 155–66
  definition of health 156
  and development 138
  and ethnicity 159
  and gender 162–3
  inequalities in health 158–60, 162
health care 160–1, 162–3
Heidensohn, F. 147
hidden curriculum 47
household 40
housework 15, 33, 37, 59, 63
human relations 60, 61

iatrogenic illness 161
identity 21, 22–3, 24, 25
ideology 22, 37, 40, 46–7, 70–3, 108, 109, 121–2, 169
ideological state apparatus 169
  see also Althusser
independent variable 6
inequality see age; ethnicity; gender; social class
  theories of inequality 96–7
  of income and wealth 88–9
Illich, I. 135, 161
income distribution 86–7, 88–9
industrial conflict 59
inner city 82
instrumentalism 58, 98, 124
integration 97, 108–9, 150, 168
interactionist perspectives 4, 14, 145, 172
interview 9, 10

job satisfaction 58

Kuhn, T. 7

labelling 4, 48, 49, 145–6, 149, 151
Laslett, P. 34
Lees, S. 24, 50
legitimation 100, 111, 120
leisure 62–3
Lemert, E. 149, 161, 173
Lockwood, D. 99
Lone-parent families 38–9, 51, 86

McRobbie, A. 25, 77
Mack, M. and Lansley, S. 82–3
Management theories 60–1
Marcuse, H. 169
market forces 55, 70
market situation 96
marriage 38–9
Marx, K. 96–9, 109, 169
Marxist theory of social class 96
mass culture 26, 29–31
mass manipulative model 70
mass media 69–80
  effects of 72–3
  and ethnicity 76
  and gender 77
  and news 74–5
  ownership and control 70–1
  and politics 75
mass production 60
material deprivation 49, 158
Mayo, E. 7, 60
Merton, R. 146
methods 6–18 see experiment; interviews; observation; participant observation; questionnaires; secondary data; survey
middle class 98–9, 124
Mills, C. W. 58, 121
modern society 175
modernization theory 132, 139
modernity 174–5
monogamy 39
moral panics 75, 148–9
mortality rates 158
Murdock, G. 12
Murray, C. 84, 171

new criminology 145
new Left realism 147
new Right 33, 47, 84, 171
new religious movements 114–5
new social movements 127
new technology 60, 65
non-work 62–3
news 74–5
nuclear family 32, 34, 40

Oakley, A. 15, 33, 37
observation 10–11
occupational classifications 94
occupational structure 95
old age 33

Parker, S. 62
Parsons, T. 34, 36, 97, 120, 132, 157, 168
participant observation 10, 11, 14
party see political parties 52, 126
patriarchy 37, 109, 170
patriarchal ideology 36
perspectives 4–5
pluralism 121
political participation 124–5
political organizations 126–7
political parties 52, 126–7
positivism 12, 13, 144, 150–1, 156, 161–2
postmodernism 21, 25, 27, 174–5
poverty 81–92
  absolute poverty 82
  culture of poverty 84
  definition of poverty 82–3
  explanations of poverty 84–5
  measuring poverty 82–3
  relative poverty 82
poverty trap 64
power 120–1
pressure groups 126–7
proletarianization 98
proletariat 96
protestant ethic 111

qualitative methods 10–11
quantitative methods 8–9
questionnaires 9

race 21, 25, 73, 76, 100–1
  see also ethnicity
racial discrimination 41, 100
racism 41, 51, 76, 100–1
Registrar General's Classification 94
reliability 6
religion 107–18
  and social change 110–11
  and social control 108
  and women 109
  decline of religion see secularization
representation in the media 76–7
research methods 6–18
reserve army of labour 32, 85, 99, 100, 102

Rex, J. 101
rich 86–7
Rosenthal, R. and Jacobson, L. 49

sampling 8
science 6
scientific method 4, 6, 7, 10, 12, 14
scientific management 60
secondary data 9, 12, 13
   see statistics
secondary sources 9, 12, 13
sects 114–5
secularization 112–13
sex 24
sexuality 24, 35, 38, 76
Sharpe, S. 25, 50, 77
Single-parent families see lone-parent families
Sklair, L. 136–7
social change 108, 111
social action theory 4
   see also interactionist theories
social class see class;
   stratification; inequality
   identity 21, 25
   measuring 94
   structure 98–9
social construction of deviance 144
social construction of health 156
social construction of suicide 150
social control 63, 108

social control theory of deviance 147
social mobility 95
social order 108
   see also deviance
social policy 86
social system 4
socialization 20–1, 22, 34, 46
state 122–3
statistics 12, 13, 64, 151, 156
status 96, 99
stereotypes 22, 41, 76
stratification 93–106
   see also age; class; ethnicity; gender
strikes 59
structuralist theories 5
structuration 23, 172
subculture 20, 25, 27, 49
suicide 150–1
survey 8

Taylor, F. 60–1
Taylorism 60–1
taxes 85, 86, 88
technology 58, 60, 75
Third World 132–9
tourism 137
Townsend, P. 82–3, 85
trade 133, 135
training 46, 52
transnational corporations
   (TNCs) 135, 136, 137, 138

underclass 98, 101, 103
underdevelopment 132–3
unemployment 49, 64–5
   and families 37
   and health 158

validity 6
variables 6
vocational education and training 52
voluntary organizations 89
voting 124–5

Wallerstein, I. 136
Wallis, R. 114
wealth 86–7, 88–9
Weber, M. 96–7, 98–9, 101, 108, 109, 111, 120
welfare state 88–9, 123, 126
Westergaard, J. and Resler, H. 101
Willis, P. 55
Willmott, P. and Young, M. 34
work 57–68
   and non-work 62–3
   and leisure 62–3
working class 49, 98, 124
working women 94, 102–3
world systems theory 136

Young, J. 148, 153
youth 24
youth culture 24